teach yourself...

Quicken

JUDY STEVENS

MIS: PRESS

A Subsidiary of
Henry Holt and Co., Inc.

First Edition—1991

ISBN 1-55828-125-8

Printed in the United States of America
10 9 8 7 6 5 4 3 2 1

MIS:Press books are available at special discounts
for bulk purchases for sales promotions, premiums,
fund-raising, or educational use. Special editions
or book excerpts can also be created to specification.

For details contact:

Special Sales Director
MIS:Press
a subsidiary of Henry Holt and Company, Inc.
115 West 18th Street
New York, New York 10011

TRADEMARKS

Billminder is a trademark of Intuit
CheckFree is a trademark of CheckFree Corporation
Hayes is a trademark of Hayes Microcomputer Products
IBM PC is a trademark of International Business Machine Corporation
Lotus 123 is a trademark of Lotus Development Corporation
MS-DOS is a trademark of Microsoft Corporation
Quicken is a trademark of Intuit
TurboTax is a trademark of ChipSoft, Inc.

Dedication

To the memory of Jeanie Sarra

Contents

PREFACE xiii

CHAPTER 1: INTRODUCTION 1

How Quicken Organizes Your Accounts 2

How to Use This Book 3

How This Book is Organized 5

Summary 6

CHAPTER 2: GETTING STARTED 7

Computer Requirements 8

Installation 9

    Installing Quicken 4.0 on a Hard Disk 10

        Hard disk installation 10

    Installing Quicken 4.0 on Floppy Disks 14

First-time Use 14

Main Menu 17

Set Up an Account 18

Exiting From Quicken 22

Summary 24

CHAPTER 3: USING QUICKEN 25

Getting Help 27

    Helpful Keys 29

Calculator 30

Correcting Mistakes 34

Main Menu 35

    Selection 1 — Write/Print Checks 36

    Selection 2 — Register 38

    Selection 3 — Reports 40

    Selection 4 — Select Account 41

Contents

Selection 5 — Change Settings 43

Selection E — Exit 45

Pull-down Menus 45

Selection [F1] — Help 46

Selection [F2] — Acct/Print 47

Selection [F3] — Edit 49

Selection [F4] — Quick Entry 50

Selection [F5] — Reports 52

Selection [F6] — Activities 53

Summary 54

CHAPTER 4: ACCOUNTS, CATEGORIES, AND CLASSES 55

Accounts 57

What Account Type Should You Use? 58

Adding an Account 60

Changing Account Information 62

Deleting an Account 62

Categories 63

Adding Categories 65

Changing Category Information 67

Deleting Categories 67

Subcategories 68

Requiring Categories in All Transactions 69

Classes 70

Adding a Class 71

Changing Class Information 73

Deleting Classes 73

Subclasses 73

Using Categories and Classes 74

Summary 74

CHAPTER 5: TRANSACTIONS AND THE REGISTER 75

The Register 77

Transactions 80
   Adding a Transaction 81
   Finding Transactions 84
      Find a transaction 85
      Go to date 87
      Key word match 88
   Changing a Transaction 89
   Deleting a Transaction 90
Transfer of Funds 91
   How to Transfer Funds 92
   Going to a Transfer Transaction 93
   Changing a Transfer Transaction 93
   Deleting a Transfer Transaction 94
Split Transactions 94
   Adding a Split Transaction 95
   Split Transactions Containing a Transfer 98
   Changing a Split Transaction 99
   Deleting a Split Transaction 99
   Other Uses of the Split Transaction Window 99
      Adding machine 99
      Long memos 100
      Recalculating the transaction total 100
Memorized Transactions 100
   Memorizing a Transaction 102
   Recalling a Memorized Transaction 103
   Changing a Memorized Transaction 104
   Deleting a Memorized Transaction 105
   Printing the Memorized Transaction List 106
Reconciling the Register 106
   First Time Reconciliation 107
   To Reconcile Accounts 107
      Marking cleared transactions 110
      Entering missing transactions 111
      Correcting errors in transactions 112
      Does it balance? 113

Contents

Printing Transactions in the Register 116
Exporting and Importing Transactions 118
  Exporting Data 119
  Importing Data 120
Transaction Groups 121
  Setting Up a Transaction Group 122
  Executing a Transaction Group 125
  Adding to a Transaction Group 127
  Changing a Transaction Group 127
  Deleting a Transaction Group 128
Summary 129

CHAPTER 6: WRITING AND PRINTING CHECKS 131
Check Writing 133
  Writing a Check 134
    Writing a post-dated check 139
  Changing a Check 141
  Deleting a Check 142
  Voiding a Check 143
Check Printing 144
  Printer Setup 145
  Positioning Checks in the Printer 145
  Printing a Sample Check 146
  Printing Checks 149
  Reprinting Checks 153
Electronic Bill Paying 153
Summary 155

CHAPTER 7: OTHER FEATURES 157
Change Settings 158
Account Groups 158
  Select/Set Up Account Groups 160
  Back Up Account Group 164
  Restore Account Group 165
  Copy/Shrink/Year-End 167
    To use the Copy/Shrink/Year-End feature 167
    To copy and shrink an account group 168

To copy an account to a different account group 169

To do year-end procedures 170

Set Account Group Location 171

Screen Colors 172

Monitor Speed 173

Printer Settings 173

Password 178

Setting the Main Password 178

Changing or Removing the Main Password 179

Setting a Transaction Password 180

Changing or Removing the Transaction Password 182

Other Settings 182

Electronic Payment 186

Billminder 187

Summary 188

CHAPTER 8: REPORTS 189

Producing a Report 190

Wide Reports 192

Printing Reports 193

Printing Wide Reports 194

Personal Reports 195

Cash Flow 196

Monthly Budget 198

Itemized Categories 202

Tax Summary 203

Net Worth 203

Business Reports 203

P & L Statement 204

Cash Flow 205

A/P by Vendor 205

A/R by Customer 206

Job/Project Report 208

Payroll Report 208

Balance Sheet 208

Contents

Investment Reports 210

    Portfolio Value 211

    Investment Performance 212

    Capital Gains 213

    Investment Income 214

    Investment Transactions 215

Memorized Reports 216

    Recalling a Memorized Report 217

Setting Report Options 219

Filtering Your Data 221

    Filter Investment Report Window 224

Custom Reports 225

    Transaction Reports 227

    Summary Reports 230

    Budget Reports 233

    Account Balances 236

Summary 238

CHAPTER 9: HOME APPLICATIONS 239

Budgeting 240

    Determine the Income and Expense Categories To Use 240

    Assign Your Transactions To Categories 241

    Determine Budget Amounts 241

    Produce Reports 242

Cash Management 243

Home Improvements 244

Loans and Mortgages 245

Managing Investments and Other Assets 246

Managing Rental Properties 248

Net Worth 249

Paycheck Deposits 249

Personal Income Taxes 251

Summary 251

CHAPTER 10: BUSINESS APPLICATIONS 253

Cash Basis Bookkeeping 254

    Accounts Payable 255

Accounts Receivable 256
Produce Reports 257
Accrual Accounting 258
Accounts Payable 258
Accounts Receivable 260
Business Budgeting 260
Cash Flow and Cash Position 260
Asset and Liability Accounting 261
Payroll 261
Writing Payroll Checks 263
Entering Payroll Checks in the Register 264
Memorizing Payroll Checks 265
Payroll Transaction Group 265
Transfers and Tax Liability 265
Printing Payroll Checks 266
Payroll Reports 266
Form W-2, Wage and Tax Statement 266
Form W-3, Transmittal of Income and Tax Statements 267
Form 940 (1989) Federal Unemployment (FUTA) Tax 267
Form 941 (1990) Employer's Quarterly Federal Tax 268
Petty Cash 268
Reporting by Client, Department, Job, Project, or Property ... 268
IRS Form 1099 270
Summary 270

APPENDIX A: KEYS 271
Quick Keys by Function 271
Quick Keys by Quick Key 272
Other Helpful Keys 273

APPENDIX B: STANDARD CATEGORIES 275
Standard Home Categories 275
Standard Business Categories 277
Both 278

APPENDIX C: MENU MAP 281

INDEX 283

Preface

As the economy continues to fluctuate, some of us need help identifying the strengths and weaknesses in our financial picture — we need to know how we are earning our money and how we are spending it. To do that effectively, we need some financial record-keeping and management tools.

If you have a PC, you have the first and most important tool — a machine with the ability to store financial records, compute the effects of financial transactions, and report the effects of those transactions. The second tool you need is a software program that uses the power of the computer to do those things. Quicken, the subject of this book, is just such a program.

Preface

Quicken is one of today's real bargains. It is a commercially available money-management software system priced well within the reach of anyone with a PC who wants to control his or her finances. It can record and report the details of your personal finances, your investments, and your small business. *teach yourself...Quicken* makes Quicken easy to install, easy to learn, and easy to use, and it teaches you how to adjust Quicken to meet your needs, instead of the other way around. This book teaches you how to use Quicken with a minimum of fuss and pain.

Chapter 1

Introduction

Quicken 4.0 is a software program that runs on the IBM PC. It helps you to organize and manage your home and business finances. With it you can maintain accounts of your finances and write and print checks. You can even use it to tie into an electronic bill paying service to automatically pay your bills! Quicken can keep track of medical and dental expenses, income and expenses for rental properties, tax information for small businesses, and much more. It can maintain a register, much like your checkbook register, for each of your checking accounts, savings accounts, credit cards, investments, and any other accounts you want to keep. In this chapter, you will learn:

- How Quicken Organizes Your Accounts
- How to Use This Book
- How This Book is Organized.

Quicken is easy to use — you don't need a degree in accounting to use it — and you can easily customize it to meet the specific needs of your personal or business finances with as little or as much detail as you want. You can use Quicken to maintain a complete and comprehensive picture of your finances, or to simply manage your checkbook and credit cards. You can start small, with something like balancing your checkbook, and work your way up. Then, having mastered your checkbook, you can add more pieces of your financial puzzle (such as credit cards, income taxes, and investments) until all of your finances are under complete control.

How Quicken Organizes Your Accounts

The orderly organization of your financial records can only be done by you. Quicken simply provides the methods and techniques to help you do it. It is up to you to use those facilities to properly describe your financial situation.

Quicken organizes your finances into accounts. An account — checking, for example — is made up of transactions and transactions can be grouped by category. Transactions are things like deposits, checks, and bank charges. You want to track these transactions to know how much you earn from salaries, interest, and investments and what you spend for groceries, car repairs, utilities, medical care, insurance, and clothing. Each check that you write, every deposit, each dividend earned — in other words, every transaction — can be assigned to one or more of your categories to relate (or group) these transactions in any way you choose. For example:

Account	Category	Category	Category	Category
Transaction		$$$		
Transaction	$$$			
Transaction				$$$
Transaction	$$$			
Transaction			$$$	
Transaction	$$$			
Transaction			$$$	

Suppose you were to set up a Quicken bank account and call it Checking. This would be the record of your personal checking account. You would enter transactions in the Quicken Register. At the local grocery store, you might write a check to pay for groceries. When you get home, you would enter the transaction in your Quicken Register. The Register contains a Category field, where you assign a category to your transaction, in this case, the category would be groceries.

A class is an additional way to group transactions. You would use classes to identify medical payments for individual family members, or for a particular illness, or to each different doctor. You could also use classes to track operating expenses for each of your automobiles.

Accounts can also be collected into account groups. Account groups enable you to maintain independent financial records within one Quicken installation. More than one member of the household can use the Quicken program, for example, without merging or mixing the details of their common types of accounts. Or, you could use account groups to separate the household expenses of your primary dwelling from those of rental properties. Whenever you need to maintain separate financial records, you should set up separate account groups.

One account group might contain your checking account, your savings account, your mortgage, your credit cards, and your retirement program. Another group might contain your rental properties and your investment accounts. A third group might contain the financial records for a part-time business that you operate.

How to Use This Book

Teach Yourself Quicken is for the person who has never used the program. There are no references to or comparisons with prior versions. The material is organized so a new user can take a logical approach to getting started with Quicken. You should be able to begin using Quicken immediately and easily find what you need to know to begin organizing your finances. In some places subjects will be touch on that are not essential to the new user (for instance, Main Menu selections like Reports and Change Settings). These items will be explained in detail in later chapters. After you have used Quicken, and have become somewhat familiar with it, you can use these capabilities to add features to your financial picture.

1 Introduction

Since it is easier to understand a new concept or feature when there are pictures to look at and study, you will find many examples of Quicken screens throughout this book. These illustrations show you exactly what you will see on your screen, to help you find your way through Quicken's menus and windows.

Quicken has two ways for you to select the features you want to use: Menus and "Quick Keys." Quicken has numerous menus that pop up on the screen. Menus are also "nested," where one menu calls another menu, which may call yet another. The second selection method uses Quick Keys — keyboard shortcuts to the menu sequences. These Quick Keys are Function keys and key combinations that allow you to execute commands.

To help you learn the fastest and easiest way for you to do things, most chapters will begin with a list of Quick Keys for the commands described in the chapter. In addition, some sections will start with a list of Quick Keys related to that subject. Keys are shown as they appear on the keyboard. When two keys must be used together, they are joined with a hyphen, such as `Ctrl`-`A` or `Ctrl`-`Enter←`. You will find a complete list of Quick Keys in Appendix A.

Note: Be aware that some Quick Keys will not work everywhere. Furthermore, some key combinations have more than one use and the Quicken screens will not always tell you which is which. For instance, `Ctrl`-`O` will call the calculator from almost anywhere in Quicken, but the function of `Ctrl`-`E` depends upon where you are in the program:

- At the Main Menu, `Ctrl`-`E` will backup all your data files and exit you to DOS.

- On the "Select Account to Use" screen or in the Category and Transfer List, `Ctrl`-`E` will edit an account or category (Edit function).

- In the Class List, `Ctrl`-`E` will edit a class on the list (Edit function again).

- At the Register or Write Checks screen, `Ctrl`-`E` will recall the list of memorized transactions.

How This Book is Organized

In Chapter 2, you will learn how to get started with Quicken. Hardware and software requirements are listed, as well as instructions for installation. Chapter 2 concentrates on first-time use of Quicken. You must set up at least one account to use Quicken, and this chapter shows you how to do that. You might use your checkbook or make up a dummy account. You can delete the account later if it is just for practice. Without an account, all you can do with Quicken is play with the calculator. But with a practice account, you'll be able to do many things, such as correcting mistakes and writing checks. You'll also learn how to exit from Quicken.

Chapter 3 explains the basics of Quicken operation. You'll learn how to get on-line help screens, use the pop-up calculator, and correct your mistakes, You'll learn about Quicken's main menu and pull-down menus, and the rest of what you will need to know to navigate the Quicken menu system and operate the various features of the program.

You begin to organize your finances in Chapter 4. You will learn more about accounts, categories, and classes. How to set them up, and how to use, add, change, and delete them. You will learn that Quicken comes with six types of accounts — bank, credit card, cash, other asset and liability, and investment accounts and you will learn about each of them. In addition, you will learn how to use Quicken's categories and classes to help you organize your finances.

Chapter 5 discusses the Register. This is the master record of every transaction in an account. You will learn how to enter transactions, how to transfer funds, and how to reconcile your accounts. You will also learn some time-saving tips, such as splitting and memorizing transactions, and setting up transaction groups.

Chapter 6 covers writing and printing checks, including writing a post-dated check and changing and deleting checks. Not everyone will use these Quicken features, but some of you will. CheckFree, an electronic bill paying service, is also discussed. This option may work for you, too.

Other Quicken features are described in Chapter 7 including year-end procedures and using Billminder. Besides accounts, Quicken supports account groups. This chapter discusses account group activities in detail. You'll learn how to set up, change, copy, backup, and restore an account group. You must be careful not to confuse account groups with accounts, which are covered in Chapter 4. Although the two are related, they have different uses, and you access them in different ways. Quicken uses accounts to organize and record your transactions. Because you can have more than one account — and no doubt you will — Quicken lets you organize your accounts into account groups, perhaps, for example, to separate your business expenses from your home expenses. This chapter also teaches you how to change various Quicken default settings and use passwords.

Reports of all kinds are covered in Chapter 8. Quicken contains forms for personal, business, and investment reports, including transaction, summary, and budget reports. And if Quicken's preset report forms don't give you the reports you need, you'll learn how to design custom reports.

Chapter 9 is about using Quicken for home applications. You'll learn how to use Quicken's features for budgeting, cash management, tracking home improvements, recording loans and mortgages, preparing personal income taxes, and managing rental properties. Quicken's Other Asset and Liability accounts can help you keep track of repairs and improvements to your home or other property, and provide accurate and up to date records of loans, investments, and net worth.

While Quicken is not a full-blown, double-entry accounting package, it can help you manage the financial resources of a small business. Chapter 10 covers some business uses of Quicken, such as business budgeting, cash-basis bookkeeping, payroll, petty cash, and reporting by client, department, job, project, or property. You can set up categories to match your chart of accounts and track income and expenses more efficiently.

Appendix A contains a complete lists of Quick Keys and other helpful keys.

Appendix B contains a list of standard home and business categories.

Summary

Teach Yourself...Quicken is a complete learning experience for the Quicken 4.0 program. It enables you to quickly and easily organize your financial picture and print out comprehensive reports.

Chapter 2

Getting Started

I t's very easy to get started with Quicken. Quicken doesn't need a hard disk, it works just fine with two floppies (although a hard disk is much faster). Quicken will even work with only one floppy drive, but you will have to do a lot of diskette swapping. The Quicken 4.0 package comes with 5 1/4-inch and 3 1/2-inch program disks, so installation is easy on any kind of system. In this chapter, you will learn:

- Computer Requirements
- How to Install Quicken 4.0 on a Hard Disk
- How to Install Quicken 4.0 on Floppy Disks
- First-time Use
- The Main Menu
- How to Set Up an Account
- How to Exit From Quicken.

This chapter covers the basics of installing Quicken 4.0 on your computer, what to expect the first-time you use Quicken, and how to exit from the Quicken program.

Computer Requirements

In order to run Quicken 4.0, you will need the following equipment:

- IBM PC, XT, AT, PS/2, or compatible computer.
- 320K RAM minimum memory with DOS 2.0 or higher.
  384K RAM minimum memory with DOS 3.0 or higher.
- One of the following, on which to install Quicken 4.0 and store data:

  - A hard disk drive.
  - Three blank formatted, 360K, 5 1/4-inch disks.
  - Two blank formatted, 720K, 3 1/2-inch disks.
  - One blank formatted high-density disk.
    (1.2 Meg, 5 1/4-inch disk or 1.44 Meg, 3 1/2-inch disk.)
- 80-column color or monochrome monitor.

Optional equipment and supplies include the following:

- Almost any printer for printing reports, and almost any non-thermal printer for printing checks. A printer that requires thermal paper cannot print checks.
- Hayes-compatible modem (required only if you are using Quicken with CheckFree).
- Quicken checks (required if you want to print checks).

Installation

CAUTION: Do not run Quicken with the diskettes that come in the Quicken package. Use these original diskettes only to install Quicken and to make safety (backup) copies.

You must install Quicken 4.0 before you can use it. These disks are not copy protected so you can make as many copies as you need for your personal use. Install Quicken with the original disks and use the copies generated by the installation process to run the program. After you have installed Quicken, keep the original disks in a safe place. If your installed copy is damaged or destroyed, use the original disks to reinstall Quicken. Reinstallation will not destroy your data files.

The Quicken program disks contain the following files:

- Q.EXE   The Quicken program
- Q.OVL   Quicken overlay program
- Q.HLP   Quicken help file
- INSTALL.EXE   Quicken installation program
- BILLMIND.EXE Program to check for due bills
- QCHECKS.DOC Blank order form for Quicken checks
- PRINTERS.DAT Predefined printer setup

The Install program creates the following files:

- Q.CFG   Configuration and setup file.
- Q3.DIR   Account group descriptions and check due dates.
- QDATA.QDT   First Account group data file.
- QDATA.QNX   First Account group index file.
- QDATA.QMT   First Account group memorized transactions file.
- QDATA.QDI   First Account group dictionary file.
- Q.BAT   Batch file that runs Quicken. If such a file exists, it is renamed QOLD.BAT.

Files with extensions of .QDT, .QNX, .QMT, and .QDI will be created for each account group.

The Quicken installation procedure is very easy to do. You need only put the correct diskettes in the drive, type INSTALL, answer a few questions, and follow the instructions as they come up on the screen.

Installing Quicken 4.0 on a Hard Disk

During installation on a hard disk drive, the Quicken program:

- Modifies or creates the CONFIG.SYS file to set BUFFERS=16 and FILES=12. The Install program will not lower these values in an existing file.

- Creates a directory named QUICKEN4 and copies all necessary files there.

- Optionally adds commands to the AUTOEXEC.BAT file for Quicken to remind you of bills due for payment (See Chapter 6 for more information on Billminder).

While it is possible to install Quicken by copying all of the files to your hard disk, this is not recommended. Quicken has system requirements that must be met in order for it to run properly. Quicken's installation procedure confirms (or installs) these requirements.

Hard disk installation

After you have booted up your computer, place the Install diskette (5 1/4-inch disk labeled Disk 1, Install/Startup Disk, or 3 1/2-inch disk labeled Program Disk) in drive A.

At the DOS prompt (C:> or D:>), type A:INSTALL, press [Enter◄┘], and follow the instructions that are displayed on the screen.

The first screen to be displayed during installation is shown in Figure 2-1. The only thing you have to do here is to press [F2] if you have a color monitor, or [Enter◄┘] if you don't.

```
┌─────────────────────────────────────────────────────────────┐
│ ███████████████████████████████████████████████████████████ │
│                       I N S T A L L                          │
│ ─────────────────────────────────────────────────────────── │
│  Quicken's Install program automatically copies the Quicken  │
│  files onto the disk(s) that you specify, and modifies       │
│  certain files so that Quicken can run properly.             │
│                                                              │
│  For a complete explanation of what Install does, press F1.  │
│  Otherwise, press ←┘ to select where to install Quicken.     │
│                                                              │
│  Current Quicken Users:                                      │
│  Installing the new version of Quicken will not harm any     │
│  Quicken data you currently have.                            │
│ ─────────────────────────────────────────────────────────── │
│          To change from monochrome to color, press F2        │
│  Esc-Cancel                   F1-Help          ←┘ Continue   │
└─────────────────────────────────────────────────────────────┘
```

Figure 2-1 — First Screen in Installation Procedure.

If you press **F1** for help, Figure 2-2 shows the Help screen you will see.

```
┌─────────────────────────────────────────────────────────────┐
│ ███████████████████████████████████████████████████████████ │
│                     INSTALL - HELP                           │
│ ─────────────────────────────────────────────────────────── │
│  If you are installing Quicken for the first time, Install:  │
│    ▪ Updates your CONFIG.SYS, to insure that the FILES and   │
│      BUFFERS settings are high enough to run Quicken properly│
│    ▪ Creates a Q.BAT file in your root directory to run Quicken.│
│      (If you already have a Q.BAT, it will be renamed QOLD.BAT)│
│    ▪ Installs Quicken's Billminder program (optional).       │
│                                                              │
│  If you are currently using Quicken on a hard disk, your existing│
│  Quicken data will not be modified.  You can:                │
│    ▪ Install the new version of Quicken in the same directory│
│      as your old version, thereby replacing the old version. │
│    ▪ Install the new version in a new directory, thereby     │
│      retaining both new and old versions of Quicken.  Features│
│      in the new version may not be fully compatible with     │
│      previous versions (see the manual for details).         │
│ ─────────────────────────────────────────────────────────── │
│                                              ←┘ Continue     │
└─────────────────────────────────────────────────────────────┘
```

Figure 2-2 — First Help Screen for Installation Procedure.

Press **Enter←┘** to continue or **esc** to cancel.

The next screen to be displayed will ask you to specify the disk drive on which you want Quicken to be installed (see Figure 2-3).

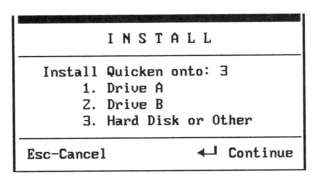

Figure 2-3 — Drive Designation Screen.

Type 3 to indicate that you want Quicken to be installed on your hard disk. Press Enter⏎ to continue (or esc to cancel) the installation process.

The next installation screen will display specific information about your hard drive and Quicken directory (see Figure 2-4). If the default drive and directory are where you want Quicken installed, press Enter⏎. If they are not, correct the information and press Enter⏎. Press esc if you wish to cancel the installation procedure.

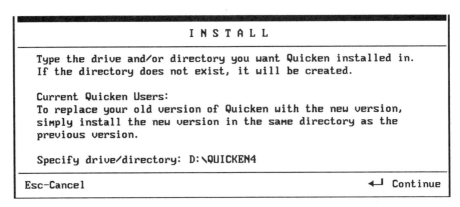

Figure 2-4 — Hard Drive Designation Screen.

The next screen (Figure 2-5), asks if you want to install Billminder. Billminder is used to remind you of bills due for payment. It can only be installed if you have a hard disk drive. Type Y if you want Billminder installed or N if you don't. If you install it and later decide not to use it, Billminder can be turned off. For more information on Billminder, see Chapter 7. Press [Enter◄─┘] to continue or [esc] to cancel.

```
┌─────────────────────────────────────────────────────────────┐
│ ▓▓▓▓▓▓▓▓▓▓▓▓▓▓▓▓▓▓▓▓▓▓▓▓▓▓▓▓▓▓▓▓▓▓▓▓▓▓▓▓▓▓▓▓▓▓▓▓▓▓▓▓▓▓▓▓▓▓▓▓ │
│                                                             │
│            Installing Quicken Billminder                    │
│  ─────────────────────────────────────────────────────────  │
│                                                             │
│   Quicken's Billminder notifies you when any of the following│
│   items are due: checks, scheduled transactions, electronic │
│   payments, or investment reminders.  Billminder alerts you │
│   of these events when you start your computer.             │
│                                                             │
│   Do you want Billminder to be installed (Y/N) ? Y          │
│                                                             │
│   Answering 'y' will cause Install to copy Billminder to    │
│   your hard disk and add a line to your AUTOEXEC.BAT file.  │
│  ─────────────────────────────────────────────────────────  │
│  Esc-Cancel                                   ◄─┘ Continue  │
└─────────────────────────────────────────────────────────────┘
```

Figure 2-5 — Billminder Installation Screen.

A message will be displayed on the screen telling you that the program is installing Quicken. The last screen to be displayed tells you the installation procedure is complete (see Figure 2-6).

```
┌─────────────────────────────────────────────────────────────┐
│ ▓▓▓▓▓▓▓▓▓▓▓▓▓▓▓▓▓▓▓▓▓▓▓▓▓▓▓▓▓▓▓▓▓▓▓▓▓▓▓▓▓▓▓▓▓▓▓▓▓▓▓▓▓▓▓▓▓▓▓▓ │
│                                                             │
│                    I N S T A L L                            │
│  ─────────────────────────────────────────────────────────  │
│            Installation of Quicken is complete.             │
│        Please store your original disk(s) in a safe place.  │
│                                                             │
│   Before you begin using Quicken, send in the Registration Card│
│   in the front of your manual.  As a registered user you get:│
│         ■ Free, unlimited technical support                 │
│         ■ Discounts on new versions of Quicken              │
│         ■ Discounts on other products from Intuit...and more│
│                                                             │
│   If the card is missing, send your name and address to:    │
│   Intuit, Dept C-I, P.O. Box 3014, Menlo Park, CA  94026    │
│  ─────────────────────────────────────────────────────────  │
│                                               ◄─┘ Continue  │
└─────────────────────────────────────────────────────────────┘
```

Figure 2-6 — Installation is Complete.

13

Press ⟦Enter←⟧ to get to the DOS prompt.

Installing Quicken 4.0 on Floppy Disks

Using your DOS boot disk, re-start your computer. Make sure you have the following diskettes ready:

- If you have 360K, 5 1/4-inch disk drives, you will need three blank formatted disks: Two disks for the Quicken software and one disk for the data files.

- If you have 720K, 3 1/2-inch drives, you will need two blank formatted disks. One for Quicken and one for data files.

- If you have a 1.2 Meg, 5 1/4-inch or 1.44 Meg, 3 1/2-inch drives, you will only need one blank formatted high-density disk.

Place the Install disk in drive A (the 5 1/4-inch disk labeled "Disk 1, Install/Startup Disk", or the 3 1/2-inch disk labeled "Program Disk").

At the DOS prompt A:>, type A:INSTALL and press ⟦Enter←⟧. Follow the instructions that are displayed on the screen.

When the installation is complete, label your disks as follows:

- 5 1/4-inch disks: Disk 1 "Installed Quicken Startup/Help"

    Disk 2 "Installed Quicken Program"
- 3 1/2-inch or 5 1/4-inch high density disks: "Installed Quicken Program"

It's a good idea to test Quicken as soon as possible to make sure it was correctly installed.

First-time Use

The first time you use Quicken, several things happen that may seem to be out of sequence. Most of these involve the setting up of accounts and account groups because, as a first time user, you have no accounts. This situation will only occur when you start Quicken for the first time.

Shortcut Keys:

| esc | Returns you to the previous screen or activity. Press esc enough times and it will take you all the way back to the main menu. |

| F1 | Help. Press this key to see a screen of helpful information about the current screen or window. See Chapter 3 for more information. |

| Ctrl - F1 | Help Index. Press this combination to see a list of all of Quicken's Help topics. Select the information you need from this list. |

To use Quicken, turn on your computer. If you installed Quicken on a hard drive, change to that drive (usually C:> or D:>). If you installed Quicken on floppy disks, change to the drive where you inserted the Quicken disk (usually A:> or B:>).

- If you're using 360K 5 1/4-inch disks, this will be the "Installed Quicken Startup/Help" disk.

- If you're using 3 1/2-inch or 5 1/4-inch high density disks, this will be the "Installed Quicken Program" disk.

Type **Q** at the DOS prompt and press Enter⏎ .

Quicken first checks your monitor type, then checks the system date.

If Quicken cannot decide what monitor you have, you will be asked for more information. Quicken will ask if you have a color monitor (see Figure 2-7). Answer "Yes" if your monitor displays several different colors (red, green, and blue). Answer "No" if you have shades of only one color (green or amber). Press Enter⏎ to continue.

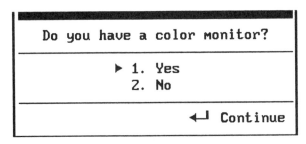

Figure 2-7 — First-time Use Screen.

If you have not already set the system date, Quicken will ask you to set the date. Type in the date in month/day/year format using numbers only (1/2/91). If you wish, you can change the format later by using the Other Settings selection on the Change Settings Menu (see Chapter 7).

The Main Menu will now be displayed (see Figure 2-8), and Quicken is ready to use.

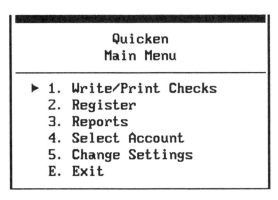

Figure 2-8 — Quicken's Main Menu.

Now that Quicken is installed, it is a good idea to go ahead and set up an account. Using Quicken is the best way to learn it — and having an account to work with makes it easy to see how to move the cursor within screens and how mistakes are corrected. However, if you do not want to continue with Quicken at this time, select Exit from the Main Menu.

Main Menu

The Main Menu has six selections and is discussed in further detail in Chapter 3.

- Write/Print Checks: see Chapter 6.

- The Register: see Chapter 5.

- Reports: see Chapter 8.

- Select Account: see Chapter 4.

- Change Settings: see Chapter 7.

- Exit: later in Chapter 2, Exiting From Quicken.

You are using Quicken for the first time and you, therefore, have no accounts to select or open. So, if you select any of the first four Main Menu choices (Write/Print Checks, Register, Reports, or Select Account), the "First Time Setup" screen will be displayed (see Figure 2-9).

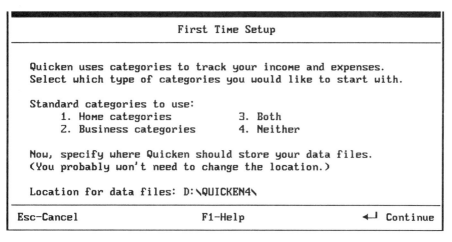

```
                           First Time Setup

   Quicken uses categories to track your income and expenses.
   Select which type of categories you would like to start with.

   Standard categories to use:
        1. Home categories        3. Both
        2. Business categories     4. Neither

   Now, specify where Quicken should store your data files.
   (You probably won't need to change the location.)

   Location for data files: D:\QUICKEN4\

 Esc-Cancel                    F1-Help                  ↵ Continue
```

Figure 2-9 — First Time Setup Screen.

Set Up an Account

The first thing you must do to set up an account, is to select the set of categories you will use. Quicken has four pre-selected sets: Home Categories, Business Categories, Both, and Neither. Unless you already have a set of categories or a chart of accounts to use, you'll want to select either Home, Business, or Both (contains Home and Business categories). Don't worry if you aren't sure which categories to use. You can add, delete, or change categories at any time. (For more information on categories, see Chapter 4.) A complete list of Quicken's standard categories (Home, Business, and Both) is included in Appendix B. Type the number of your selection and press ⌷Enter◄━⌷, or press ⌷esc⌷ to cancel.

Next you must set the location of your data files. Press ⌷Enter◄━⌷ to use the drive and directory location shown in the window. If you want the files stored somewhere else, type the location including drive and directory (if applicable), over the existing location. If the directory doesn't exist, Quicken will create it. Remember that you can change the location at any time; Quicken makes it easy (see Chapter 7). Press ⌷Enter◄━⌷ to continue or ⌷esc⌷ to cancel.

You can also get to the First Time Setup screen in another way — by choosing selection 5 on the Main Menu, you get the Change Settings Menu (see Figure 2-10). Selection 1 gets you to the Account Group Activities Menu (see Figure 2-11). The first selection on this menu, Select/Set Up Account Group, will give you the First Time Setup screen (Figure 2-9).

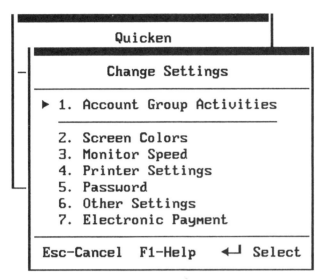

Figure 2-10 — Main Menu Selection 5 - Change Settings.

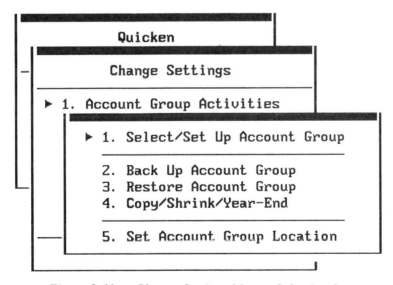

Figure 2-11 — Change Settings Menu - Selection 1.

The next screen to be displayed will allow you to set up your first account.

```
                    Set Up New Account
  ─────────────────────────────────────────────────────
  Account Type: 1
       1. Bank Account          4. Other Asset
       2. Credit Card           5. Other Liability
       3. Cash                  6. Investment Account

  Name for this account:

  Balance:              as of:  1/1/91
  (Enter the balance in your bank account)

  Description (optional):
  ─────────────────────────────────────────────────────
             Please type account information
  Esc-Cancel                F1-Help          ↵ Continue
```

Figure 2-12 — Set Up New Account Window.

Select one of the six choices for your account type. For your first account, you may find it easiest to set up a bank account. This account type includes both checking and savings accounts. You can make up the data for this account, or you can use your own checkbook. Type the appropriate number (1 through 6) and press [Enter←] to position the cursor at the next field.

You now need to enter an account name. The account must have a name, and to avoid confusion later, it should be a unique and meaningful one. You can use up to 15 characters, excluding the left bracket ([ ), right bracket ( ]), forward slash (/), and colon (:). If, for instance, you have more than one checking account, you may find it helpful to give each account a name that clearly and distinctly identifies it. Checking1 or Checking2 may not give enough information to properly identify the account you want to find. Use the name of the bank, if the accounts are in different banks, or include your name, or your spouse's. The same goes for Credit Card Accounts; if you have two VISA cards, use the bank name as part of the account name. Type the name of the account and press [Enter←] to position the cursor at the next field.

Enter a beginning balance for the account. Quicken requires a valid number here, so if you're not sure, enter 0.00 or make a good guess. If you have an accurate checkbook register, enter the last balance or the balance at the beginning of the period (such as the first day of a new year or month). You can correct the amount later from the register if you need to. Type the balance of the account and press [Enter←] to position the cursor at the next field.

You can use the date shown or change it. If you entered a balance from your checkbook, use the corresponding date. Press [Enter←] to position the cursor at the next field.

An account description is optional, but you may find it very helpful later on. Enter a brief description of the account — no more than 21 characters. You may want to use the account number or another specific piece of information to distinguish the account. Press [Enter←], and the account is set up.

Quicken creates a new account with the information you just entered, and puts it into an account group named QDATA. Any other accounts you create will be placed in this same account group. You can rename the account group or set up other account groups. For more information about accounts and account groups, see Chapters 4 and 7.

The next screen you see will depend on the selection you made at the Main Menu. You may see the Write Checks screen, the Register screen, or the Select Account To Use screen (for more information, see Chapters 6, 5, and 4, respectively).

Exiting From Quicken

Shortcut Keys:

From the Main Menu (use [esc] to get to the Main Menu) use:

[E]   to exit the Quicken program

[Ctrl]-[E]   to backup files on disk and exit Quicken

[Ctrl]-[B]   to backup your files

To exit the Quicken program, press [esc] until you reach the Main Menu.

Use the arrow keys to move the cursor to E. Exit, and press [Enter←]. Or type [E] (pressing [Enter←] isn't necessary). This causes Quicken to close all files and gets you back to the DOS prompt. A message "Saving Index Files" will be displayed at the bottom of the screen, telling you that the exit process is working.

You can automatically back up your data files when you exit Quicken by pressing [Ctrl]-[E] instead of selecting E (from the menu). The "Select Backup Drive" screen (see Figure 2-13) will be displayed, asking you to type the letter of the drive on which you want your back-ups to be saved.

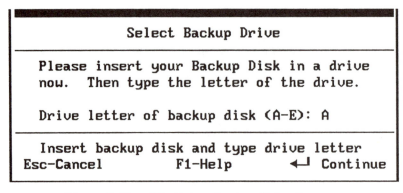

```
              Select Backup Drive

   Please insert your Backup Disk in a drive
   now.  Then type the letter of the drive.

   Drive letter of backup disk (A-E): A

   Insert backup disk and type drive letter
Esc-Cancel           F1-Help        ←┘ Continue
```

Figure 2-13 — The Select Backup Drive Screen.

Insert your backup diskette in a drive and type the drive letter. Press [Enter←] to continue, or press [esc] to get back to the Main Menu.

The Select Account Group screen asks you to select the account group you want to back up (see Figure 2-14). Unless you have set up another account group, there will be only one choice — QDATA — the default account group set up by the Quicken install program.

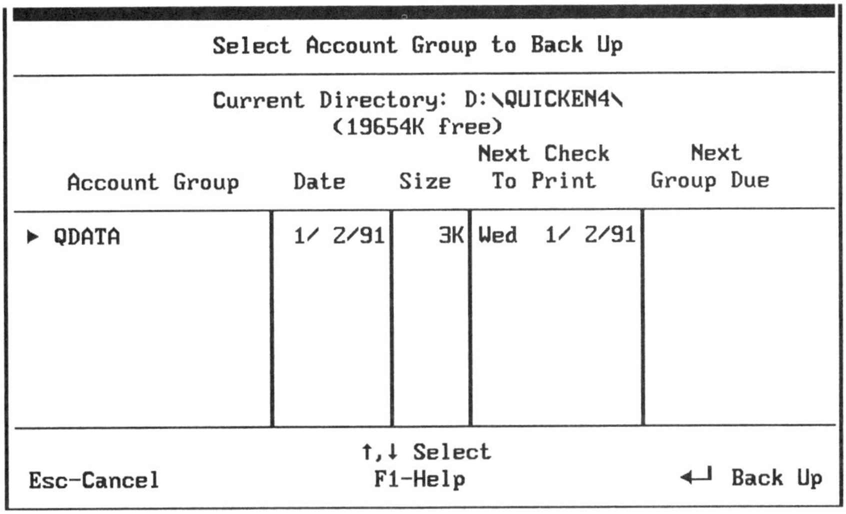

```
┌──────────────────────────────────────────────────────────────┐
│              Select Account Group to Back Up                  │
├──────────────────────────────────────────────────────────────┤
│           Current Directory:  D:\QUICKEN4\                    │
│                     (19654K free)                            │
│                                  Next Check      Next         │
│      Account Group    Date   Size  To Print   Group Due       │
│     ─────────────────────────────────────────────────────    │
│   ▶ QDATA           1/ 2/91    3K│Wed   1/ 2/91               │
│                                  │                            │
│                                  │                            │
│                                  │                            │
│                                  │                            │
│                                  │                            │
│     ─────────────────────────────────────────────────────    │
│                       ↑,↓ Select                             │
│     Esc-Cancel        F1-Help              ←┘  Back Up        │
└──────────────────────────────────────────────────────────────┘
```

Figure 2-14 — The Select the Account Group to be Backed Up Screen.

Position the cursor on the group to be backed up and press [Enter←]. A message will be displayed stating that the account group has been backed up successfully (see Figure 2-15).

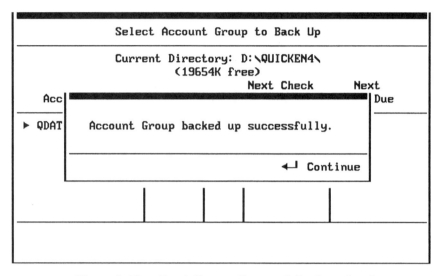

Figure 2-15 — Back Up was Successfully Completed.

Press Enter⏎ and the Select Account Group screen is again displayed (see Figure 2-14), allowing you to back up more than one account group or to make more than one backup copy. Or press esc to get to the DOS prompt.

You can easily back up your files from the Main Menu without exiting Quicken. Press Ctrl-B and follow the instructions to back up your files to any location.

Always exit the Quicken program through the Main Menu so the necessary index files can be saved. If you experience a power outage, all is not lost. Your data files are safe because Quicken saves data as you work. Quicken can rebuild incomplete index files when you next load Quicken, and all that takes is some extra time.

Summary

In this chapter you learned how to install Quicken, get the program started, and to exit the program. You are now ready to begin using Quicken and to discover how Quicken can help you to organize your finances.

Chapter 3

Using Quicken

T he best way to learn Quicken is to play with it — to set up an account and make up transactions as you go along. This dummy exercise is valuable because mistakes will not matter. You will not find yourself going back and recreating valuable data which was accidentally removed. But if you are a person who can only work on something "real," then go ahead and set up a valid account. In this chapter, you will learn about:

- Getting Help
- Helpful Keys
- The Calculator, Ctrl - O
- Correcting Mistakes
- The Main Menu
- Pull-down Menus.

Shortcut Keys discussed in this chapter:

[esc]	Returns you to previous screen or activity
[Fl]	Help key
[Ctrl]-[Fl]	Help Index
[Ctrl]-[O]	Calculator
Arrow Keys	Move the cursor one space or line at a time

There are many things you should do before you begin to enter your financial information. Familiarize yourself with some of the features of Quicken by looking through the Help screens and playing with the calculator, [Ctrl]-[O]. You should also practice using the Quick Keys to get yourself to different places within Quicken.

If you set up an account during your first-time use, you're ready to continue. If not, set one up now (see Chapter 2).

Getting Help

Use the Quicken Help key, ⌨F1, if you need help with the current screen, window, or menu. Some messages are too long for one window and can be viewed by pressing ⌨PgDn or ⌨↓ (see Figure 3-1). To exit the Help window, press ⌨esc.

```
                    How to Use Help

   You can get help with most tasks as you use Quicken.
   When you have a question, just press F1. Quicken's
   Help will show you information about the current
   screen or window.

   To see more help on a topic
     If there's more help on a topic, the bottom of the
     Help window will tell you to press one of the arrow
     keys or the PgUp and PgDn keys.

     To scroll more information into view, line by line,
     use ↑ or ↓.

     To see the next screenful of information, press
     PgDn. To move back up through the text, press PgUp.

   For information on a different topic, press F1 to
   display the Help Index. (You can reach the Help Index

 Esc-Cancel            F1-Help Index          ↓,PgDn-More
```

Figure 3-1 — The How to Use Help Screen.

[Ctrl]-[F1] will get you to the Help index, a list of all of the topics for which help screens are available. By using the Help index (see Figure 3-2), you can get information about any topic in Quicken, not just the current screen or window.

```
┌─────────────────────────────────────────────────────┐
│ ███████████████████████████████████████████████████ │
│                 Select Help Topic                    │
│ ──────────────────────────────────────────────────── │
│ ▶ Account Group Activities                           │
│   Account group, selecting one to use                │
│   Account group, setting up new one                  │
│   Account types                                      │
│   Account, setting up new one                        │
│   Acct/Print Menu                                    │
│   Action List                                        │
│   Activities Menu                                    │
│   Balance Sheet, business report                     │
│   Beginning to use Quicken, part 1                   │
│   Beginning to use Quicken, part 2                   │
│   Business Reports Menu                              │
│   Calculator, using                                  │
│   Change Settings Menu                               │
│ ──────────────────────────────────────────────────── │
│ Esc-Cancel   PgDn,PgUp-More Topics    ↵ Select       │
└─────────────────────────────────────────────────────┘
```

Figure 3-2 — The Select Help Topic List.

You can also get to the Help index by pressing [F1] twice. To look through the list:

- Use [↑] and [↓] to move through the list one line at a time.

- Use [PgUp] and [PgDn] to move one screen at a time.

- Type a letter of the alphabet to see the first listing of the topic beginning with that letter. This works in both directions; try it. Press [Ctrl]-[A] and the Select Help Topic screen appears with the cursor at the first topic, Account Group Activities. Watch the screen as you type S, N, A, I, Q, T, B. Or choose your own letters.

    You can select a topic from this list and read about it at any time.

- Press [esc] to get out.

Helpful Keys

Quick Keys, a combination of Ctrl and another key, can save you time. You'll find the Quick Keys listed on most menus and windows. All of the Quick Keys are covered in this book in chapters relating to the function of the Quick Key.

Ctrl-O is a Quick Key — it activates the calculator from almost anywhere in Quicken (see the section later in this chapter on the Calculator). Some Quick Keys have more than one use depending on where you are. Ctrl-E is one example: at the Main Menu it will backup your accounts and exit to DOS; at the Register or Write Checks screen it will give you a list of memorized transactions; from the account, category, or class lists, it allows you to edit the setup information.

As you become more familiar with Quicken, Quick Keys will save you time. You'll find it faster and easier to press Ctrl-R to go directly to the Register, or Ctrl-W to write checks, rather than going through the Main Menu.

Other helpful keys make moving around in windows and correcting mistakes much easier.

- Use ↑ and ↓ to move the cursor one line at a time.
- Use ← and → to move the cursor one character at a time.
- Press Ctrl and ← or → to move the cursor to the beginning of the previous or next word.
- Use home to move the cursor to the beginning of a field.
- Press home twice to move the cursor to the beginning of the first field in the current screen or window.
- Press Ctrl-home to move the cursor to the beginning of the Register or to the first check in the Write Checks screen.
- Use end to move the cursor to the end of a field.
- Press end twice to move the cursor to the end of the last field in the current screen or window.
- Press Ctrl-end to move the cursor to the end of the Register or to the last check in the Write Checks screen.

- Use ⌨tab and ⌨Enter⏎ to move the cursor forward from field to field.
- Use ⌨⇧Shift -⌨tab to move the cursor backward through the fields.
- Use ⌨delete to delete the character at the cursor.
- Use ⌨←BkSp to delete the key to the left of the cursor.
- Use ⌨Ctrl-⌨←BkSp to delete the contents of the entire field.
- Use ⌨Ctrl-⌨Enter⏎ or ⌨F10 to confirm the current screen and move on to the next.

A complete list of these keys is included in Appendix A.

Calculator

Shortcut Keys:

⌨Ctrl-⌨O	Calculator
⌨F9	Paste calculation in transaction
⌨C	Clear calculator

Quicken's built-in calculator allows you to add, subtract, multiply, divide, calculate percentages, and add or subtract percentages without exiting the current transaction. To activate the calculator from almost anywhere, press ⌨Ctrl-⌨O (see Figure 3-3). You can also select Calculator from the ⌨F6-Activities menu at the top of the Write Checks or Register screens, but the Quick Key is faster.

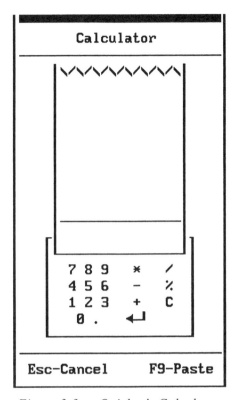

Figure 3-3 — Quicken's Calculator.

The numeric lock, [num lock], on the key pad is automatically set when the calculator is selected, so you can immediately begin to use the numbers on the key pad. The calculator is easy to operate and is accurate to eight decimal places. If you enter an invalid or over-large number, you get an error message that says you can enter a number from –9,999,999 to 9,999,99.

Use the [+] operator to add, [–] to subtract, [*] to multiply, and [/] to divide. Press [Enter←] or [=] to finish the calculation. If you are adding a series of like numbers, for instance 2+2+2+2, enter 2, +, +, +, +, and [=] or [Enter←] to complete the equation (see Figure 3-4).

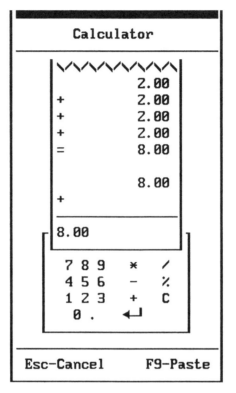

Figure 3-4 — Calculator Showing Calculations.

Use [%] to calculate percentages. If you want to add or subtract a percentage, first calculate or type the amount. Then type the appropriate operator (+ or –), type the percentage number, type

%

and press [Enter⏎] to complete the calculation.

To do multiple calculations, complete one calculation, type an operator (+, *, /) for the new calculation, and press [Enter⏎]. Quicken uses the results of the previous calculation as the beginning number of the next calculation. Note that this does not seem to work with the [–] operator.

Press ⬚F9 to paste the result in the current transaction. The cursor must be in the blank where the calculation is to be pasted or you get an error message (see Figure 3-5).

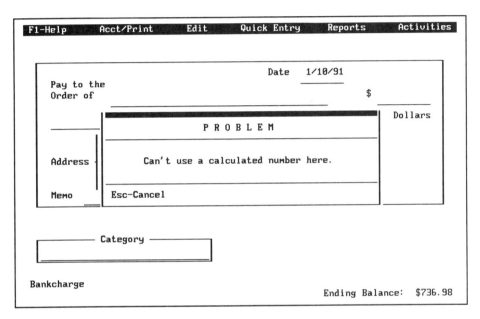

Figure 3-5 — Error Message.

Type **C** to clear all calculations.

Correcting Mistakes

Quicken makes it easy to correct mistakes you made while writing checks or entering transactions in the Register. There are some basic keystrokes that make it faster.

- Use the arrow keys to move the cursor around. Each stroke will move the cursor one line or space.
- Use ⟦Ctrl⟧ with the ⟦←⟧ or ⟦→⟧ to move the cursor from word to word.
- Use ⟦tab⟧ and ⟦Enter←⟧ to move the cursor forward from blank to blank.
- Use ⟦⇧Shift⟧-⟦tab⟧ to move it backward through the blanks.
- Use ⟦home⟧ to move the cursor to the beginning of the current blank.
- Press ⟦home⟧ twice to move the cursor to the beginning of the first blank.
- Press ⟦end⟧ to move the cursor to end of the current blank.
- Press ⟦end⟧ twice to move the cursor to the end of the last blank.
- Use the above keystrokes to position the cursor where you want to delete, insert or replace characters.

To delete characters:

- Use ⟦delete⟧ to delete the character at the cursor.
- Use ⟦←BkSp⟧ to delete the key to the left of the cursor.
- Use ⟦Ctrl⟧-⟦←BkSp⟧ to delete the contents of the entire field.
- In Overwrite (Ins off) mode, press ⟦space⟧ to delete the character at the cursor and replace it with a space.

To insert characters, press ⟦ins⟧ (the cursor will change to a blinking rectangle), and type the new information you want to insert.

To replace characters, press ⟦ins⟧ again (the cursor will change to a blinking line) and type over the characters you want to replace.

When you've finished correcting the mistakes, press ⟦F10⟧ or ⟦Ctrl⟧-⟦Enter←⟧ to record the changes you've made.

Main Menu

Shortcut Keys:

`esc`	Returns you to previous screen or activity
`F1`	Help key
`Ctrl`-`F1`	Help Index
`Ctrl`-`A`	Select or setup an account
`Ctrl`-`B`	Use to backup your files (only at Main Menu)
`Ctrl`-`E`	Use to backup files on disk and exit
`Ctrl`-`G`	Select or setup an account group (only at Main Menu)
`Ctrl`-`O`	Calculator
`Ctrl`-`R`	Register
`Ctrl`-`W`	Write Checks Screen

There are six selections on the Main Menu (see Figure 3-6). You'll need some information about each choice in order to decide where to start, so each one will be briefly discussed here. More complete information on each selection can be found in other chapters.

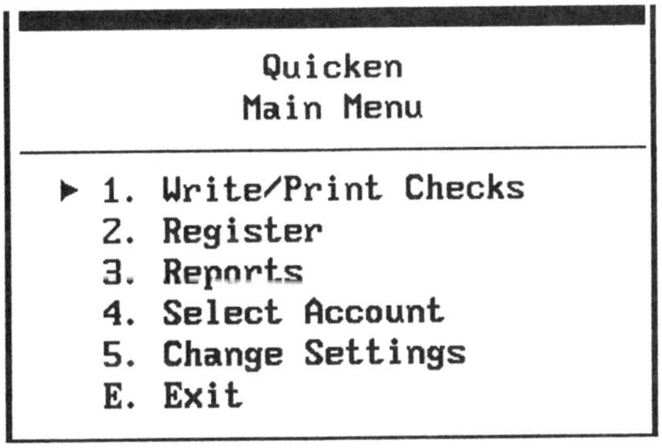

```
                 Quicken
                 Main Menu

   ▶ 1. Write/Print Checks
     2. Register
     3. Reports
     4. Select Account
     5. Change Settings
     E. Exit
```

Figure 3-6 — Quicken's Main Menu.

If you're typing in a lot of transactions and want to backup your files periodically, press Ctrl-B at the Main Menu. Your files will be backed up to a diskette and you won't have to exit Quicken.

Use the arrow keys to move the cursor to the selection you want or use appropriate Quick Keys, and press Enter←. Or type the number of your choice (pressing Enter← isn't necessary).

Selection 1 — Write/Print Checks

Shortcut Keys:

esc	Returns you to previous screen or activity
F1	Help key
Ctrl-F1	Help Index
Ctrl-A	Select or setup an account
Ctrl-B	Find previous transaction (only from Write Checks)
Ctrl-C	Select or setup a category
Ctrl-D	Delete transaction
Ctrl-E	Edit item
Ctrl-F	Find transaction
Ctrl-G	Go to Date
Ctrl-J	Changes to Register/Select transaction group
Ctrl-L	Select or setup a class
Ctrl-M	Memorize the transaction
Ctrl-N	Find next transaction
Ctrl-O	Calculator
Ctrl-P	Print checks
Ctrl-R	Go to Register
Ctrl-S	Split transaction
Ctrl-T	Memorized Transactions List

Ctrl-U   Back to Main Menu

Ctrl-V   Void a check

Ctrl-X   Go to Transfer

You use the Write/Print selection, Ctrl-W, to write and review checks before you print them using Quicken's Print Checks option (see Figure 3-7).

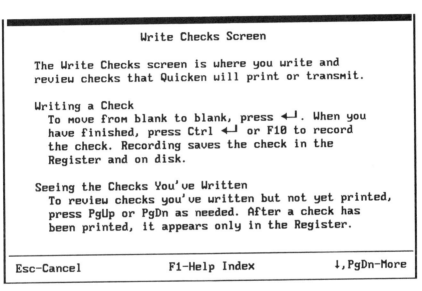

```
         ┌─────────────────────────────────────────────────────┐
         │▐▀▀▀▀▀▀▀▀▀▀▀▀▀▀▀▀▀▀▀▀▀▀▀▀▀▀▀▀▀▀▀▀▀▀▀▀▀▀▀▀▀▀▀▀▀▀▀▀▀▀▀▀▐│
         │             Write Checks Screen                     │
         │                                                     │
         │  The Write Checks screen is where you write and     │
         │  review checks that Quicken will print or transmit. │
         │                                                     │
         │  Writing a Check                                    │
         │    To move from blank to blank, press ◄┘. When you  │
         │    have finished, press Ctrl ◄┘ or F10 to record    │
         │    the check. Recording saves the check in the      │
         │    Register and on disk.                            │
         │                                                     │
         │  Seeing the Checks You've Written                   │
         │    To review checks you've written but not yet printed, │
         │    press PgUp or PgDn as needed. After a check has   │
         │    been printed, it appears only in the Register.   │
         │                                                     │
         ├─────────────────────────────────────────────────────┤
         │ Esc-Cancel         F1-Help Index        ↓,PgDn-More │
         └─────────────────────────────────────────────────────┘
```

Figure 3-7 — Help Screen for Write Checks.

There are three ways to choose this selection:

- Press Ctrl-W.

- Type 1.

- Position the cursor on this selection and press Enter↵.

At the Write/Print Checks screen, you print checks by selecting **2** (Print Checks) from the F2-Acct/Print menu, or by pressing Ctrl-P. For more information on writing and printing checks, see Chapter 6.

Selection 2 — Register

Shortcut Keys:

`esc`	Returns you to previous screen or activity
`F1`	Help key
`Ctrl`-`F1`	Help Index
`Ctrl`-`A`	Select or setup an account
`Ctrl`-`B`	Find previous transaction (only from Register)
`Ctrl`-`C`	Select or setup a category
`Ctrl`-`D`	Delete transaction
`Ctrl`-`E`	Memorized Transactions list
`Ctrl`-`F`	Find transaction
`Ctrl`-`G`	Go to Date
`Ctrl`-`J`	Select transaction group
`Ctrl`-`L`	Select or setup a class
`Ctrl`-`M`	Memorize the transaction
`Ctrl`-`N`	Find next transaction
`Ctrl`-`O`	Calculator
`Ctrl`-`P`	Print Register
`Ctrl`-`S`	Split transaction
`Ctrl`-`T`	Memorized Transactions List
`Ctrl`-`U`	Back to Main Menu
`Ctrl`-`V`	Void a check
`Ctrl`-`W`	Record changes and leave transaction
`Ctrl`-`X`	Go to Transfer

Use the Register selection, [Ctrl]-[R], to enter checks you've already written or to continue using your present checkbook. The Register will help you keep an accurate record of the transactions in your checkbook, including ATM withdrawals, bank charges, and deposits. For other accounts, such as credit cards, the Register will be the way you enter most transactions associated with that account.

```
                        Using the Register

    The Register shows all transactions in the current
    account. You can review and change existing
    transactions and enter new ones.

    Use this quick key          To move
    ─────────────────────────────────────────────────────
    ↵, Tab                 To the next blank in a transaction
    Shift-Tab              To the previous blank in a
                              transaction
    ↑, ↓, ←, →             A space at a time
    Ctrl-→                 A word to the right
    Ctrl-←                 A word to the left
    Home, End              To the start/end of a blank
    Home-Home, End-End     To the first/last blank
    PgUp, PgDn             Up or down a screen's worth
    ─────────────────────────────────────────────────────
    Esc-Cancel              F1-Help Index          ↓,PgDn-More
```

Figure 3-8 — Help Screen for Using the Register.

There are three ways to choose this selection:

- Press [Ctrl]-[R].

- Type 2.

- Position the cursor on Register and press [Enter↵].

For more information on using the Register, see Chapter 5.

Selection 3 — Reports

Shortcut Keys:

`esc`	Returns you to previous screen or activity
`F1`	Help key
`Ctrl`-`F1`	Help Index
`Ctrl`-`A`	Select or setup an account
`Ctrl`-`O`	Calculator
`Ctrl`-`R`	Register
`Ctrl`-`W`	Write Checks Screen
`F7`	Edit budget amounts
`F8`	Customize report

The Reports menu (Main Menu selection 3) lets you choose the type of financial report you want to view and/or print (see Figure 3-9). There are five standard report forms for personal use, seven forms for business use, and five forms for investment use. In addition, Quicken provides four custom report types and allows you to customize any of the standard forms.

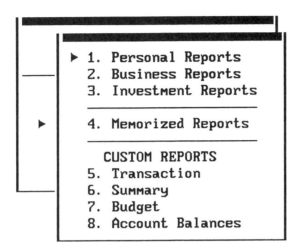

Figure 3-9 — The Reports Menu.

There are two ways to choose this selection:

- Type 3.

- Position the cursor on this selection and press [Enter←].

You can also access the reports menu by pressing [F5] from the Write Checks or Register windows. For more information on all types of reports, see Chapter 8.

Selection 4 — Select Account

Shortcut Keys:

[esc]	Returns you to previous screen or activity
[F1]	Help key
[Ctrl]-[F1]	Help Index
[Ctrl]-[D]	Delete transaction
[Ctrl]-[E]	Memorized Transactions list
[Ctrl]-[R]	Register
[Ctrl]-[W]	Write Checks Screen

Use Select Account, [Ctrl]-[A], to create a new account and to select an existing one (see Figure 3-10). Quicken has six account types: bank accounts, credit card accounts, cash accounts, other asset accounts, other liability accounts, and investment accounts.

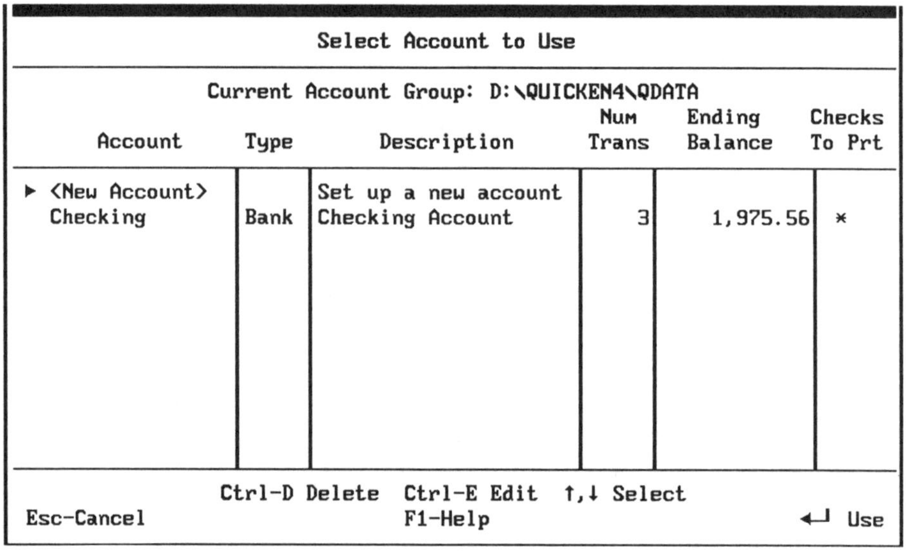

```
╔══════════════════════════════════════════════════════════════════╗
                          Select Account to Use
 ──────────────────────────────────────────────────────────────────
            Current Account Group: D:\QUICKEN4\QDATA
                                            Num   Ending    Checks
            Account    Type      Description  Trans  Balance   To Prt
 ──────────────────────────────────────────────────────────────────
  ► <New Account>            Set up a new account
    Checking       Bank   Checking Account      3    1,975.56    *




                  Ctrl-D Delete   Ctrl-E Edit  ↑,↓ Select
    Esc-Cancel                    F1-Help                    ←┘ Use
```

Figure 3-10 — The Select Account to Use Window.

There are three ways to choose Select Account:

- Press [Ctrl]-[A].
- Type 4.
- Position the cursor on Select Account and press [Enter←┘].

This is one of the few places where you cannot use [Ctrl]-[O] to call the calculator. For more information on setting up and using accounts, see Chapter 4.

Selection 5 — Change Settings

Shortcut Keys:

`esc`	Returns you to previous screen or activity
`F1`	Help key
`Ctrl`-`F1`	Help Index
`Ctrl`-`A`	Select or setup an account
`Ctrl`-`G`	Select or setup an account group (only at Main Menu)
`Ctrl`-`O`	Calculator
`Ctrl`-`R`	Register
`Ctrl`-`W`	Write Checks Screen

The Change Settings menu (Main Menu selection 5) allows you to customize Quicken for your own use. You can set the monitor screen colors and speed, set up printers and passwords, set up and maintain additional account groups, and use electronic bill payment (see Figure 3-11). For more information on Quicken settings and how to change them, see Chapter 7.

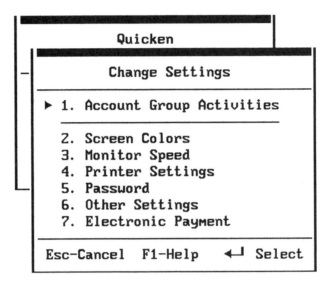

Figure 3-11 — Change Settings.

There are two ways to choose this selection:

- Type 5.
- Position the cursor on Change Settings and press Enter.

Selection E — Exit

Shortcut Keys:

Ctrl-B	Use to backup your files (only at Main Menu)
E	Use to exit the Quicken program
Ctrl-E	Use to exit and backup files on disk

Use Exit, (Main Menu selection E) to save all of your files, make backup copies, and exit to DOS. As previously discussed in Chapter 2, always exit the Quicken program from here.

There are two ways to exit the Quicken program:

- Press Ctrl-E to back up your data files and exit.
- Press E to exit without backup.

Pull-down Menus

The pull-down menus provide easy access to Quicken functions, options, and features (see Figure 3-12). The menus are accessible from the Write Checks window (Ctrl-W or Main Menu selection 1) and the Register window (Ctrl-R or Main Menu selection 2).

The bar at the top of the screen lists the function keys and menu titles. Press the appropriate function key to see a list of selections. Once you have a pull-down menu displayed, you can see other menu choices by pressing ← and →, or by pressing the appropriate function key.

Selection ⒡ — Help

Press ⒡, the first function key, to see a help screen of either the Write Checks or Register window (see Figure 3-12). You can press ⒡ at anytime to receive helpful information about the current window or screen.

```
                          Pull-down Menus

    Many of Quicken's features are available from "pull-down"
    menus listed at the top of the screen.

    To see a pull-down menu, press the function key, shown
    next to its name, such as F6 for the Activities menu.

    To select an item from a menu, type its number.

    To select an item without displaying the menu, press the
    appropriate "quick key." Quick keys are shown on the pull-
    down menus. They consist of Ctrl and a letter, such as
    Ctrl-S. That means to hold down the Ctrl key and press
    the S key.

    For a description of the items on a pull-down menu,
    press its function key and then press F1.

    Esc-Cancel              F1-Help Index
```

Figure 3-12 — Help Screen for pull-down menus.

For information about other Quicken features, press ⒞⒯⒭⒧-⒡ to see the Help index. Select a topic from the list to learn about something other than the current screen.

Selection ⁅F2⁆ — Acct/Print

This selection on the Pull Down Menu allows you to select accounts, print checks or the Register, change printer settings, back up all accounts, and export or import data (see Figure 3-13).

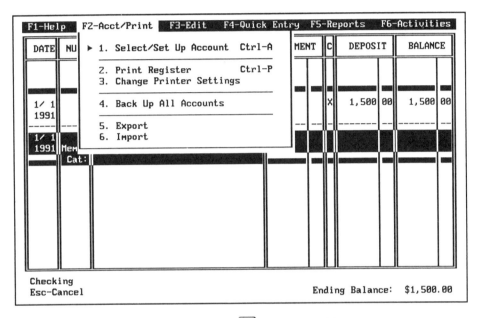

Figure 3-13 — The ⁅F2⁆-Acct/Print Menu.

1. **Select/set up account, ⁅Ctrl⁆-⁅A⁆**: Use this selection to create a new account and to select an existing one. For more information, see Chapter 4.

2. **Print Register (or Checks), ⁅Ctrl⁆-⁅P⁆**: Use this selection to print the Register and/or checks you have written. For more information on the Register, see Chapter 5. Writing and printing checks is discussed in detail in Chapter 6.

3. **Change printer settings**: This selection allows you to set up as many as three different printers. You can have one printer for printing checks, another for printing reports, and an alternate printer. This selection is the same as using the Change Settings selection on the Main Menu (see Figure 3-11). For more information, see Chapter 7.

4. **Back up all accounts**: Use this selection to back up your accounts while you are working in the Register or writing checks. If you are at the Main Menu, press [Ctrl]-[B] to back up your accounts without leaving the Quicken program.

5. **Exporting data**: Quicken allows you to export Register transactions into an ASCII file called QIF (Quicken Interchange Format). To do this, you specify a range of dates; all transactions within that range are exported.

6. **Importing data**: Quicken also allows you to import data from an ASCII file into a Quicken Register. If you use Quicken to transmit payments to CheckFree, you can import data from a CheckFree Register. For more information on using CheckFree, see Chapter 6.

There are several uses for exporting and importing data:

- Move data from one account to another. This is useful if you type transactions into the wrong Register. For example, you typed transactions into the Savings Register instead of the Checking Register. Instead of retyping the transactions in the Checking Register and deleting them from the Savings Register, export them from the Savings Register to an ASCII file and import the file into your Checking Register. Be sure to delete them from the Savings Register when you're finished.

- Change the account type or merge account groups. You can consolidate transactions from different places into one place.

- Add transactions from another program.

For more information on importing and exporting transactions, see Chapter 5.

Selection F3 — Edit

The Quicken commands listed on this selection of the pull-down menu make editing of transactions faster and easier (see Figure 3-14).

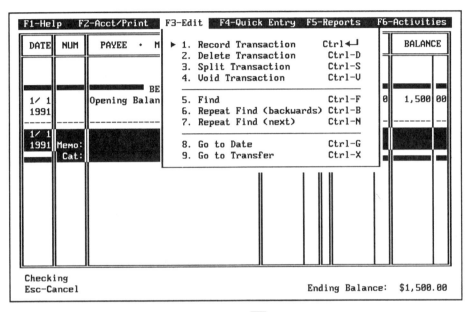

Figure 3-14 — The F3-Edit Menu.

1. **Record Transaction**, Ctrl - Enter⏎ : Tells the Quicken program you are finished and you want the transaction recorded.

2. **Delete Transaction**, Ctrl - D : Deletes the specified transaction.

3. **Split Transaction**, Ctrl - S : Allows you to split the amount of the transaction (check or deposit) between two or more categories and/or classes.

4. **Void Transaction**, Ctrl - V : Marks a check as void but retains a record of the check number. Use this command if you made a mistake while handwriting a check or stopped payment on a check.

5. **Find**, Ctrl - F : Allows you to search backward or forward for a specific transaction.

6. **Repeat Find — Backwards**, Ctrl-B: Allows you to search backwards to find a transaction.

7. **Repeat Find — Next**, Ctrl-N: Allows you to find the next transaction.

8. **Go to Date** Ctrl-G: Allows you to go to a specified date in the Register or Write Checks screen.

9. **Go to Transfer** Ctrl-X: When the cursor is positioned on a transfer transaction in a Register or Write Checks screen, this command will display the Register of the transfer transaction.

You will find more information on these Quick Keys in Chapter 5.

Selection F4 — Quick Entry

The Quick Entry menu helps you save time when entering repeated transactions such as rent or mortgage payments, utility bills, car payments, etc. (see Figure 3-15).

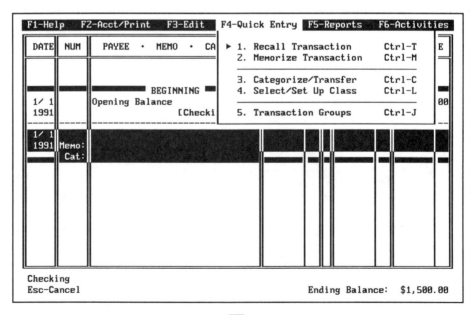

Figure 3-15 — The F4-Quick Entry Menu.

1. **Recall Transaction**, [Ctrl]-[T]: Lists all of the transactions you have memorized.

2. **Memorize Transaction**, [Ctrl]-[M]: Allows you to make a copy of a transaction from the Register or Write Checks screen. It can be one you just typed or one you entered earlier. The memorized transaction can be recalled at any time, entered into any account, and edited if necessary (as in the case of utility bills where the amount changes each month). For more information, see Chapter 5.

3. **Categorize/Transfer**, [Ctrl]-[C]: Displays a list of all categories and accounts. From the list, you can select a category for expenses, select an account for transfer, or set up a new category. For more information, see Chapters 4 and 5.

4. **Select/Set Up Class**, [Ctrl]-[L]: Displays a list of the classes you've set up. You can select a class or add a new one. See Chapter 4 for more information.

5. **Transaction Groups**, [Ctrl]-[J]: Displays a list of Transaction Groups you have set up. Transaction groups are groups of transactions that occur at the same time, such as payments due on the first or fifteenth of each month. Using Transaction Groups can save you time and keystrokes. For more information, see Chapter 5.

Selection F5 — Reports

This pull-down menu selection is the same as selection 3 of the Main Menu, and lets you choose the type of financial report you want to view and/or print (see Figure 3-16).

For more information on Reports, see Chapter 8.

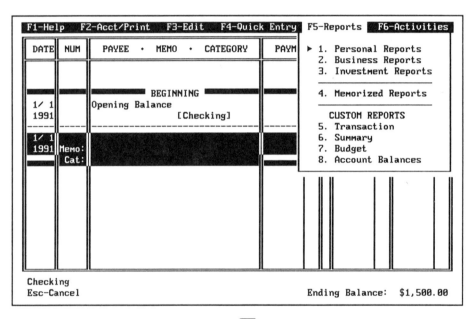

Figure 3-16 — The F5-Reports Menu.

Selection ⬚ — Activities

This pull-down menu gives you several options (see Figure 3-17). You can go to the Write Checks screen or the Register (depending on which window you're in), reconcile the Register, order Quicken checks, or use the calculator and DOS.

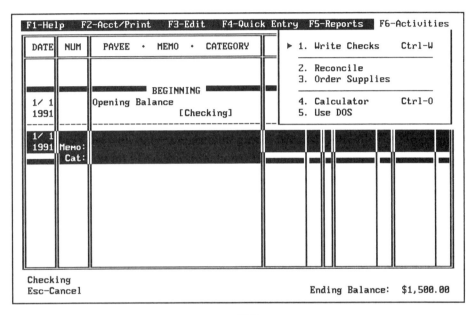

Figure 3-17 — The ⬚*-Activities Menu.*

1. **Write Checks or Register**, `Ctrl`-`W`: This selection gets you from the Write Checks screen to the Register or vice versa. For more information, see Chapters 5 and 6.

2. **Reconcile**: This selection allows you to reconcile the Quicken Register with your bank statement. See Chapter 5 for more information.

3. **Order Supplies**: This selection will allow you to print an order form (see Figure 3-18) for Quicken checks, envelopes, and other supplies, as well as product information and ordering instructions.

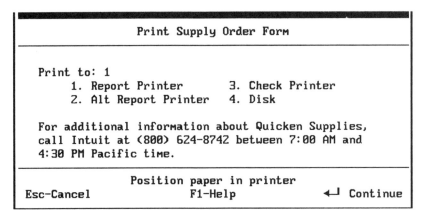

Print Supply Order Form

```
Print to: 1
        1. Report Printer      3. Check Printer
        2. Alt Report Printer  4. Disk

For additional information about Quicken Supplies,
call Intuit at (800) 624-8742 between 7:00 AM and
4:30 PM Pacific time.

              Position paper in printer
Esc-Cancel            F1-Help            ↵ Continue
```

Figure 3-18 — Print Supply Order Form.

4. **Calculator**, Ctrl-O: This selection will pop up the Calculator. See the section earlier in this chapter on the Quicken Calculator.

5. **Use DOS**: If you have at least 512K RAM, this selection allows you to temporarily leave Quicken without exiting the program. Choose this selection if you want to format disks for backup purposes or use another DOS function. To return to Quicken, type EXIT at the DOS prompt.

Summary

In this chapter you learned the basics of using Quicken. This done, you are encouraged to experiment with your dummy accounts, to play around with Quicken and become familiar with its features and the way it organizes your finances.

Chapter 4

Accounts, Categories, and Classes

Structuring your financial system may seem complicated. For example, you can have a transaction assigned to an account, a category, a subcategory, a class, and one or more subclasses. While this does indeed sound complex, Quicken does not require you to do all those things up front, so don't worry. Start out slowly and do what you can. If you're not sure what category or class to use, don't use one. You can assign them later, and you can change your mind at any time.

4 Accounts, Categories, and Classes

In this chapter, you will begin to get your financial house in order. You will learn how to define your income and expenses using: accounts, categories, subcategories, classes and subclasses. You will learn about:

- Accounts and Account types
- Adding and Deleting Accounts
- Changing Account Information
- Adding and Deleting Categories
- Changing Category Information
- Subcategories
- Requiring Categories in all transactions
- Adding and Deleting Classes
- Changing Class Information
- Subclasses
- Using Categories and Classes.

Shortcut Keys discussed in this chapter:

Ctrl-A	Select or setup an account
Ctrl-C	Select or setup a category
Ctrl-D	Delete an account, category, or class
Ctrl-E	Edit an account, category, or class
Ctrl-L	Select or setup a class
Ctrl-P	Print category or class list

Helpful Keys:

esc	Returns you to previous screen or activity
F1	Help key
Ctrl-F1	Help Index

Accounts, categories and classes will be discussed before you learn the details of transactions in the Register. This is for a good reason. It is important for you to understand these tools as you are entering your transactions. You will then be able to make better decisions about your transaction assignments.

Quicken will let you add, change, and delete things whenever you want. You can set up a category or class as you are entering a transaction. You can also edit a transaction you recorded earlier, assigning it to categories and/or classes that you set up after you recorded it. When you make a change, Quicken updates all appropriate records.

Start with your checking account. You will have a better understanding of how Quicken works, and how to better organize your accounts, after you have worked with your checkbook for a while. Figuring out categories and classes should become obvious as you work with your incomes and expenses.

Accounts

Quicken has six account types: bank accounts, credit card accounts, cash accounts, other asset accounts, other liability accounts, and investment accounts. You can set up as many accounts as you need, but you are limited to 255 accounts per account group.

It is best to start with only one account group, because you will want to produce reports based on all of your transactions. If you have business transactions that are separate from your personal transactions, however, you will probably want a different account group for each. If you do have more than one account group, be sure you've selected the right group before you set up a new account — Quicken always places a new account in the currently active account group. For more information about account groups, see Chapter 7.

Each account must have a name. The name must be unique (different from any other account or category on the list). The name should be meaningful, so you can properly identify it later from the Quicken menu. The name may consist of up to 15 characters, including letters, numbers, or other characters, except the left bracket ([ ), right bracket ( ]), forward slash (/), and colon (:).

If you try to give an account the same name as an existing Category, Quicken won't accept it (see Appendix B, for names of Quicken's standard categories). Give each account a name that clearly identifies it, such as "Tyler Checking," or "First Bank Chkg." This will avoid confusion. Use bank names if the accounts are in different banks, or use your name and your spouse's. The same goes for Credit Card Accounts; if you have two VISA cards, use the bank name as part of the account name, such as "First Visa."

What Account Type Should You Use?

Quicken's account types are as follows:

Bank Accounts:

> Set up separate Bank accounts for each of your checking, savings, and money market accounts. Most of us have a checking account, so it's best to start with that when you're learning how to use Quicken. After you've used Quicken for a while, you can set up other accounts.

Credit Card Accounts:

> Set up Credit Card accounts if:
>
> - You want records of every credit card transaction.
> - You want to know your credit card balance at all times.
> - You want records of some, but not all, credit card transactions.
> - You want to keep separate records for each year or other accounting period.
>
> If you pay your credit card balance in full every month, you may not need a separate account. You can handle your credit card payments with a category in the Register. If you want to keep records of a few credit card purchases, do it through the Register using a Split Transaction to charge different categories (see Split Transactions in Chapter 5).

Cash:

> Set up a Cash account if you want to keep detailed records of petty cash or cash expenditures.

- If you don't have a checking account, use a cash account to keep records of your spending. Save cash receipts and use them for entering transactions.

- If you want to track some cash expenses but don't want detailed records, set up a category to handle the petty cash records you want to keep. Assign all transactions involving cash to that category.

Generally speaking, the following account types should only be used by experienced Quicken users. For more information on these account types, see Chapter 9.

Other Asset:

> Set up an Other Asset account to track major assets — things like your house, automobile, accounts receivables, or capital equipment.

Other Liability:

> Set up an Other Liability to track major liabilities (things you owe) — things like mortgages or major bank loans.

Investment Accounts:

> Set up an Investment Account to keep track of your investments — things like stocks, bonds, mutual funds, and certificates of deposit.

Adding an Account

Shortcut Keys:

Ctrl - A   Select or setup an account

From the Main Menu, choose 4 (Select Account), or press Ctrl - A. The Select Account to Use screen will be displayed. Position the cursor at the first selection (New Account) and press Enter. The Set Up New Account screen will be displayed (see Figure 4-1).

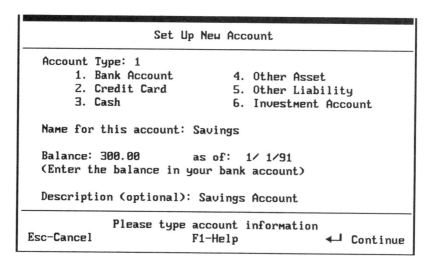

```
                    Set Up New Account

Account Type: 1
        1. Bank Account          4. Other Asset
        2. Credit Card           5. Other Liability
        3. Cash                  6. Investment Account

Name for this account: Savings

Balance: 300.00        as of:  1/ 1/91
(Enter the balance in your bank account)

Description (optional): Savings Account

              Please type account information
Esc-Cancel                 F1-Help              ↵ Continue
```

Figure 4-1 — The Set Up New Account Screen.

Enter your information, at the following prompts, to set up a new account.

- Account Type: Type the number (1 through 6) of the kind of account you want to set up.

- Name for this account: Use up to 15 characters, including letters, numbers, and spaces, and make the name unique and meaningful. Two accounts cannot have the same name and an account name cannot be the same as a category name.

- Enter a balance: Quicken requires a valid number here. If you aren't sure, enter 0.00 or make a guess. You can change it later. The following suggestions may help you decide.

    - Bank Accounts: enter the amount at the beginning of the accounting period (the first of the year or month); if it's a new account, enter the amount of the opening deposit; or enter the ending balance from your last bank statement.

    - Credit Card Accounts: enter the balance due from the last statement less any payments.

    - Cash Accounts: Enter the amount of cash you have on hand.

    - Other Asset Accounts: Enter the current value of the asset.

    - Other Liability Accounts: Enter the amount currently owed, principle and unpaid but accrued interest.

- As of what date?: Quicken will insert the current date, but you can change it. If you are entering transactions that have already occurred, use the date for the beginning of the period, such as 1/1/91.

- Description: (optional) You can use up to 20 characters. A description of your account is not required but you'll find it helpful to include something that further explains the account. If you are setting up bank or credit card accounts, you might use the account number as a description.

- Press [Enter⏎] to set up the account.

- If you are setting up a credit card account, you will be asked to enter the credit limit for this account. This information is optional. If you enter a credit limit, it will appear at the bottom of the Register when you select that account.

- Press [Enter⏎] to add this new account to the list of accounts.

Changing Account Information

Shortcut Keys:

[Ctrl]-[A] Select or setup an account

[Ctrl]-[E] Edit an account

If you want to change an account name, description, or credit limit, Quicken makes it easy.

- Press [Ctrl]-[A] to see the Select Account to Use list. Use [↑] and [↓] to position the cursor on the account you want to edit.
- Press [Ctrl]-[E] and the Edit Account Information window is displayed.
- Make changes to the account name and description and press [Enter←].
- If you selected a Credit card account, the Modify Credit window will be displayed. Make changes, if needed, and press [Enter←].

Quicken will update the account to reflect the new information. If you change the name of an account, Quicken will record the new name in all transactions assigned to it.

Deleting an Account

Shortcut Keys:

[Ctrl]-[A] Select or setup an account

[Ctrl]-[D] Delete an account

CAUTION: Be careful with this feature — once an account has been deleted, you can not get it back.

To delete an account:

- Press `Ctrl`-`A` for the Select Account to Use list. Use `↑` and `↓` to position the cursor on the account you want to edit.

- Press `Ctrl`-`D` to delete the account. A warning message will be displayed, showing the name of the account and asking you if you want to permanently delete the account.

- To delete the account, you must type "YES" in the blank and press `Enter←`. If you don't type "YES," the account will not be deleted.

- Press `F1` for Help or `esc` to cancel.

Categories

Quicken uses categories to help you specifically identify your income and expenses. Each transaction can be assigned to a category, making it possible for you to produce reports on every aspect of your finances.

Shortcut Keys:

`Ctrl`-`C`	Select or setup a category
`Ctrl`-`D`	Delete category
`Ctrl`-`E`	Edit a category
`Ctrl`-`P`	Print category list

The first time you used Quicken, you selected a predefined set of categories (home, business, or both) to use for your account. After working with Quicken for a while, however, you may have noticed that this predefined list was not exactly right for your needs. There were categories you never used, and categories you may have wished you had. Now is the time to make this list into exactly what you need. For reference, a complete list of standard categories is listed in Appendix B.

- From the Register or Write Checks screen, press Ctrl-C to see the Category and Transfer List (Figure 4-2).

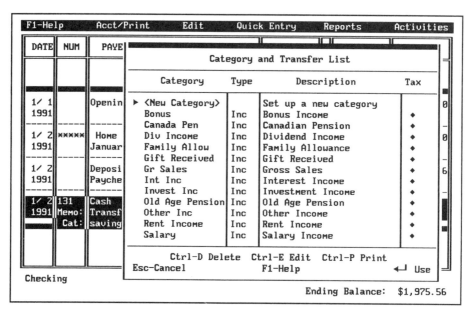

Figure 4-2 — The Category and Transfer List.

- Use ↑ and ↓ to scroll through the list. Each category has a name, type, description, and tax notation. Categories are listed alphabetically, with income categories first, followed by expenses, subcategories, and accounts. Accounts appear on this list to enable you to make transfers to them. For more information on Transfer of Funds, see Chapter 5.

- If you want to print a paper copy of the Category and Transfer List, press Ctrl-P. Answer the questions as to where to print the list (see Figure 4-3) and press Ctrl-Enter.

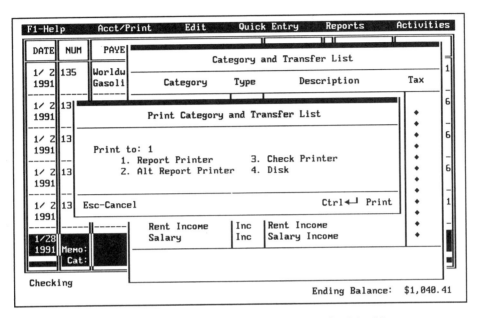

Figure 4-3 — The Print Category and Transfer List Menu.

Adding Categories

To add categories.

- From the Register or Write Checks screen, press [Ctrl]-[C] to see the Category and Transfer List. Or press [F4] (Quick Entry Menu) and choose selection 3 — Categorize/Transfer.

- The first line of the Category and Transfer List says <New Category>. Position the cursor here, and press [Enter◄—].

- The Set Up Category screen will be displayed (see Figure 4-4).

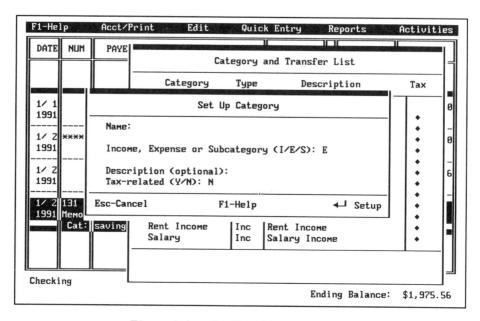

Figure 4-4 — Set Up a New Category.

All categories are classified as income, expense, or subcategory and each has a tax status. Type in the following information for each new category.

- Name: Use up to 15 characters, including numbers, letters, spaces, and characters, except the left bracket ([ ), right bracket ( ]), forward slash (/), and colon (:). Make the name unique and meaningful.

- Income, Expense, or Subcategory: All categories need a classification. Quicken uses classifications for printing reports that include totals for income and expenses. Type:

  - **I** for an Income category, includes salary or wages, bonus, dividends, and interest or gifts received.

  - **E** for an Expense category, includes medical, gasoline, food, insurance, and utilities.

  - **S** for a Subcategory, used to give more detailed information about your transaction. Subcategories are described in more detail later in this chapter.

- Description: (Optional) Use up to 25 characters to describe the category. Although Quicken doesn't require you to fill in this field, you may find it helpful later on.

- Tax-related: Type Y if the category is tax-related, or N if the category is not tax-related. Interest income, salary, charitable donations, and medical expenses are used when preparing taxes. By marking the category as tax-related, Quicken will help you identify these transactions and provide totals. For more information, see Chapter 7. Business users should note that all business categories are tax-related.

- Press  to set up the category.

Changing Category Information

If the category description you used isn't exactly clear, or you want to change the category name, or you made a typing error, Quicken makes it easy to edit the information in a Category:

- From the Register or Write Checks screen, press Ctrl-C to see the Category and Transfer List.

- Use ↑ and ↓ to scroll through the list. Position the cursor on the category you want to change.

- Press Ctrl-E to see the category information. Type in your changes, and press Enter to record the new information.

Deleting Categories

If you find that you no longer need a Category, you can delete it.

Caution: Make very certain you want to delete a category, because once it is deleted, it is gone and can not be brought back.

- From the Register or Write Checks screen, press Ctrl-C to see the Category and Transfer List.

- Use ↑ and ↓ to scroll through the list. Position the cursor on the category you want to delete.

- Press ⌈Ctrl⌉-⌈D⌉. A warning message appears on the screen (see Figure 4-5).

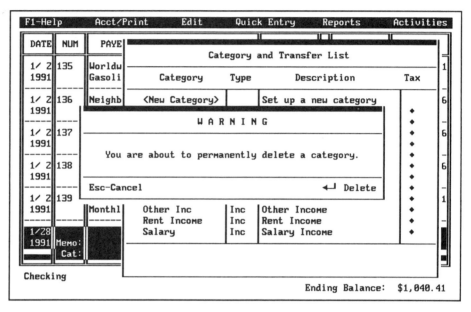

Figure 4-5 — Delete Category Warning Message.

- To delete the category, press ⌈Enter◄─┘⌉.
- If you do not want to delete this category, press ⌈esc⌉.

Subcategories

Subcategories can help you to further identify income and expenses. One good example is Utilities. Quicken has a separate category for telephone expenses, so these can be tracked. The rest of your utilities, including electricity, water, sewer, gas, and cable television, are only tracked as a lump sum total. If you want to know exactly how much you are spending on each utility, you must set up a subcategory for each separate utility.

To set up a subcategory, begin by following the instructions for setting up a category. At the line Income, Expense, or Subcategory (I/E/S): type S. Subcategories have no further classification and can be used with either income or expense categories. The first time you set up a subcategory, you'll see a special screen (see Figure 4-6).

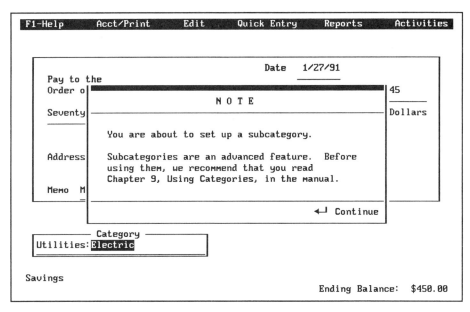

Figure 4-6 — The Subcategory Special Screen.

To assign a subcategory to a transaction entered at the Register or Write Checks screen, position the cursor in the Category blank. Enter the category name, a colon [:], and the subcategory name. Do not use spaces. For example, Utilities:Phone or Utilities:Water.

Subcategories can be used to identify many things. If you own rental properties, use subcategories to separate income and expenses for each property. You can use subcategories to identify income and expenses for each member of the family.

Requiring Categories in All Transactions

You can set Quicken to require a category in every transaction except transfers. This is because Transfers use the name of another account in the Category blank (see Transfer of Funds in Chapter 5). When Quicken is set to require a category and you leave the Category blank, it will ask you to confirm that you want no category in the transaction.

To make this setting, use the Other Settings selection at the Change Settings menu. For more information, see Chapter 7.

Classes

Shortcut Keys:

[Ctrl]-[D] Delete a class

[Ctrl]-[E] Edit a class

[Ctrl]-[L] Select or setup a class

[Ctrl]-[P] Print class list

Quicken classes are similar to categories but they're used to identify the who, what, where, or when of a transaction. Classes have no classification, such as income, expense, or tax-related, and can be used alone or with categories to help you to identify transactions more specifically (see Figure 4-7).

```
                              Classes

     Classes work together with categories to provide
     additional flexibility in organizing and reporting on
     your transactions. Unlike categories, which specify what
     a transaction is for, classes are used to specify who,
     where, or when.

     For example, you could set up classes for the names of
     each of several properties that you manage.

     To enter a class, type it in the category blank following
     the category itself, separated from it by the '/'
     character. For example, Utilities/Elm Road.

     Alternatively, you can have Quicken insert the class for
    ─────────────────────────────────────────────────────────
     Esc-Cancel              F1-Help Index          ↓,PgDn-More
```

Figure 4-7 — Help Screen for Quicken Classes.

You can add, delete, or make changes to classes at any time.

Adding a Class

There are no standard classes in Quicken so you must set up your own. Quicken makes this task easy. Setting up a class is similar to setting up a category, but less information is needed.

Note: When naming classes, remember that the Category blank will only hold 31 characters. If you use a category, a subcategory, a class, and one or more subclasses (each of which can have a name up to 15 characters long), you will quickly run out of space. If classes are to be used, it is advisable to keep the names short and rely on a good description to discern which class does what.

At the Register or Write Checks screen, press Ctrl-L to see the Class List (see Figure 4-8). Or press F4 (Quick Entry Menu) and choose selection 4 — Select/Set Up Class.

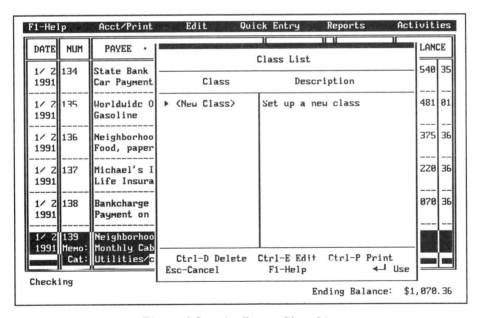

Figure 4-8 — An Empty Class List.

- The first line of the Class List says <New Class>. Position the cursor here and press ⌜Enter⏎⌝.

- The Set Up Class screen will appear (see Figure 4-9).

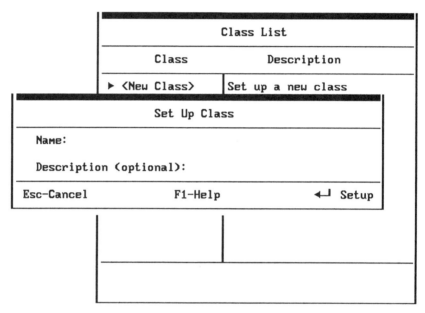

Figure 4-9 — Set Up a Class.

- Type a Name: Use up to 15 characters, including numbers, letters, spaces, and characters, except the left bracket ([ ), right bracket ( ]), forward slash (/), and colon (:). Make the name unique and meaningful.

- Type a Description: (Optional) Use up to 25 characters to describe the class. Although Quicken doesn't require you to fill in this field, you may find it helpful later.

- Press ⌜Enter⏎⌝ to set up the Class.

If you want to print a copy of the Class List, press ⌜Ctrl⌝-⌜P⌝. Answer the question as to where to print the list, and press ⌜Ctrl⌝-⌜Enter⏎⌝.

Changing Class Information

If you need to edit the information in a Class, because the description isn't clear or you made some typing errors, Quicken makes it easy to do.

- From the Register or Write Checks screen, press Ctrl-L to see the Class List.

- Use ↑ and ↓ to scroll through the list. Position the cursor on the class you want to change.

- Press Ctrl-E to see the class information. Type in any desired changes and press Enter↵ to record the new information.

Deleting Classes

If you find that you don't need a Class any more, you can delete it. But make sure you really don't need it. Once it is gone, you can not bring it back.

- From the Register or Write Checks screen, press Ctrl-L to see the Class List.

- Use ↑ and ↓ to scroll through the list. Position the cursor on the class you want to delete.

- Press Ctrl-D. A warning message appears on the screen similar to the one in Figure 4-5.

- If you don't want to delete this class, press esc.

- To delete the class, press Enter↵.

Subclasses

You set up a subclass the same way you set up a class. Subclasses are typically used to produce reports that group and subtotal similar classes.

There is nothing to differentiate a class from a subclass except in the way you use it.

Using Categories and Classes

At the Register or Write Checks screen, position the cursor in the Category blank.

- To use a category with a class:
    - Type the name of the category in the Category blank.
    - Type a forward slash [/].
    - Type the name of the class.
- To use a class with no category:
    - Type a forward slash [/].
    - Type the name of the class.

In the Category blank, Quicken treats anything typed after a [/] as a class. If there is no [/], Quicken treats it as a category.

To use categories and subcategories in the Category blank, separate them with a colon [:].

To use classes and subclasses in the Category blank, separate them with a colon [:]. You can use more than one subclass in a transaction but remember that the category field in the Register and on a check is only 31 characters long. If you try to type too many classes and subclasses, it won't fit. Use the most general class first because Quicken uses the first class name as the primary class, when preparing class reports. For example, if Tyler had expenses at the dentist and Elizabeth at the doctor, you would type Medical/Tyler:Dentist or Medical/Dentist:Tyler (depending on which is to be the primary class) and Medical/Elizabeth:Doctor or Medical/Doctor:Elizabeth.

Summary

Accounts are sets of transactions grouped by categories, subcategories, classes and subclasses. Additionally, accounts may, themselves, be grouped into account groups. All these classifications are designed to help you differentiate your transactions into meaningful reports: Total income and expenses, by category; Itemized expenses, by class; and so on. And if the reports you get are not what you want, all of these groupings are easily changed and/or rearranged.

Chapter 5

Transactions and the Register

The Register is the backbone of any accounting system. Whether on paper or computer, the Register is the worksheet upon which the transactions, or entries, are recorded. In this chapter you will learn about:

- The Register
- Entering and Manipulating Transactions
- How to Transfer Funds
- Split Transactions, Ctrl - S
- Memorized Transactions
- Reconciling and Balancing the Register
- Printing Transactions in the Register
- Exporting and Importing Transactions
- Transaction Groups.

Shortcut Keys discussed in this chapter:

[esc]	Returns you to previous screen or activity
[F1]	Help key
[Ctrl]-[F1]	Help Index
[Ctrl]-[A]	Select or setup an account
[Ctrl]-[B]	Find previous transaction (only from Register)
[Ctrl]-[C]	Select or setup a category
[Ctrl]-[D]	Delete transaction
[Ctrl]-[E]	Edit a Transaction Group
[Ctrl]-[F]	Find transaction
[Ctrl]-[G]	Go to Date
[Ctrl]-[J]	Select transaction group
[Ctrl]-[L]	Select or setup a class
[Ctrl]-[M]	Memorize the transaction
[Ctrl]-[N]	Find next transaction
[Ctrl]-[O]	Calculator
[Ctrl]-[P]	Print Register
[Ctrl]-[R]	Go to Register
[Ctrl]-[S]	Split transaction
[Ctrl]-[T]	Memorized Transactions List
[Ctrl]-[X]	Go to Transfer
Arrow Keys	Move cursor one line or space at a time
[+] (Plus)	Increase date or check number
[-] (minus)	Decrease date or check number
[PgUp], [PgDn]	Move up or down one screen at a time
[Ctrl]-[PgUp]	Go to beginning of previous month
[Ctrl]-[PgDn]	Go to beginning of next month
[Ctrl]-[home]	Go to beginning of Register

`Ctrl`-`end`	Go to end of Register
`F10`	Record the transaction
`Ctrl`-`Enter←`	Record the transaction
`.``.` (two periods)	Represents the unknown portion of a field
`?`	Represents an unknown character
`~`	Used in reports to exclude certain transactions
`"`	Repeats Category and Class name in a Split

The Register

The Quicken Register contains the record of all transactions in an account, just as your paper register contains all of the transactions in your checking account. The Register is used the same way, too. All transactions, such as checks written by hand, deposits, ATM withdrawals, and bank charges must be entered in the Register so your account balance will be accurate.

Quicken's Register has several advantages over your paper register.

- Quicken does all the arithmetic calculations for you, so there are no mistakes in addition or subtraction.

- Quicken automatically arranges your transactions in chronological order by date and check number no matter how you enter them.

- You can add, change, or delete transactions at any time. Quicken will recalculate your balance.

- You can print a copy of the Register at any time (see Printing the Register, later in this chapter).

Use the Register option, `Ctrl`-`R`, to enter checks you've already written, even if you want to continue using your present hand written check register book. The Register will help you keep an accurate record of the transactions in your checkbook, including ATM withdrawals, bank charges, and deposits. For other accounts, such as credit cards, the Register is the way you enter transactions into the account.

If you are going to use Quicken's check writing feature to automatically print checks, enter any checks that you've already written into the Register. When you start using the Write/Print Checks option, the checks you write with Quicken will be automatically entered in the Register. That way, you'll have all of your transactions recorded and can accurately produce the reports you want.

Every Quicken account has a Register and all registers work the same. In this chapter, we will work only with the Check Register (see Figure 5-1).

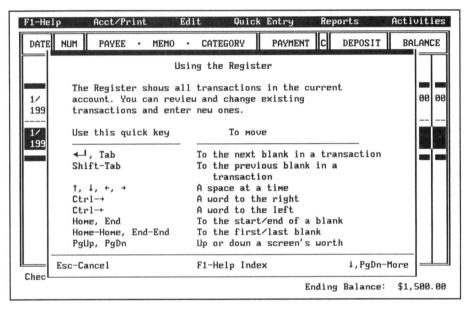

Figure 5-1 — Quicken's Help Screen for the Register.

As you can see from Figure 5-2, the Charge Card Register, and Figure 5-3, the Cash Account register, the three registers differ only in the names of three of their fields.

All three registers have fields for date, payee, memo, category, cleared, and balance. The Check Register has named the three remaining fields Num, Payment, and Deposit; the Charge Card register calls them Ref, Charge, and Payment; and the Cash Account register calls them Ref, Spend, and Receive.

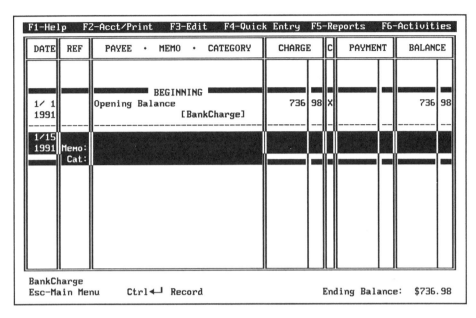

Figure 5-2 — A Charge Card Register.

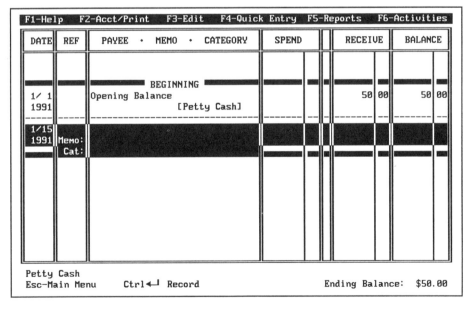

Figure 5-3 — A Cash Account Register.

Transactions

A transaction is the basic unit in your financial picture. Quicken uses transactions to organize your data. The following are examples of transactions:

- a check you wrote.
- a bank deposit.
- a bank service charge.
- a purchase you charged to your credit card.
- an ATM withdrawal.

Shortcut Keys:

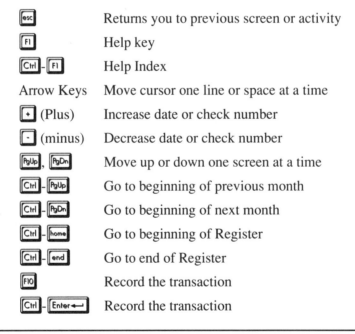

[esc]	Returns you to previous screen or activity
[F1]	Help key
[Ctrl]-[F1]	Help Index
Arrow Keys	Move cursor one line or space at a time
[+] (Plus)	Increase date or check number
[-] (minus)	Decrease date or check number
[PgUp], [PgDn]	Move up or down one screen at a time
[Ctrl]-[PgUp]	Go to beginning of previous month
[Ctrl]-[PgDn]	Go to beginning of next month
[Ctrl]-[home]	Go to beginning of Register
[Ctrl]-[end]	Go to end of Register
[F10]	Record the transaction
[Ctrl]-[Enter←]	Record the transaction

Each transaction belongs to account. You can't write or print a check or enter a deposit or service charge in the Register until you open an account. When you first use Quicken, you are asked to select an account, [Ctrl]-[A]. On each subsequent use, however, Quicken will assume you want to use the last account you worked with.

If you ended the last Quicken session working with an account named Checking1, and you want to continue working with that account, you only have to start Quicken and you're there. Press [Ctrl]-[R], at the Main Menu, and the Register for Checking1 will be displayed. If you want to work with a different account, press [Ctrl]-[A], select the account you want to work with, and press [Enter◄─┘]. The Register for that account will be displayed.

You can start your Quicken accounts from any date, even one from a year or more ago. Pick a starting date, such as the first of the month or a new year. Type in the transactions that occurred on and after that day and ignore all others.

Note: Always enter new transactions at the blank line at the end of the Register. Don't worry if your transactions aren't in chronological order. Quicken will place them in order according to the date and check number (if applicable) within that date. And Quicken will automatically calculate or recalculate your balance with every transaction.

Adding a Transaction

Press [Ctrl]-[R] to see the Check Register. Enter your transaction as follows:

- **Date**: At the beginning of each session, Quicken enters the current date here. After the session is begun, the last date used will be displayed. To change the date, press [+] (plus) to increase it or [-] (minus) to decrease it. Or type in the date you want, including the [/] between month, day, and year. Press [Enter◄─┘] to move to the next blank.

  - You enter post-dated items as you would any other entry. When the transaction is recorded, it will appear in the Register with the date highlighted and a double line separating it from the rest of the transactions.

- **Num**: When entering checks you've already written, type the check number here. If you previously entered some of your checks, press [+]. Quicken will automatically enter the number of the last check plus one in this blank. For subsequent checks, use the [+] and [-] keys to increase or decrease the number. Press [Enter◄─┘] to move to the next blank.

  - You can have Quicken warn you when you use duplicate check numbers. For more information, see Chapter 7.

- **Payee**: If you're entering a check, type the name of the payee. For other transactions, type some word or phrase to identify the transaction, such as deposit, bank charge, service charge, ATM withdrawal, or check charge. Press ⟦Enter⬑⟧ to move to the next blank.

- **Payment**: If you are entering a check or other payment such as bank or service charge, type the amount. (If you are entering a deposit, don't type anything here. Press ⟦Enter⬑⟧ to continue.)

  The maximum amount allowed for a transaction is $9,999,999.99. You don't need to type dollar signs and commas. You need to type the decimal point only if the number is a combination of dollars and cents. For example:

  - to enter $1,500.00, type 1500

  - to enter $123.45, type 123.45

  - to enter $50.00, type 50

- **C**: (for Cleared) This column will show an X or an * (asterisk) when transactions have cleared your bank (see Reconciling the Register, later in this chapter). When entering transactions, you won't usually type anything in this field. Press ⟦Enter⬑⟧ to move to the next blank.

- **Deposit**: If this transaction is a deposit, type the amount using the same guidelines as for a payment. If you are entering a check or other payment, don't type anything in this blank. Press ⟦Enter⬑⟧ to move to the next blank.

- **Memo**: (Optional) Type any word or phrase to describe the transaction. Quicken doesn't require that you use this field, but you may later find it helpful if you provide a brief description. Press ⟦Enter⬑⟧ to move to the next blank.

- **Category**: (Optional) This is where you type the category information, but remember that you're limited to 31 characters. You have several options here:

- You can assign the transaction to one or more of the following: category, subcategory, class, and subclass. Press [Ctrl]-[C] to see the Category and Transfer List and [Ctrl]-[L] to see the Class List. For more information on categories and classes, see Chapter 4.

- You can make the transaction a transfer. For more information, see the section on Transfer of Funds, later in this chapter.

- You can split the transaction, [Ctrl]-[S], and assign it to two or more categories. A Split Transaction can include a transfer. For more information, see the section on Split Transactions, later in this chapter).

If you type in a category or class that doesn't exist, Quicken will tell you that it could not be found (see Figure 5-4). You can add it to the list at this time or select another.

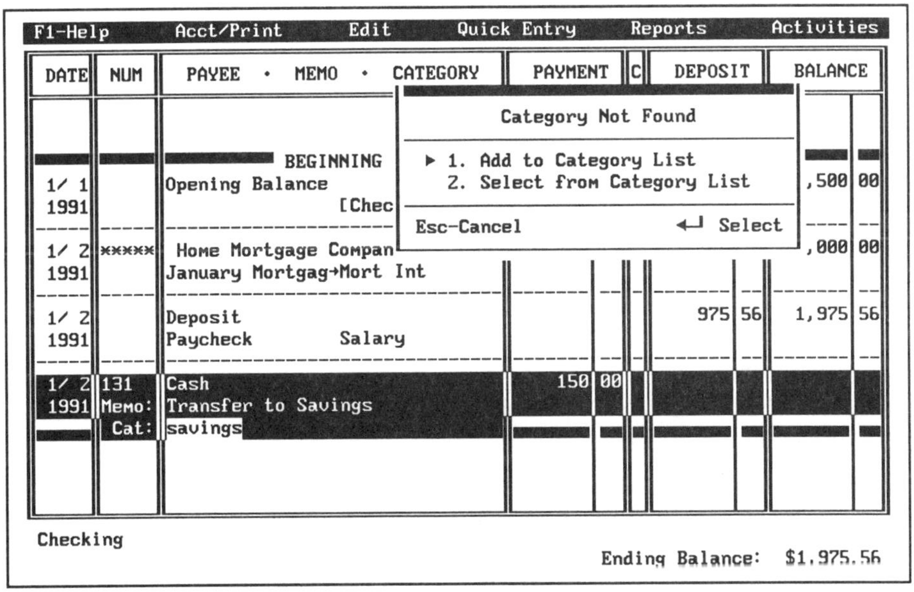

F1-Help		Acct/Print	Edit	Quick Entry	Reports		Activities
DATE	NUM	PAYEE • MEMO •	CATEGORY	PAYMENT	C	DEPOSIT	BALANCE

```
                                    Category Not Found

                    BEGINNING   ▶ 1. Add to Category List
 1/ 1       Opening Balance        2. Select from Category List    ,500 00
 1991                   [Chec   
                                  Esc-Cancel              ↵ Select
 1/ 2 xxxxx Home Mortgage Compan                                    ,000 00
 1991       January Mortgag→Mort Int

 1/ 2       Deposit                                      975 56   1,975 56
 1991       Paycheck        Salary

 1/ 2 131   Cash                              150 00
 1991 Memo: Transfer to Savings
      Cat:  savings
```

Checking

Ending Balance: $1,975.56

Figure 5-4 — Quicken Can Not Find the Category.

- Press [F10] or [Ctrl]-[Enter↵] to record the transaction. Quicken will ask you to confirm the record (see Figure 5-5). Or press [esc] to cancel and return to the transaction for editing or [Enter↵] to record it.

```
┌─────────────────────────────────────────────────────────────────────┐
│ F1-Help      Acct/Print      Edit      Quick Entry    Reports   Activities │
│ ┌──────┬─────┬──────────────────────────────────┬─────────┬─┬─────────┬─────────┐ │
│ │ DATE │ NUM │ PAYEE  ·  MEMO  ·  CATEGORY      │ PAYMENT │C│ DEPOSIT │ BALANCE │ │
│ │      │     │                                  │         │ │         │         │ │
│ │      │     │        BEGINNING                 │         │ │         │         │ │
│ │ 1/ 1 │     │Opening Balance                   │         │X│ 1,500 00│ 1,500 00│ │
│ │ 1991 │     │                                  │         │ │         │         │ │
│ │ 1/ 2 │xxxxx│Home Mort    OK to Record Transaction?        │         │ 1,000 00│ │
│ │ 1991 │     │January Mo                        │         │ │         │         │ │
│ │      │     │           ▶ 1. Record transaction            │         │         │ │
│ │      │     │             2. Do not record                 │         │         │ │
│ │ 1/ 2 │Memo:│Deposit                           │         │ 975 56│         │ │
│ │ 1991 │Cat: │Paycheck   Esc-Cancel F1-Help  ↵ Select       │         │         │ │
│ │      │     │Salary                            │         │ │         │         │ │
│ └──────┴─────┴──────────────────────────────────┴─────────┴─┴─────────┴─────────┘ │
│ Checking                                                                │
│                                        Ending Balance:  $1,000.00      │
└─────────────────────────────────────────────────────────────────────┘
```

Figure 5-5 — OK to Record Transaction?

When you record the transaction, Quicken will place it where it belongs in the Register (chronologically by date and then by check number if there is one) and recalculate the balance. As Quicken does this, you'll hear a beep and see the word "Recording" flash at the lower left corner of the screen. If the transaction has to be moved to the correct date, you may see the word "Moving". You may not see these messages if your computer is very fast, but you will hear the beep.

Finding Transactions

You can look through and review transactions in the Register at any time. If you are looking for a specific transaction, Quicken has two Quick Keys to help you find it: Ctrl-F to find a transaction, and Ctrl-G to go to a date.

84

Find a transaction

Shortcut keys:

Ctrl-F	Find a Transaction
Ctrl-B	Search backward
Ctrl-D	Erase contents of window
Ctrl-N	Search forward

This feature is listed on the F3-Edit menu but it is much faster to use the Quick Keys. Press Ctrl-F to see the Transaction to Find window (see Figure 5-6).

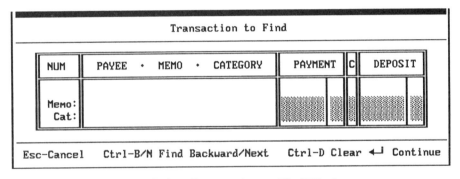

Figure 5-6 — Transaction to Find Window.

The Transaction to Find window contains the following fields:

- **NUM**: If you want to find a specific check, type the check number here. Press Enter to continue.

- **Payee**: This field is the first line of the second column. Type the exact name of the payee if you're looking for a check; the exact description if it was a deposit or a bank charge; or a key word match. (See the section on Key Word Matching, later in this chapter.) Press Enter to continue.

- **Memo**: Use the second line of the second column to type the text of the memo in the transaction you want to find. You can also use a key word match here. Press Enter to continue.

- **Category**: Use the third line of the second column to search for a category and class. If you don't remember the entire category and class assignment, use a key word match. You can search for an account if the transaction involved a transfer, but you don't need to type brackets. Press [Enter⬅] to continue.

- **Payment**: If you are looking for a specific amount, type it here. Press [Enter⬅] to continue.

- C (Cleared): You can look for cleared transactions by typing X in this column. Type a period [.] to look for uncleared transactions. Type an asterisk [*] to find transactions marked with an asterisk. Press [Enter⬅] to continue.

- **Deposit**: Type the amount in this column if you are looking for a specific deposit. Press [Enter⬅] to continue.

Quicken now queries which way you want to search (see Figure 5-7). Move the cursor to the desired choice, or press [Ctrl]-[B] to search backward or [Ctrl]-[N] to find the next. After you've found the first occurrence of the search criteria, you can continue by pressing [Ctrl]-[B] if you're searching backwards, or [Ctrl]-[N] if you're searching forward.

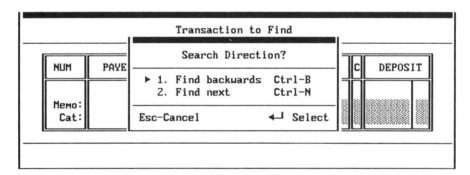

Figure 5-7 — Search Direction for Finding a Transaction.

If you use the Transaction to Find window more than once during a Quicken session, it may retain information from a previous use. Press [Ctrl]-[D] to erase the old data and enter your new information.

Go to date

This Quicken feature will help you find a transaction when you know the date. Press [Ctrl]-[G] or select Go to Date from the [F3]-Edit menu. The Go to Date window will be displayed (see Figure 5-8).

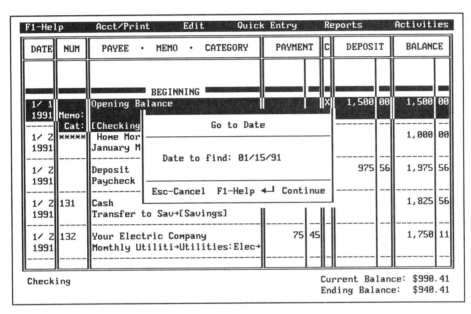

Figure 5-8 — Go to Date Window.

Type the date you want to find and press [Enter←]. Quicken will highlight the first transaction in the Register with that date, or the transaction closest to it if there are no transactions with that date.

Key word match

Shortcut keys:

⟦.⟧⟦.⟧   (Two periods) Represents the unknown portion of a field

⟦?⟧   (Question mark) Represents an unknown character

⟦~⟧   (Tilde) Used in reports to exclude certain transactions

---

In order to find a specific transaction, you need to know precisely what you're looking for. If you remember exactly how the transaction was worded, you will have no trouble finding it. But, if you can't remember the exact sequence of words and letters, Quicken will not be able to find your match.. To help you find the transaction, you can use what Quicken calls a "key word match."

If you want to look for a check that you wrote to someone named Jones but can't remember his first name, the "key word match" will help you find it. When searching for a match, Quicken ignores any spaces before or after the key phrase and ignores upper and lower case.

Use two periods [..] to represent the unknown portion of a name. Typing:

..Jones   will find Casey Jones and John H. Jones.

Jones..   will find Jones Hardware and Jones Plumbing.

..Jones..   will find Robert A. Jones, M.D., as well as the first four examples.

Use a question mark [?] as a substitute for one character. You can use this if you have categories that represent two or more cars, such as Car1 or Car2. Or you might be looking for a Transfer transaction assigned to Checking1 or Checking2. Typing:

Car?   will find Car1 and Car2.

Bank???   will find Bankers and Banking, but not Bank.

You can also use key word matches when you are preparing custom reports. You might want to produce a report that includes some transactions but not all. You can tell Quicken to exclude certain transactions by using a tilde [~] in the Memo or Category fields.

~.. In the Category field will find transactions not assigned to categories.

~.. In the Memo field will find transactions with nothing in that field.

Changing a Transaction

There will be times when you'll need to change part of a transaction. Quicken makes this easy to do. You can edit any field in a transaction except the Balance. To change that you must enter a payment or deposit.

- Press [Ctrl]-[R] to see the Check Register. Position the cursor on the transaction you want to change. Use [Ctrl]-[F] (Find Transaction), [Ctrl]-[G] (Go to Date), or the [PgUp], [PgDn], and arrow keys to find it.

- Press [Enter←] or [tab] to position the cursor on the field you want to change. If needed, use the arrow keys to position the cursor on a character within the field.

- Make the necessary additions or corrections:

    - To overwrite existing characters, turn [ins] off and type the new information. Use [space] and [delete] as needed.

    - To insert characters, turn [ins] on and type the information.

- Press [F10] or [Ctrl]-[Enter←] to record the changes. Quicken will ask you if you want to record the transaction. Press [esc] to cancel and return to the transaction for more editing or [Enter←] to record it.

If you make changes in a transaction and use [↑] and [↓] to leave the transaction (instead of [Enter←]), a screen will appear informing you that you are leaving the transaction (see Figure 5-9). Type 1 to record the changes and leave or 2 to cancel the changes and leave.

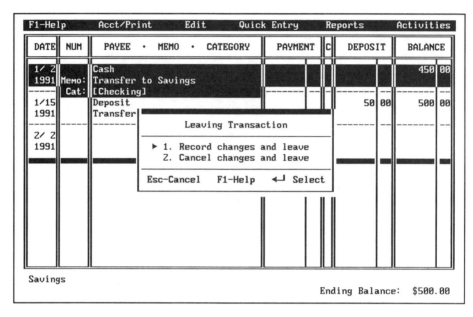

Figure 5-9 — Leaving an Edited Transaction.

Deleting a Transaction

CAUTION: If you delete a transaction, it is gone forever and you cannot recover it.

If you must delete a transaction:

- Press Ctrl-R to see the Check Register. Position the cursor on the transaction you want to delete. Use Ctrl-F (Find Transaction), Ctrl-G (Go to Date), or the PgUp, PgDn, and arrow keys to find it.

- Press Ctrl-D or select Delete Transaction on the F2-Edit menu.

- The OK to Delete Transaction window (see Figure 5-10) will appear. Notice that Delete transaction is highlighted.

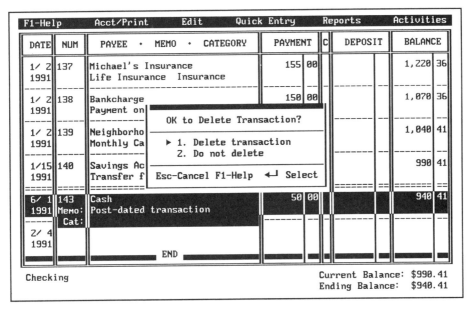

Figure 5-10 — Deleting a Transaction.

- To delete the transaction, press 1 or Enter⏎. Quicken deletes the transaction and recalculates the balance as necessary. Press esc or 2 to cancel and Quicken will return you to the Register.

Transfer of Funds

This is one of the time-saving features. It is especially nice if you regularly write checks to transfer money from one account to another. Suppose you write a check to deposit money into your savings account. Or maybe you and your spouse have two checking accounts, with one used as a holding or savings account (as in an interest bearing checking account), and the other for paying expenses. You may also have a Petty Cash account that occasionally needs replenishing. With the Quicken transfer feature, you won't have to enter the transaction twice. Quicken will do it for you.

You cannot assign a category to the transaction when it is transferred. Transfer is the category, and Quicken won't let you assign it to another category. If you need to have all transactions assigned to income or expense categories, enter each part (the check and the deposit) as a separate transaction. Assign each transaction to one or more categories as appropriate.

How to Transfer Funds

If you wrote a check to deposit money into your savings account:

- Enter the transaction in your checking account register as usual. Type in the date, check number, payee, payment, and memo (perhaps "Transfer of Funds" or "To Savings").

- At the Category blank, type the name of your savings account. Don't type any symbols or other characters. Press Enter⏎.

  - Quicken will insert square brackets ([ ]) before and after the account name and ask if it's okay to record the transaction.

  - If you have not yet set up this account, you'll see the Category Not Found screen. Set up your savings account at this time, so you can complete the transfer.

  - There are three other ways to type an account name in the Category field:

    - Type the first three or four letters of the account name and press Enter⏎.

    - Type a right-facing bracket ([ ) and the first two or more characters of the account name and press Enter⏎. If Quicken can find the category using the characters you typed, the complete category name will appear in the Category field. Otherwise Quicken announces that it can't find the category and prompts you to add or select.

    - Type a right-facing bracket ([ ), press Ctrl-C, and the Category and Transfer List will appear with the cursor on the first account name on the list.

  - To bypass the OK to Record message, press Ctrl-Enter⏎ after entering the Category name.

Quicken will record the transaction in your account and create a corresponding transaction in your savings account for the deposit.

You can also record the transaction in a "reverse" way. Enter the deposit transaction in your savings account and Quicken will create the corresponding transaction in your checking account. If you do it this way, you'll have to add the correct check number in your Checking Account Register. You may also have to edit the Payee field (depending on what you entered in the field; it may say "Deposit").

Going to a Transfer Transaction

When you want to see the corresponding transaction in a transfer;

- In the Register, position the cursor on the transaction involving a transfer.
- Press `Ctrl`-`X`. The screen will change to the Register of the corresponding transaction in the transfer. You can also use selection 9 — Go to Transfer — on the `F3`-Edit menu.

Changing a Transfer Transaction

There may be times when you'll need to change a transaction that includes a transfer. When you make a change, Quicken changes the transaction in the other account as well.

- If you want to change the date, amount, or category in the transaction, Quicken changes those fields in both accounts.
- If you rename an account used in a transfer transaction, Quicken will change the account name in the transfer.

The rules for changing a Transfer Transaction are the same as for a regular transaction with one exception. If the transfer is part of a Split Transaction (see Changing a Split Transaction, later in this chapter), you must change it in the original transaction. You can use `Ctrl`-`X` (Go to Transfer) to help you find the original transaction.

- Press `Ctrl`-`R` to see the Check Register. Position the cursor on the transaction you want to change. Use `Ctrl`-`F` (Find Transaction), `Ctrl`-`G` (Go to Date), or the `PgUp`, `PgDn`, and arrow keys to find it.
- Press `Enter←` or `tab` to position the cursor on the field you want to change. If needed, use the arrow keys to position the cursor on a character within the field.

- Make the necessary additions or corrections:
  - To overwrite existing characters, turn [ins] off and type the new information. Use [space] and [delete] as needed.
  - To insert characters, turn [ins] on and type the information.
- Press [F10] or [Ctrl]-[Enter←] to record the changes. Quicken will ask you if you want to record the transaction. Press [Enter←] to record the transaction or [esc] to cancel and return to it for more editing.

Quicken makes the changes in both accounts.

Deleting a Transfer Transaction

You can delete a Transfer Transaction:

- Press [Ctrl]-[R] to see the Check Register. Position the cursor on the transaction you want to delete. Use [Ctrl]-[F] (Find Transaction), [Ctrl]-[G] (Go to Date), or the [PgUp], [PgDn], and arrow keys to find it.
- Press [Ctrl]-[D] or select Delete Transaction on the [F2]-Edit menu and the OK to Delete Transaction window will appear.
- Press [esc] or [2] to cancel and you will be returned to the Register. To delete the transaction, press [1] or [Enter←].

Quicken deletes the transaction in both accounts and recalculates all balances as necessary.

Split Transactions

You will sometimes have a transaction that covers more than one income or expense item, such as a deposit consisting of your paycheck and a refund check. To keep your records accurate, you should assign each check to a different category, but the Register has room for only one. Quicken's Split Transaction window will help you do this.

Split transactions are a good way to keep accurate and detailed records of your income and expenses. Each transaction can be separated into individual parts and assigned to the correct category and/or class.

Like other transactions, split transactions can be reviewed, added, changed, or deleted at any time.

Shortcut Keys:

Ctrl-S	Split Transactions
Ctrl-A	Select or setup an account
Ctrl-C	Select or setup a category
Ctrl-D	Delete an account, category, or class
Ctrl-L	Select or setup a class
Ctrl-end	Go to the next blank line in a Split Transaction
Ctrl-home	Go to top line in a Split Transaction
"	Repeats Category and Class name in a Split
F9	Recalculate transaction total
esc	Cancel

Adding a Split Transaction

Select your account, Ctrl-A, and press Ctrl-R to see the Check Register. Enter your transaction as usual: Date, Num, Payee, Payment or Deposit, and Memo.

Press Ctrl-S or select Split Transaction from the F3-Edit menu, and the Split Transaction window will appear (see Figure 5-11). This window will hold up to 30 lines of category information unless you print voucher checks. Then, only 16 lines will print.

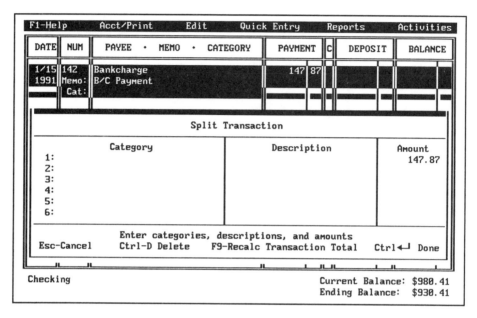

Figure 5-11 — The Split Transaction Screen.

Quicken copies the Payment to the first line in the Amount column. If you had typed in category information, this would be on the first line as well.

Enter the rest of the transaction information as follows:

- **Category**: Type the name of each category and class on a separate line. You can type the full name, a partial name and press [Enter←], or call the Category, [Ctrl]-[C], or Class, [Ctrl]-[L], lists. Remember to separate your categories, subcategories, and class the correct way. For example: "category:subcateg/class:subclass". Press [Enter←].

  - If a category already appears on the first line, make any necessary changes and press [Enter←].

  - On subsequent entries, you can save yourself some time and keystrokes. You can copy the category and class from the previous line by pressing the ["] (double quote) key that Quicken calls the ditto key. You don't have to use [⇧ Shift] to make this work. Use this when you want to assign parts of a transaction to the same category but different classes, such as miscellaneous expenses.

- **Description** (optional): You don't have to enter anything here but it may be helpful later if you do. Press [Enter◄─] to continue.

- **Amount**: The total amount of the transaction appears here. Type the amount to be assigned to the first category, including the decimal point and cents. For example:

  - for $25.00 — type 25.00

  - for $41.45 — type 41.45

  - for $150.00 — type 150.00

Press [Enter◄─]. Quicken will subtract the first amount from the total and show the balance on the next line.

Add categories, descriptions, and amounts until you have completed the transaction. If you did it right, there will be no remaining amount (see Figure 5-12).

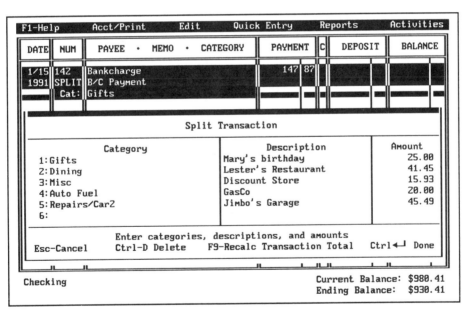

Figure 5-12 — Completed Split Transaction Screen.

Press ⌈Ctrl⌉-⌈Enter↵⌉ to record the transaction. Quicken puts you back at the Register, ready to type in another transaction. Notice that the word SPLIT appears in the NUM column under the check number (replacing the word Memo:) and the first category you entered appears in the Category field.

You can change an existing transaction to a Split Transaction by following this same procedure.

Split Transactions Containing a Transfer

You can include a transfer in a Split Transaction. For instance, you want to deposit two checks and get cash back (see Figure 5-13).

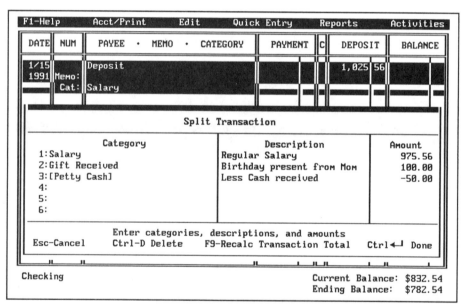

Figure 5-13 — Split Transaction with a Transfer.

You can assign a transfer to a class. You may want to keep track of your spouse's petty cash expenditures and well as your own. But you can not assign it to a category.

Changing a Split Transaction

You can review and change the information in a Split Transaction at any time.

- Position the cursor on the split transaction you want to change and press Ctrl - S to open the Split Transaction window.

- Make the changes you want.

- Press Ctrl - Enter← to record the changes.

Deleting a Split Transaction

You can delete one or all of the contents or category assignments in a Split Transaction at any time. Remember that once deleted, it is gone forever.

- Position the cursor on the split transaction you want to change and press Ctrl - S to open the Split Transaction window.

- Press Ctrl - D to delete each line. You have to delete it one line at a time.

- When all lines are deleted, press Ctrl - Enter← to close the Split Transaction window.

- The word SPLIT will disappear from the Num column but any information you typed, such as Date, Num, Payee, Payment, or Deposit, will remain.

If you want to delete the entire transaction at this time, press Ctrl - D.

Other Uses of the Split Transaction Window

The Split Transaction window has several other functions that you may find useful.

Adding machine

- Press Ctrl - S before you enter an amount in the payment or deposit column.

  Type the category and amount information and Quicken will display the total in Deposit column. Type a minus [–] before the amounts and the total will appear in the Payment column.

- Enter the Payment or Deposit amount before you press [Ctrl]-[S]. As you enter each line item, the balance will reflect the difference. If there is still a balance when you're finished, you know you made a mistake.

Long memos

- If you have a transaction that requires a large description (more than 31 characters), use the Description column in the Split Transaction window. You'll have to press [Enter←] three times at the end of each line to get back to the Description column on the next line. To record the transaction, press [Ctrl]-[Enter←].

Recalculating the transaction total

Use this feature when you want to change the total amount of the transaction because of information you added in the split.

- Enter the amounts of a Split Transaction in the window.
- Delete the balance amount that Quicken adds on the last line. Position the cursor on the balance and press [Ctrl]-[D].
- Press [F9] (Recalc Transaction Total).
- Quicken will recalculate the amount of the transaction and enter it in the Payment or Deposit field of the Register.
- Press [Ctrl]-[Enter←] to record the transaction.

Memorized Transactions

Most of us have some bills that we pay regularly, such as rent or mortgage payment, telephone bill, electricity bill, and a car payment. Quicken has a feature that will save you a lot of time and keystrokes every month. It's called Memorizing Transactions.

You can memorize any transaction from a Register or Write Checks screen, even transactions with transfers and splits. You can also memorize a transaction without recording it.

Shortcut Keys:

`Ctrl`-`E`	Quick recall of Memorized Transactions list
`Ctrl`-`D`	Delete a memorized transaction
`Ctrl`-`M`	Memorize the transaction
`Ctrl`-`P`	Print the Memorized Transactions List
`Ctrl`-`T`	Memorized Transactions List

After you've entered your first month's transactions, or as you are typing them, you can memorize the information for later use. The next time you want to enter a check, deposit, or service charge in the Register or write a check at the Write Checks screen, simply recall the transaction and let Quicken do the typing for you. If the amount changes from month to month, as in the case of utility bills, you only have to type the new payment amount.

Memorizing a Transaction is usually done as you are writing checks or entering the transaction in the Register. You can also memorize a check you've already written or a transaction already in the Register.

There are several ways to memorize transactions.

- For transactions, such as utilities and bank card payments where the amount differs every month, leave the payment or deposit field empty. Recall it when necessary and add the amount.

- For transactions where the payment or deposit is set, such as rent or mortgage payments, include the payment or deposit in the memorized transaction.

- You can memorize a transaction to record bank service charges and Quicken will include the C (cleared) field. This can save you time when you reconcile the Register with your bank statement. For more information, see the section on Reconciling later in this chapter.

- If you regularly make payments of the same amount to different people, memorize a transaction without the payee. Recall it when you need it and add the payee name.

Memorizing a Transaction

To memorize a transaction:

- At the Register, position the cursor on the transaction you want to memorize. It may be one you just typed or one that's been there for some time.

- Press [Ctrl]-[M]. Quicken will highlight some of the fields, such as payee, payment, **C** (cleared), deposit, memo, and category fields.

    - If the payment, deposit, and **C** (cleared) fields are blank, they won't be highlighted.

    - If just the name, or the name and memo are entered, the name and memo fields will be highlighted.

A verification window will be displayed on the screen (see Figure 5-14).

```
 F1-Help       Acct/Print      Edit      Quick Entry     Reports      Activities
╔══════╦══════╦══════════════════════════╦═════════╦═╦══════════╦══════════╗
║ DATE ║ NUM  ║ PAYEE · MEMO · CATEGORY  ║ PAYMENT ║C║ DEPOSIT  ║ BALANCE  ║
╠══════╬══════╬══════════════════════════╬═════════╬═╬══════════╬══════════╣
║ 1/ 1 ║      ║ Opening Balance          ║         ║X║ 1,500 00 ║ 1,500 00 ║
║ 1991 ║      ║          [Checking]      ║         ║ ║          ║          ║
╠══════╬══════╬══════════════════════════╩═════════╩═╩══════════╩══════════╣
║ 1/ 2 ║*****║ Home Mortgage Company                                        ║
║ 1991 ║      ║ January Mortgag→Mort Int      The marked information is      ║
║ 1/ 2 ║      ║ Deposit                       about to be memorized.         ║
║ 1991 ║      ║ Paycheck       Salary                                        ║
║ 1/ 2 ║ 131  ║ Cash                      Esc-Cancel        ↵ Memorize       ║
║ 1991 ║      ║ Transfer to Sav→[Savings]                                    ║
╠══════╬══════╬══════════════════════════╦═════════╦═╦══════════╦══════════╣
║ 1/ 2 ║ 132  ║ Your Utility Company     ║   75 45 ║ ║          ║ 1,750 11 ║
║ 1991 ║Memo: ║ Monthly Utilities        ║         ║ ║          ║          ║
║      ║Cat:  ║ Utilities                ║         ║ ║          ║          ║
║ 1/ 2 ║      ║                          ║         ║ ║          ║          ║
║ 1991 ║      ║              END         ║         ║ ║          ║          ║
╚══════╩══════╩══════════════════════════╩═════════╩═╩══════════╩══════════╝
 Checking
                                             Ending Balance:  $1,750.11
```

Figure 5-14 — Memorizing a Transaction in the Register.

- Press [Enter←┘] to memorize the transaction and add it to the list of Memorized Transactions, or [esc] to cancel.

- If you want to record the transaction, press [Ctrl]-[Enter←], or press [Ctrl]-[D] to clear the screen without adding the transaction to the Register.

- Press [Ctrl]-[T] or [Ctrl]-[E] to see the Memorized Transactions List.

Recalling a Memorized Transaction

To recall a memorized transaction, you must be in a Register or at the Write Checks screen. You recall a memorized Register transaction from the Register screen, and a memorized check from the Write Checks screen. You might mess up existing transactions if you do it backwards.

- In the Register, position the cursor on the first blank line at the end. This is very important; you don't want to overwrite an existing transaction with a memorized transaction.

- Press [Ctrl]-[T] or select Recall Transaction from the [F4]-Quick Entry menu to see the Memorized Transactions List (see Figure 5-15).

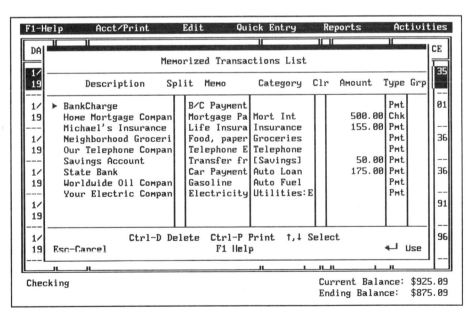

Figure 5-15 — Memorized Transactions List.

103

Each line contains a transaction and shows the description (payee), whether or not it is split (the letter **S** will display in the column), memo, category, whether or not it is cleared, amount, type (check or payment), and whether or not it is in a group.

- Use ⬆ and ⬇ to highlight the transaction you want. Or you can type the first letter of the transaction and Quicken will highlight the first occurrence of that letter.

- Press [Enter←] to display the transaction in the Register.

- Make any necessary additions or changes and press [Ctrl]-[Enter←] to record the transaction in the Register.

To save time, type a few letters of the payee name and press [Ctrl]-[E]. Quicken will fill in the rest of the transaction for you. You must type enough characters to make the name unique. If there are two or more transactions that match the letters you typed, Quicken will display the Memorized Transactions List.

If you type a letter or two and press [Ctrl]-[T], Quicken will position the cursor on the first memorized transaction beginning with those letters. If it's the right transaction, press [Enter←]. Otherwise, use the arrow keys to position the cursor on the transaction you want, and press [Enter←].

You can set up several memorized transactions in a Transaction Group. For more information, see Transaction Groups, later in this chapter.

Changing a Memorized Transaction

To change a memorized transaction:

- Position the cursor on a blank line in the Register. This is very important; you don't want to overwrite an existing transaction with a memorized transaction.

- Press [Ctrl]-[T] or select Recall Transaction from the [F4]-Quick Entry menu to see the Memorized Transactions List.

- Use 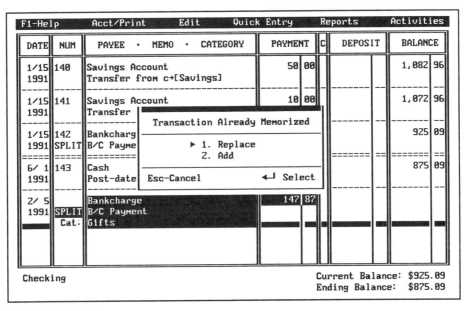↑ and ↓ to highlight the one you want. Or you can type the first letter of the transaction you want and Quicken will highlight the first occurrence of that letter.

- Press Enter↲ to display the transaction in the Register.

- Make any necessary additions or changes and press Ctrl-M. Quicken will highlight the information to be memorized.

- Press esc to cancel or Enter↲ to memorize the new information. Because the memorized transaction already exists, Quicken will ask if you want to add or replace it (see Figure 5-16).

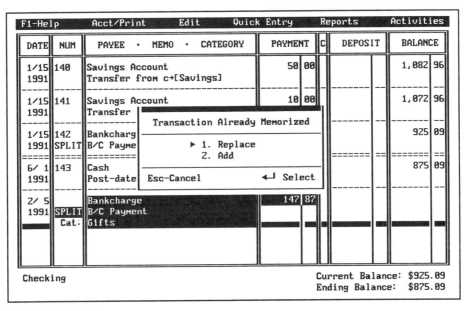

F1-Help		Acct/Print	Edit	Quick Entry		Reports	Activities
DATE	NUM	PAYEE · MEMO · CATEGORY		PAYMENT	C	DEPOSIT	BALANCE
1/15 1991	140	Savings Account Transfer from c→[Savings]		50 00			1,082 96
1/15 1991	141	Savings Account Transfer		10 00			1,072 96
1/15 1991	142 SPLIT	Bankcharg B/C Payme	Transaction Already Memorized				925 09
6/ 1 1991	143	Cash Post-date	▶ 1. Replace 2. Add				875 09
2/ 5 1991	SPLIT Cat:	Bankcharge B/C Payment Gifts	Esc-Cancel ↲ Select	147 87			

Checking

Current Balance: $925.09
Ending Balance: $875.09

Figure 5-16 — Transaction Already Memorized Window.

Deleting a Memorized Transaction

If you delete a memorized transaction, it is permanently removed and can not be recovered. If the memorized transaction you want to delete is part of a transaction group, it will be removed from the transaction group, as well as from the list of memorized transactions. For more information, see Transaction Groups later in this chapter.

To delete a memorized transaction:

- Press ⌈Ctrl⌉-⌈T⌉ or select Recall Transaction from the ⌈F4⌉-Quick Entry menu to see the Memorized Transactions List.
- Use the ⌈↑⌉ and ⌈↓⌉ to highlight the one you want.
- Press ⌈Ctrl⌉-⌈D⌉ to delete the memorized transaction. Quicken will warn you that you are about to delete a Memorized transaction.
- Press ⌈Enter◄──⌉ to delete the transaction or ⌈esc⌉ if you want to keep it.

Printing the Memorized Transaction List

You may find it helpful to have a paper copy of the Memorized Transactions List.

- Press ⌈Ctrl⌉-⌈T⌉ or select Recall Transaction from the ⌈F4⌉-Quick Entry menu to see the Memorized Transactions List.
- Press ⌈Ctrl⌉-⌈P⌉ and the Print Memorized Transactions List window will be displayed.
- Tell Quicken which printer to use, or to print it to disk. Press ⌈Ctrl⌉-⌈Enter◄──⌉ to print, or ⌈esc⌉ to cancel.

Reconciling the Register

Reconciling is the act of matching, or verifying, two accounts — such as your Quicken account Register and the monthly statement from your bank. You should reconcile the Register each time you get a statement from your bank. This will take only a few minutes and will verify that your records are the same as the bank's. If you have more than one bank statement for your account, reconcile them one at a time, beginning with the earliest one.

Reconciling your account is easier if you fixed a beginning date and worked forward as you entered transactions. You can start with last month's transactions and then include earlier ones at a later time, but it may cause you some problems with reconciliation. If you want to do things that way, skip the reconciliation process until you have all of the earlier transactions entered in the Register. Begin reconciling with the earliest bank statement, completing one month at a time until you are current.

First Time Reconciliation

The first time you reconcile your Quicken account, you might run into some discrepancies, especially with the opening balance. If you set up your account with the balance shown in your checkbook register on the first day of a new month, the opening balance shown on your bank statement will not be the same. This is because you made deposits and wrote checks last month that did not clear the bank before they sent out your statement. These uncleared items will appear on later statements, but for now, they will be the reason your balance doesn't match. Be sure to check earlier months for uncleared items, as well.

You can solve the problem with uncleared transactions as follows:

- Enter all of the transactions you wrote that have not yet cleared the bank. If you find an uncleared error during reconciliation, you don't have to leave the reconciliation process to enter items in the Register. For more information, see Marking Cleared Transactions, later in this chapter.

- Change the opening balance to include these uncleared transactions. Quicken can do this for you at the end of the reconciliation process. See Does It Balance?, later in this chapter.

To Reconcile Accounts

- Select the account, [Ctrl]-[A], you want to reconcile and its Register, [Ctrl]-[R].

- At the Register, select [F6]-Activities menu. Position the cursor on Reconcile and press [Enter◄┘] or Type 2.

- The Reconcile Register with Bank Statement screen appears (see Figure 5-17).

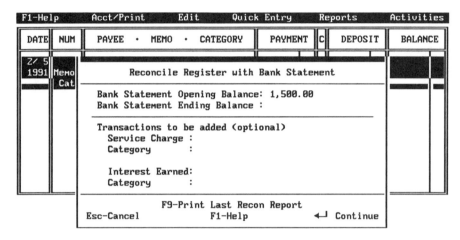

Figure 5-17 — Reconciling the Register.

If you want to print the last Reconciliation Report you did, press ⟦F9⟧. The Print Reconciliation Report screen will be displayed (see Figure 5-18). Type in the information and press ⟦Ctrl⟧-⟦Enter◀─┘⟧ to print, or press ⟦esc⟧ to cancel.

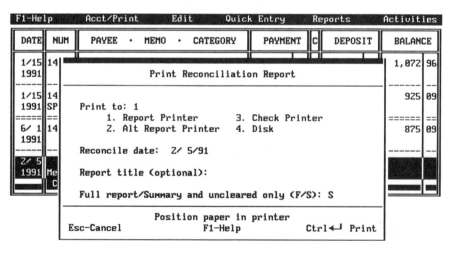

Figure 5-18 — Print the Reconciliation Report.

Enter the following information in the Reconcile Register with Bank Statement window:

- **Bank Statement Opening Balance**: The amount shown should be the same as the one on your bank statement. The number may be different if you're reconciling the account for the first time or if you haven't done it for months. If the amounts are different, type the opening balance from the bank statement and press [Enter←].

- **Bank Statement Ending Balance**: Type the ending balance from your bank statement and press [Enter←].

- **Transactions to be added** (optional): If you have not entered the following transactions in the Register, enter them here. Make sure you don't enter them twice. If you're not going to enter any of this optional information, you can continue by pressing [Ctrl]-[Enter←] from any field.

  - **Service Charge**: Type the total of any service charges that appear on your bank statement and press [Enter←]. Use the Quicken Calculator, [Ctrl]-[O], if there is more than one. Quicken will create a record in the Register for this transaction.

  - **Category**: Type the name of the category you'd like to assign the transaction to and press [Enter←].

  - **Interest Earned**: Type the amount of any interest you earned and press [Enter←]. Quicken will create a record in the Register for this transaction.

  - **Category**: Type the name of the category you'd like to assign the transaction to.

- Press [Enter←] to continue or [esc] to cancel.

The Reconciliation screen will be displayed (see Figure 5-19).

```
┌─────────────────────────────────────────────────────────────────────────┐
│ F1-Help      Acct/Print      Edit      Quick Entry    Reports    Activities│
├──────┬──┬──────────┬─────────┬──────────────────────┬─────────────────────┤
│ NUM  │C │  AMOUNT  │  DATE   │       PAYEE          │        MEMO         │
├──────┼──┼──────────┼─────────┼──────────────────────┼─────────────────────┤
│►     │  │   975.56 │ 1/ 2/91 │Deposit               │Paycheck             │
│ 131  │  │  -150.00 │ 1/ 2/91 │Cash                  │Transfer to Savings  │
│ 132  │  │   -75.45 │ 1/ 2/91 │Your Electric Company │Electricity          │
│ 133  │  │   -34.76 │ 1/ 2/91 │Our Telephone Company │Telephone Expenses   │
│ 134  │  │  -175.00 │ 1/ 2/91 │State Bank            │Car Payment          │
│ 135  │  │   -59.34 │ 1/ 2/91 │Worlduide Oil Company │Gasoline             │
│ 136  │  │  -105.65 │ 1/ 2/91 │Neighborhood Groceries│Food, paper products,│
│ 137  │  │  -155.00 │ 1/ 2/91 │Michael's Insurance   │Life Insurance       │
│ 138  │  │   -57.45 │ 1/ 2/91 │Our Telephone Company │Telephone Expenses   │
│ 139  │  │   -29.95 │ 1/ 2/91 │Neighborhood Cable    │Monthly Cable fees   │
├──────┴──┴──────────┴─────────┴──────────────────────┴─────────────────────┤
│ ■ To Mark Cleared Items, press Space Bar  ■ To Add or Change Items, press F9│
├───────────────────────────────────────────────────────────────────────────┤
│                         RECONCILIATION SUMMARY                             │
│      Items You Have Marked Cleared (*)                                     │
│      ─────────────────────────────────────  Cleared (X,*) Balance  1,500.00│
│          0    Checks, Debits        0.00    Bank Statement Balance   925.09 │
│          0    Deposits, Credits     0.00    Difference               574.91 │
├───────────────────────────────────────────────────────────────────────────┤
│ F1-Help          F8-Mark Range        F9-Uiew as Register     Ctrl F10-Done│
└───────────────────────────────────────────────────────────────────────────┘
```

Figure 5-19 — Reconciliation Summary, Marking Cleared Transactions.

Marking cleared transactions

You are now ready to mark the transactions that have cleared your bank. You can mark the cleared transactions in two ways — select and clear the transactions one at a time, or select an unbroken range of check numbers and clear them all.

To select and clear individual transactions:

- Use the arrow keys to move from line to line, highlighting each transaction.

  - If it appears on the bank statement, press [space] to mark it as cleared. An asterisk will appear in the column marked **C**.

  - Or, press [Enter⤶] to mark the transaction as cleared and move to the next one. If the next one hasn't cleared yet, use the arrow keys to move on.

  - Or, press [F5] to move the cursor up and [F6] to move it down. Press [space] to mark the item as cleared.

To select and clear an unbroken range of check numbers:

- Press ⃞F8⃞ and another window displays (see Figure 5-20).

```
 F1-Help       Acct/Print      Edit      Quick Entry      Reports       Activities
┌────────┬─┬─────────┬────────┬──────────────────┬─────────────────────┐
│  NUM   │C│ AMOUNT  │  DATE  │      PAYEE       │        MEMO         │
├────────┼─┼─────────┼────────┼──────────────────┼─────────────────────┤
│▶       │ │  975.56 │ 1/ 2/91│Deposit           │Paycheck             │
│  131   │ │ -150.00 │ 1/ 2/91│Cash              │Transfer to Savings  │
│  132   │ │  -75.45 │ 1/ 2/91│Your Electric Company│Electricity       │
│  133   │ │  -34.76 │ 1/ 2/91│Our Telephone Company│Telephone Expenses│
│  134   │ │         │        │                      │           nt      │
│  135   │ │     Mark Range of Check Numbers as Cleared    │           │
│  136   │ │                                               │ er products,│
│  137   │ │  ─────────────────────────────────────────    │ rance       │
│  138   │ │     Mark items numbered      to      with an *.│  Expenses  │
│  139   │ │                          ─────    ─────        │ able fees  │
├────────┼─┼───────────────────────────────────────────────┼────────────┤
│ ■ To Mark│ Esc-Cancel         F1-Help      ↵ Continue    │s, press F9 │
└────────┴─────────────────────────────────────────────────┴────────────┘

                        RECONCILIATION SUMMARY
           Items You Have Marked Cleared (*)
        ─────────────────────────────────────  Cleared (X,*) Balance  1,500.00
            0    Checks, Debits        0.00     Bank Statement Balance   925.09
            0    Deposits, Credits     0.00        Difference            574.91
```

Figure 5-20 — Having Quicken Clear a Range of Check Numbers.

- Type the beginning check number, press ⃞Enter↵⃞, then type the ending number.

- Press ⃞Enter↵⃞ to continue. Quicken will mark each item with an asterisk.

The bottom of the screen contains a Reconciliation Summary (see Figure 5-20). Totals appear on the left side of the screen for checks and deposits marked as cleared. The right side contains totals for the cleared balance, the bank statement balance, and any difference between the two. Quicken automatically updates these totals as you mark items as cleared.

Entering missing transactions

If you have transactions on the bank statement that don't appear on the list of uncleared transactions, you can enter them without leaving the reconciliation process.

111

- With the list of uncleared transactions on the screen, press [F9] to see a small version of the Register (see Figure 5-21).

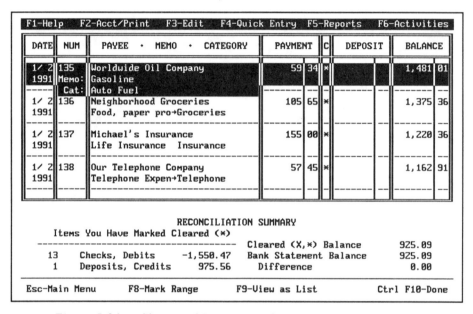

| F1-Help | F2-Acct/Print | F3-Edit | F4-Quick Entry | F5-Reports | F6-Activities |

DATE	NUM	PAYEE · MEMO · CATEGORY	PAYMENT	C	DEPOSIT	BALANCE
1/ 2 1991	135 Memo: Cat:	Worldwide Oil Company Gasoline Auto Fuel	59 34	*		1,481 01
1/ 2 1991	136	Neighborhood Groceries Food, paper pro→Groceries	105 65	*		1,375 36
1/ 2 1991	137	Michael's Insurance Life Insurance Insurance	155 00	*		1,220 36
1/ 2 1991	138	Our Telephone Company Telephone Expen→Telephone	57 45	*		1,162 91

RECONCILIATION SUMMARY
Items You Have Marked Cleared (*)

			Cleared (X,*) Balance	925.09
13	Checks, Debits	-1,550.47	Bank Statement Balance	925.09
1	Deposits, Credits	975.56	Difference	0.00

Esc-Main Menu   F8-Mark Range   F9-View as List   Ctrl F10-Done

Figure 5-21 — Shortened Register and Reconciliation Summary.

- Position the cursor in the blank highlighted space at the bottom of the Register and type in the missing transaction.
    - Type all fields, including an asterisk (*) in the column marked **C** (Cleared). This marks the transaction as cleared.
- Press [Ctrl]-[Enter←] to record the transaction.
- Add any other missing transactions. Press [F9] to return to the list of uncleared transactions.

Correcting errors in transactions

If you find a transaction on the statement that differs from the one in the Register, you can correct it now.

- Move the cursor to the transaction containing the error.
- Press [F9] to see the same transaction in the Register.

- Correct the error in the transaction.

- Press F9 to record the changes and return to the list of uncleared transactions.

Does it balance?

As mentioned before, Quicken automatically updates the totals listed in the Reconciliation Summary as you mark the items that are cleared. After you have finished marking all of the cleared items, the difference should be zero (see Figure 5-21). If it is, you've successfully reconciled your account.

To complete the reconciliation process:

- Press Ctrl-F10 from the list of uncleared items or the Register. A congratulatory message appears asking if you want to print the Reconciliation Report (see Figure 5-22).

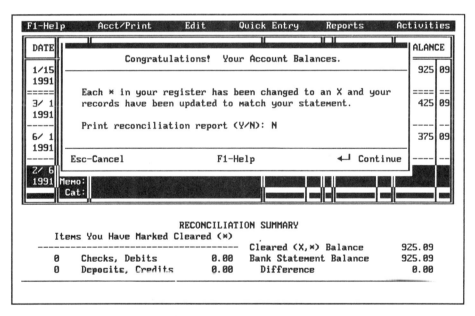

Figure 5-22 — A Successful Reconciliation.

- Type Y to print the report and answer the questions. Type N or press Enter↵ if you do not want to print.

Quicken replaces the asterisks in the **C** (cleared) column of the Register with an **X**. The reconciliation process is now complete.

If it does not balance — if the difference on the Reconciliation Summary is not zero, you have to find and resolve the problem. There are several reasons why your balance may be off:

1. Opening Balance Differs — You may have a different opening balance, for reasons discussed earlier (uncleared items in your checkbook, for example). When there is an opening balance difference, Quicken displays the amount.

   If the account is out of balance by an amount equal to the difference in the opening balance, your account is in balance for the month, and the error is in a previous period. In this case, you can complete the reconciliation process by pressing `Ctrl`-`F10` from the List of Uncleared Items or from the Register.

   Quicken will ask if you want to create an adjusting transaction for the difference. Type Y to have Quicken make the opening balance adjustment. Type N to complete reconciling without adjusting the transaction. Press `Enter←`.

   You will have the option of printing the Reconciliation Statement, as previously mentioned. When Quicken has finished reconciling, the cleared items in the Register will have an **X** in the Cleared column.

2. If the account is out of balance, and this is not due to a difference in the opening balance, the transactions are out of balance — you probably have too many or too few deposits or payments, or you have made typing errors in the dollar amounts of one or more transaction. To fix an out of balance account, you have two options:

   1. Find the error or errors in the Register and/or bank statement and make corrections. This is the preferable choice but it could take some time.

      - Check the number of debits on the bank statement with the number on the Reconciliation Summary. If they differ, you may have mistakenly marked an item as cleared, missed an item that has cleared, or forgotten to enter an item in the Register.

- Do the same with credits (interest earned and other deposits). If they differ, you may have mistakenly marked a deposit as cleared, missed a deposit that has cleared, or forgotten to enter a deposit in the Register.

- Check the total amount of the debits (checks, service charges, and other payments) on the bank statement with the total on the Reconciliation Summary. If the amounts are different, check each item on the statement with the corresponding item in your Register to find the error.

- Do the same with credits.

2. Allow Quicken to create an adjusting transaction and modify your balance. You may consider this the easiest way out, but it will usually cause problems later. You should make a strong effort to find and correct any errors to keep your records accurate. If you want Quicken to make an adjusting entry:

- Press [F10]. If there is a difference between the opening balance on the statement and the one in your account, Quicken will ask if you want to make an adjustment.

- Type Y to have an adjustment made in your opening balance or N to complete the reconciliation with no adjustment. Press [Enter←].

- If there is still a difference, Quicken will display a window showing the amount of the difference and some ways to correct it.

  - Press [F9] to see the list of uncleared items, or

  - Press [esc] to cancel, or

  - Press [Enter←] to have Quicken adjust the difference.

  - A window will display asking for verification, and an optional category assignment.

- Type N to return to the Reconciliation process,

    or

- Type Y to have the adjustment made, and press [Enter←]. Type the category name, and press [Enter←]. Quicken will add the adjusting transaction to the Register and complete the Reconciliation process.

While your records should be accurate, you are the one who decides the accuracy you require. If the account is for your personal use, you might not want to track down the error — let Quicken make an adjusting entry. If you are using Quicken to help you to properly organize your finances, however, you cannot compromise your results by taking the easy way out and corrupting your data.

Fortunately, you don't have to make that choice immediately. You can leave the Reconciliation process uncompleted. If you have spent a lot of time unsuccessfully looking for the error, it sometimes helps to put everything away for a while. When you return, you can usually find the problem. If you had Quicken make an adjusting entry, you can always delete it after you find the error.

When the problem is found and your account is in balance, follow the steps in "Does It Balance?" to complete the reconciliation process.

Printing Transactions in the Register

Shortcut keys:

[Ctrl]-[P]   Print the Register

[+], [-]   Increase or decrease date

Quicken's print option allows you to print all, or part, of your Register.

1.   Select your account and press [Ctrl]-[R] to see the Register.

2.   Press [Ctrl]-[P] or select Print Register from the [F2]-Acct/Print menu. The Print Register window will be displayed (see Figure 5-23).

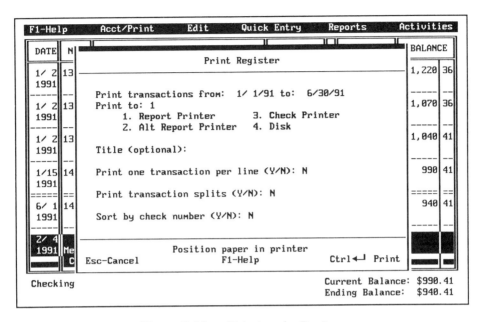

Figure 5-23 — Printing the Register.

3. Fill in the following information:

    Print transactions from: Type the beginning and ending dates of the transactions you want to print, or use ⊕ and ⊖ to increase or decrease the dates shown. Quicken will print all transactions within that period. Press ⌨Enter↲ to continue.

    Print to: Type the number of the printer to use (1, 2, or 3) or type 4 to write an ASCII file to disk. For more information, see Importing and Exporting Transactions later in this chapter. Quicken's default is 1. Press ⌨Enter↲ to continue.

    Title (optional): Type the title you'd like printed on the report. If you don't specify one, Quicken will print "Check Register". Press ⌨Enter↲ to continue.

    Print one transaction per line (Y/N): If you type N, Quicken will use three lines for each transaction. If you want one transaction per line, type Y and Quicken will abbreviate the transaction to fit on a single line. Quicken's default is N. Press ⌨Enter↲ to continue.

Print transaction splits (Y/N): If you want your split transaction printed, type Y. Otherwise Quicken will not print the contents of split transactions. Quicken's default is N. Press [Enter←] to continue.

Sort by check number (Y/N): Type Y to have checks sorted by number first and date second. If a check number is missing, Quicken will display an asterisk to the left of the next number. Quicken will not print your running balance. Type N to print checks sorted by date first and number second. Quicken's default is N.

4.   Make certain your printer is turned on and the paper is correctly positioned.

5.   Press [Ctrl]-[Enter←] to begin printing the Register. If the printer is not ready, Quicken will tell you. Press [esc] if you want to cancel the print option.

Exporting and Importing Transactions

Quicken has another feature that can save you time. You can export Register transactions into a special ASCII file with a format called QIF (Quicken Interchange Format). By specifying a beginning and ending date, all transactions within that range are exported to the QIF file.

You can also import data from an ASCII file into a Quicken Register. If you use Quicken to transmit payments to CheckFree, you can import data from a CheckFree Register. For more information on using CheckFree, see Chapter 6.

There are several uses for exporting and importing data:

•   You can move data from one account to another. This is useful if you type transactions into the wrong Register. For example, if you typed ten transactions in the Savings Register instead of the Checking Register, export them from the Savings Register to an ASCII file and import the file into your Checking Register. Be sure to delete them from the Savings Register when you're finished.

•   You can change the account type or merge account groups, consolidating transactions from different places into one place.

•   You can add transactions from another program.

Exporting Data

To export Quicken transactions to the special file, you need to know the dates of the transactions you will export. Select the account containing those transactions, Ctrl - A .

- From the Register or Write Checks screen, select the F2 -Acct/Print menu.

- Type 5 or position the cursor on Export and press Enter← . The Export Transactions to QIF file window will appear (see Figure 5-24).

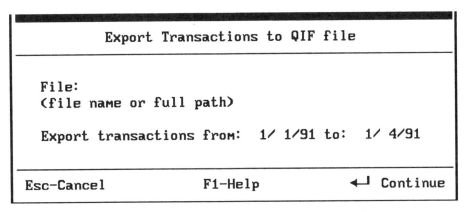

```
┌─────────────────────────────────────────────────────┐
│█████████████████████████████████████████████████████│
│                                                      │
│         Export Transactions to QIF file              │
│                                                      │
├──────────────────────────────────────────────────────┤
│                                                      │
│  File:                                               │
│  (file name or full path)                            │
│                                                      │
│  Export transactions from:  1/ 1/91 to:  1/ 4/91     │
│                                                      │
├──────────────────────────────────────────────────────┤
│  Esc-Cancel           F1-Help          ↵ Continue    │
└──────────────────────────────────────────────────────┘
```

Figure 5 24 — Export Transactions to QIF File.

- Type in the name of the QIF file to be created. Quicken does not assign a .QIF extension, so you can use up to eight characters plus the three letter extension to name the file. Include the path if you want the file in a location other than where you store your Quicken data. Press Enter← .

- Type in a beginning date and an ending date. If you want to export all transactions for January 1991, type 1/1/91, press Enter← , type 1/31/91.

- Press Enter← and the file is created.

Importing Data

To import data, select the account into which you want the data inserted, use
⌈Ctrl⌉-⌈A⌉. From the Register or Write Checks screen, select the ⌈F2⌉-Acct/Print
menu.

- Type 6 or position the cursor on Import and press ⌈Enter◄─⌉. The Import
  from QIF file or CheckFree window will appear (see Figure 5-25).

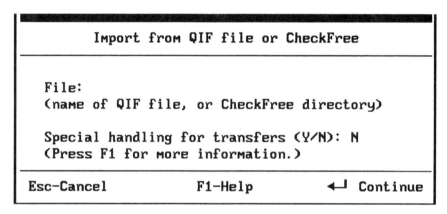

```
            Import from QIF file or CheckFree
    ─────────────────────────────────────────────────

    File:
    (name of QIF file, or CheckFree directory)

    Special handling for transfers (Y/N): N
    (Press F1 for more information.)
    ─────────────────────────────────────────────────
    Esc-Cancel              F1-Help           ◄┘ Continue
```

Figure 5-25 — Import Transactions to QIF File.

- Type in the name of the file to be imported or the CheckFree directory
  (for more information, see Chapter 6). Press ⌈Enter◄─⌉.
- Press ⌈Enter◄─⌉ at the "Special handling for transfers" field to import the
  file. A message will appear on the screen informing you how many items
  were successfully imported.
- Press ⌈Enter◄─⌉ to continue.

Transaction Groups

Shortcut Keys:

Ctrl - D	Delete Transaction Group
Ctrl - E	Edit a Transaction Group
Ctrl - J	Select Transaction Group

If you have a group of bills that are due at the same time of the month, or if you pay your bills only once or twice a month, you can save time by using Transaction Groups. A transaction group is nothing more than one or more Memorized Transactions that you can recall all at once. A Transaction Group can be set up to be used in any account or to be account specific. Quicken will remind you when the group is due, but it won't automatically pay it.

Once a Transaction Group has been set up, Quicken allows you to add, change, or delete it. You can also set the time interval (in days) ahead of the due date, for Quicken's reminder.

Quicken will allow you to set up a maximum of twelve (12) Transaction Groups. You can use them:

- To pay bills due on the first (or any other day) of the month.
- To record quarterly or semi-annual payments for insurance, Quarterly Estimate payments to the IRS, or other periodic payments.

When the Main Menu is displayed, Quicken places a reminder at the bottom of the screen of Transaction Groups due to be paid (see Figure 5-26).

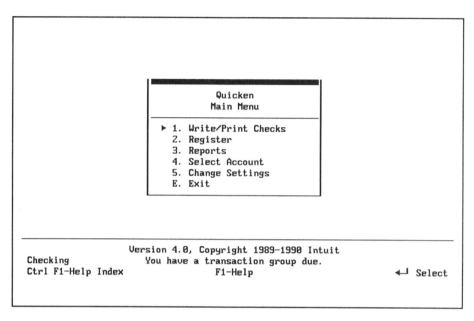

Figure 5-26 — Reminder of Transaction Due for Payment.

Setting Up a Transaction Group

You must memorize a transaction, Ctrl - M, before you can use it in a Transaction Group. Use a transaction memorized at the Register to record items in the Register. Use transactions memorized at the Write Checks screen for writing and printing checks.

- When all the transactions you want to use are memorized, press Ctrl - J to see the Select Transaction Group to Execute window (see Figure 5-27).

```
┌─────────────────────────────────────────────────────────────┐
│          Select Transaction Group to Execute                │
├─────────────────────────────────────────────────────────────┤
│                                                              │
│         Group        Size    Frequency      Next Scheduled  │
│                                                              │
│  ▶  1. <unused>                                              │
│     2. <unused>                                              │
│     3. <unused>                                              │
│     4. <unused>                                              │
│     5. <unused>                                              │
│     6. <unused>                                              │
│     7. <unused>                                              │
│     8. <unused>                                              │
│     9. <unused>                                              │
│    10. <unused>                                              │
│    11. <unused>                                              │
│    12. <unused>                                              │
│                                                              │
├─────────────────────────────────────────────────────────────┤
│         Ctrl-D Delete  Ctrl-E Edit   ↑,↓ Select             │
│  Esc-Cancel                F1-Help              ↵ Continue   │
└─────────────────────────────────────────────────────────────┘
```

Figure 5-27 — Select Transaction Group to Execute Window.

- Use the arrow keys to position the cursor on the first unused group and press Enter↵ . This will display the Describe Group 1 window (see Figure 5-28).

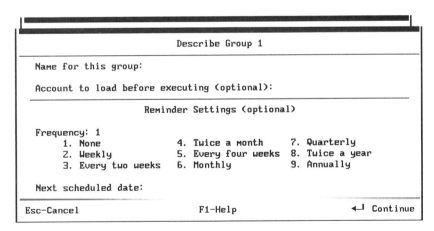

Figure 5-28 — Describe Group 1.

123

- **Name**: Type the name of this group, using a maximum of 20 characters. Press [Enter↵].

- **Account (optional)**: To assign this group to a specific account, type the account name here. If you want to use it in more than one account, leave this field blank. Press [Enter↵].

- **Frequency**: Type the number to indicate how often this group is to be paid. If the group has no regular schedule, leave it set to 1 (none). Press [Enter↵].

- **Next scheduled date**: If you want to be reminded when the group is due for payment, type in the date for the next reminder. After this first entry, Quicken will adjust the reminder date according to the selected frequency.

- Press [Enter↵] to display the Assign Transactions to Group 1 window or [esc] to cancel (see Figure 5-29).

```
┌─────────────────────────────────────────────────────────────────────┐
│            Assign Transactions to Group 1:First of month             │
├─────────────────────────────────────────────────────────────────────┤
│    Description    Split  Memo       Category   Clr  Amount  Type Grp │
├─────────────────────────────────────────────────────────────────────┤
│ ▶ Bankcharge       S B/C Payment Gifts              147.87 Pmt       │
│   BankCharge         B/C Payment                           Pmt       │
│   Deposit            Paycheck    Salary             975.56 Dep       │
│   Home Mortgage Compan Mortgage Pa Mort Int         500.00 Chk       │
│   Michael's Insurance Life Insura Insurance         155.00 Pmt       │
│   Neighborhood Groceri Food, paper Groceries               Pmt       │
│   Our Telephone Compan Telephone E Telephone               Pmt       │
│   Savings Account    Transfer fr [Savings]           50.00 Pmt       │
│   State Bank         Car Payment Auto Loan          175.00 Pmt       │
│   Worldwide Oil Compan Gasoline   Auto Fuel                Pmt       │
│   Your Electric Compan Electricity Utilities:E             Pmt       │
├─────────────────────────────────────────────────────────────────────┤
│                    Space Bar-Assign/Unassign                         │
│  Esc-Cancel              F1-Help                            ↵ Done   │
└─────────────────────────────────────────────────────────────────────┘
```

Figure 5-29 — Assign Transactions to Group 1.

- Use the [↑] and [↓] to position the cursor on the transactions you want to include in this group. Press [space] and the number 1 will appear in the Group column. If you do not want the transaction in this group, press [space] again to remove or unassign it.

- Check the column called Type. If the transaction was memorized from the Register, "Pmt" will appear here. Use this type of transaction for Register use only. If you need this transaction to write and print checks, you must rewrite and rememorize the transaction from the Write Checks screen.

- You can assign a transaction to more than one group by memorizing the same transaction more than once. For instance, you may have two cars insured under two different policies with the same company. Memorize two transactions, one for each car. If the payments are due at different times, such as semi-annual payments for Car1 in January and July and for Car2 in April and October, you can put them in two different semi-annual groups. If the payments are due at the same time, include both in the same group.

- Repeat these steps until all of the transactions you want are assigned to the group.

- Press 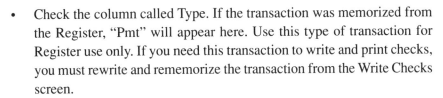 to complete Group 1.

Your first transaction group is set up. Repeat the process if you want to set up other groups.

Executing a Transaction Group

When you recall a Transaction Group, Quicken types all of the information in the Register or the Write Checks Screen, saving you time and keystrokes. If you specified an account with the group, Quicken enters the transactions in that account. You only need to make any necessary changes, such as dollar amounts, and record them.

To recall and execute a transaction group:

- From the Register or Write Checks Screen, press Ctrl-J or select Transaction Groups on the F4-Quick Entry menu. The Select Transaction Group window will be displayed.

- Use ↑ and ↓ to position the cursor on the group you want to use and press Enter. If the group you selected is assigned to another account, Quicken will load that account.

- The Transaction Group Date window will be displayed (see Figure 5-30). If you assigned a date to this group, it will appear in the window. If necessary, use 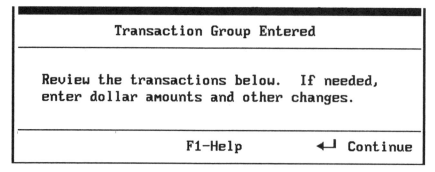 or ⊟ to increase or decrease the date. Press [Enter←].

```
F1-Help        Acct/Print      Edit      Quick Entry     Reports      Activities

DATE  NUM   PAYEE  ·  MEMO  ·  CATEGORY    PAYMENT  C   DEPOSIT     BALANCE

1/21 145   The News                          15 00               1,702 13
1991       Newspaper        Entertain

1/21 146   Neighborhood Groceries            42 85               1,659 28
1991       Food, paper
                        Transaction Group Date
1/22 147   The Departm                                           1,516 62
1991       Clothing/Ty
                    Date of group:  2/ 1/91
1/25 148   The Drug St                                           1,474 73
1991       Misc. Suppl
                    Esc-Cancel      ←┘ Continue
1/25 149   Neighborhoo                                           1,434 76
1991       Food, paper pro→Groceries

2/1        Memo:
1991       Cat:

Checking
                                              Ending Balance:  $1,434.76
```

Figure 5-30 — Transaction Group Date Window.

- The Transaction Group Entered message will be displayed (see Figure 5-31). Press [Enter←] to continue.

```
         Transaction Group Entered
─────────────────────────────────────────────
   Review the transactions below.  If needed,
   enter dollar amounts and other changes.
─────────────────────────────────────────────
            F1-Help          ←┘ Continue
```

Figure 5-31 — Transaction Group Entered Window.

Make any necessary changes now, such as adding dollar amounts and check numbers. Press ⌈Ctrl⌉-⌈Enter⏎⌉ to record each transaction. If you wrote any checks that need to be printed, see Chapter 6.

Adding to a Transaction Group

You can add transactions at any time to a group you've set up.

- Memorize the transactions you want to add.
- From the Register or Write Checks Screen, press ⌈Ctrl⌉-⌈J⌉ to see the Select Transaction Group window.
- Use ⌈↑⌉ and ⌈↓⌉ to position the cursor on the group you want to use and press ⌈Ctrl⌉-⌈E⌉. The Describe Group screen for that group will be displayed (see Figure 5-28).
- Press ⌈Ctrl⌉-⌈Enter⏎⌉ to see the Assign Transactions to Group window (see Figure 5-29).
- Use the ⌈↑⌉ and ⌈↓⌉ to position the cursor on the transaction you want to include in this group. Press ⌈space⌉ and the number of the group will appear in the Group column. If you don't want this transaction in the group, press ⌈space⌉ again to remove or unassign it. Repeat this step until all of the transactions you want in this group are assigned to it.
- Press ⌈Enter⏎⌉ to assign the new transactions to the Group.

Changing a Transaction Group

You may want to change something about a group, the description, the assigned account, or remove a transaction when a loan is paid off.

- From the Register or Write Checks Screen, press ⌈Ctrl⌉-⌈J⌉ to see the Select Transaction group window.
- Use ⌈↑⌉ and ⌈↓⌉ to position the cursor on the group you want to use and press ⌈Ctrl⌉-⌈E⌉. The Describe Group screen for that group will be displayed (see Figure 5-28).

- Make any necessary changes to the name, account, frequency, or date and press ⌜Enter←⌟ to see the Assign Transactions to Group window (see Figure 5-29).

- Use ⌜↑⌟ and ⌜↓⌟ to position the cursor on the transaction you want to include in or exclude from this group. Press ⌜space⌟ to change the assignment. Repeat this step until all of the transactions you want in this group are assigned to it.

- Press ⌜Enter←⌟ to complete the Group.

Deleting a Transaction Group

If you delete a transaction group, it is permanently removed. Any memorized transactions included in it remain in the Memorized Transactions List. If you delete a memorized transaction from the Memorized Transactions List, Quicken will also remove it from the transaction group.

- From the Register or Write Checks Screen, press ⌜Ctrl⌟-⌜J⌟ to see the Select Transaction group window.

- Use ⌜↑⌟ and ⌜↓⌟ to position the cursor on the group you want to delete.

- Press ⌜Ctrl⌟-⌜D⌟ to delete the group. Quicken will warn you that you are about to permanently delete a transaction group (see Figure 5-32).

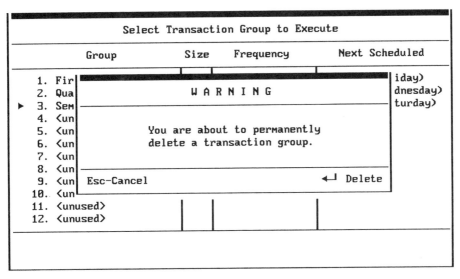

Figure 5-32 — Deleting a Transaction Group.

- Press [Enter←] to delete the transaction group or [esc] to cancel.

Summary

In this chapter you learned about Registers and Transactions: how to enter transactions in the Register, how to transfer funds, and reconcile your accounts. There were time-saving tips about transactions — how to split and memorize them, and how to import and export them to and from a file. Transaction Groups were discussed, what they are, and how they should be used.

Chapter 6

Writing and Printing Checks

Writing checks to pay bills can be a time-consuming and disagreeable job. Quicken can help you minimize the time and effort involved in this process by writing and printing the checks for you. Then, all you need to do is sign the checks, put them in stamped window envelopes, and mail them. Quicken treats the writing and printing of checks as separate procedures. This lets you write checks at any time you want, then print them as they are needed.

This chapter teaches you about

- writing checks
- printing checks
- paying bills electronically.

Shortcut Keys:

[esc]	Returns you to previous screen or activity
[F1]	Help key
[Ctrl]-[F1]	Help Index
[Ctrl]-[A]	Select or set up an account
[Ctrl]-[B]	Find previous transaction
[Ctrl]-[C]	Select or set up a category
[Ctrl]-[D]	Delete a check
[Ctrl]-[F]	Find transaction
[Ctrl]-[G]	Go to Date
[Ctrl]-[J]	Select a transaction group
[Ctrl]-[L]	Select or set up a class
[Ctrl]-[M]	Memorize a transaction
[Ctrl]-[N]	Find next transaction
[Ctrl]-[P]	Print checks
[Ctrl]-[S]	Split transaction
[Ctrl]-[T]	Memorized Transaction List
[Ctrl]-[V]	Void a check
[Ctrl]-[W]	Write Checks screen
Arrow keys	Move the cursor one space or line at a time
[PgUp]	Go to the preceding check
[PgDn]	Go to the next check
[Ctrl]-[home]	Go to the first check
[Ctrl]-[end]	Go to the last check
[+]	Increase date
[-]	Decrease date
["]	Ditto key

Check Writing

Writing a check with Quicken is similar to handwriting or typing a paper check. Some of the advantages of letting Quicken write and print your checks are:

- Typing errors can be fixed before the check is printed.

- When you fill in the amount, Quicken automatically spells it out on the next line.

- Regular payments can be memorized so you do not have to type them in every time.

- Periodic payments can be grouped together, and you can tell Quicken to write the group with one command.

These are the check-writing features in Quicken:

- **The Check Register**: When you write and record a check, Quicken automatically creates a transaction in the Register. Instead of assigning a check number, Quicken places five Asterisks (*****) in that column. Quicken will assign a check number to the transaction when you print the check.

  If you write a post-dated check, Quicken places it at the end of the Register and separates it from the others with a double line.

  When you use Quicken to write and print checks, you have to use the Register to record other transactions in your account, such as handwritten checks, previous transactions, deposits, and bank charges.

- **Categories and Classes**: Assign your checks to categories, subcategories, classes, and subclasses just like you did with transactions in the Register.

- **Transactions**: You can do the same things to a transaction in the Write Checks screen as you can to a transaction in the Register. Memorize it, split it, use a transfer in it, and put it in a Transaction Group. But remember one thing: if you want to use a memorized transaction or transaction group in the Write Checks screen, memorize it at the Write Checks screen.

Writing a Check

Use the Write Checks screen (see Figure 6-1) only for checks you want to print with Quicken. Enter handwritten checks, deposits, and service charges in the Register (see Chapter 5 for more information).

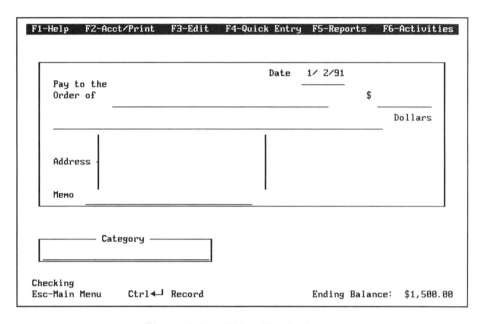

```
 F1-Help   F2-Acct/Print   F3-Edit   F4-Quick Entry  F5-Reports   F6-Activities


                                          Date    1/ 2/91
         Pay to the                              ─────────
         Order of
                      ──────────────────────────────  $  ─────────
                                                          Dollars
         ─────────────────────────────────────────────

                      │                          │
         Address  ┤   │                          │
                      │                          │
         Memo         ────────────────────       │


              ─── Category ───
         ┌──────────────────────────┐
         │──────────────────────────│
         └──────────────────────────┘

    Checking
    Esc-Main Menu     Ctrl↵  Record           Ending Balance:  $1,500.00
```

Figure 6-1 — Write Checks Screen.

The screen looks like a blank check except for three things:

- There will be no Check Number. Quicken does not number checks until the check is printed.

- The name of your Quicken account appears in the lower left of the screen.

- The lower right corner of the screen will display up to three lines. These lines show: the dollar total of the checks to print, the current balance, and the ending balance.

Figure 6-1 only shows the Ending Balance line, which is always on the screen. This number represents the last balance of your account. Figure 6-2 shows all three lines.

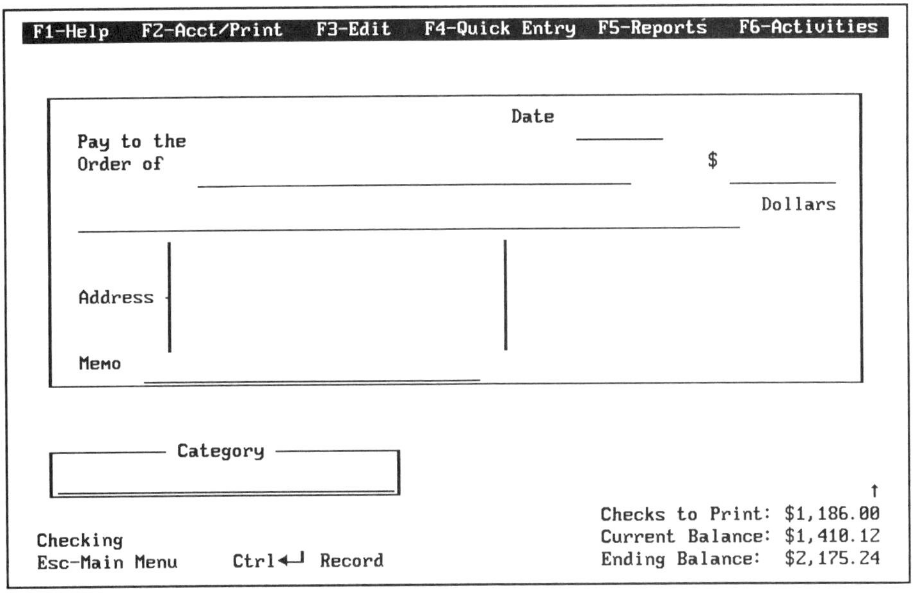

```
 F1-Help   F2-Acct/Print   F3-Edit   F4-Quick Entry  F5-Reports   F6-Activities


                                        Date
        Pay to the                     _____
        Order of      _____        $  _____

                                                              Dollars
        _____

                    |                         |
        Address  -  |                         |
                    |                         |
        Memo        |                         |
                _____


            ┌─────── Category ───────┐
            │                        │                                    ↑
            └────────────────────────┘               Checks to Print: $1,186.00
        Checking                                      Current Balance: $1,410.12
        Esc-Main Menu       Ctrl↵  Record             Ending Balance:  $2,175.24
```

Figure 6-2 — Write Checks Screen Showing Three Totals Lines.

- The first line shows the Checks to Print amount. This number is the sum of all checks written but not printed.

- The second line shows the Current Balance. This number is displayed if you've written post-dated checks and represents the total of all transactions through today's date.

- The third line shows the Ending Balance. Quicken adjusts this total every time you record a check.

To write a check, select the account you want to use. Press [Ctrl]-[W] or select Write/Print Checks from the Main Menu.

Date: Type the date of the day you plan to print and mail the check, or use ⊞ and ⊟ to increase or decrease the date shown. If you want a different date, type numbers only; Quicken inserts the slash character. For example:

- To enter 1/1/91   type 0, 1, 0, 1, 9, 1
- To enter 5/14/91   type 0, 5, 1, 4, 9, 1
- To enter 12/12/91   type 1, 2, 1, 2, 9, 1

Press ⌈Enter←⌉. If you type any zeros, Quicken removes them.

Pay to the Order of: Type the name of the payee, using up to 40 characters, and press ⌈Enter←⌉.

Amount: Type the amount of the check up to $9,999,999.99. You do not need to type dollar signs and commas. You need to type the decimal point only if the number is a combination of dollars and cents. For example:

- to enter $1,500.00 type 1, 5, 0, 0.
- to enter $123.45   type 1, 2, 3, ., 4, 5.
- to enter $50.00   type 5, 0.

Press ⌈Enter←⌉ and Quicken spells out the amount on the next line,

Address (optional): This feature saves time if you are using window envelopes. Use up to 30 characters per line, and up to five lines for the payee's name, address, city, state, and ZIP code.

- Use ditto (⌈"⌉ or ⌈'⌉) to have Quicken copy the payee name into the first line of the address field. Note that the Payee line contains 40 characters, but the address line has only 30. You have to type the remainder of the address yourself.
- Press ⌈Enter←⌉ at the end of each line.
- If you do not want to type an address, press ⌈Enter←⌉.

Memo (optional): Use up to 31 characters on this line for identifying the payment, such as with an account number or other special notation. The line will be printed on the check.

- Quicken allows you to set up and print another memo line. The line appears to the right of the address but will not be recorded with the transaction. For more information, see Chapter 7.

Category (optional): Use up to 31 characters (a single category name is limited to a maximum of 15 characters) to assign the transaction to:

- A category, subcategory, and one or more classes. Always separate the category and class names with a slash (/). Separate categories from subcategories and classes from subclasses with a colon (:). For more information on categories, `Ctrl`-`C`, and classes, `Ctrl`-`L`, see Chapter 4.
- A Split Transaction, `Ctrl`-`S`, with more than one category or class. See Chapter 5 for more information.
- A Transfer. Use this to write a check to be deposited in your savings account or for a payment to a credit card account. For more information, see Chapter 5.

At the Category field, press `Enter⏎` to record the check. Or press `Ctrl`-`Enter⏎` from anywhere in the Write Checks screen to record the transaction.

Quicken creates a transaction in the Register and places five Asterisks (*****) in the Num column to denote an unprinted check (see Figure 6-3). Quicken assigns a check number to this transaction when you print the check.

```
┌──────────────────────────────────────────────────────────────────────┐
│ F1-Help   F2-Acct/Print   F3-Edit   F4-Quick Entry  F5-Reports   F6-Activities │
│ ┌────┬─────┬──────────────────────────┬─────────┬─┬─────────┬─────────┐ │
│ │DATE│ NUM │ PAYEE  ·  MEMO  ·  CATEGORY│ PAYMENT │C│ DEPOSIT │ BALANCE │ │
│ │    │     │                          │         │ │         │         │ │
│ │    │     │                          │         │ │         │         │ │
│ │    │     │ ══════ BEGINNING ══════  │         │ │         │         │ │
│ │1/ 1│     │Opening Balance           │         │X│ 1,500 00│ 1,500 00│ │
│ │1991│     │            [Checking]    │         │ │         │         │ │
│ │                                                                     │ │
│ │1/ 2│*****│ Home Mortgage Company    │ 500 00  │ │         │ 1,000 00│ │
│ │1991│     │January Mortgag→Mort Int  │         │ │         │         │ │
│ │                                                                     │ │
│ │1/ 2│Memo:│                          │         │ │         │         │ │
│ │1991│ Cat:│                          │         │ │         │         │ │
│ │                                                                     │ │
│ └────┴─────┴──────────────────────────┴─────────┴─┴─────────┴─────────┘ │
│ Checking                                                               │
│ Esc-Main Menu      Ctrl↵  Record          Ending Balance:  $1,000.00   │
└──────────────────────────────────────────────────────────────────────┘
```

Figure 6-3 — Register Showing Written but Unprinted Check.

If this is a check you will write regularly, such as the mortgage or rent payment, car loan payment, or utility payment, memorize the transaction now, Ctrl-M (see Figure 6-4). The next time you want to pay this bill, recall the memorized transaction, with Ctrl-T, to save keystrokes. For more information, see Chapter 5.

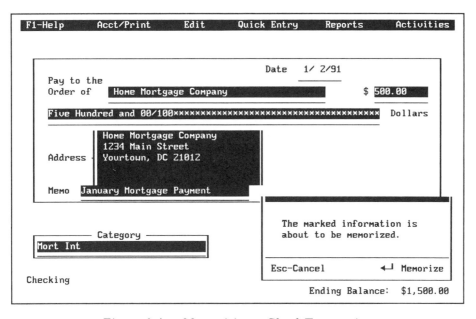

Figure 6-4 — Memorizing a Check Transaction.

Additionally, you can group your regularly paid bills into a Transaction Group. You can recall them with one command, `Ctrl`-`J`, and let Quicken fill in the checks (see Chapter 5).

Writing a post-dated check

You can write a post-dated check like you write any other kind of check.

- In the Date field, type the date that you plan to print and mail the check. Or use `+` or `-` to change the date shown. Press `Enter←`.
- Fill in the rest of the check as described above.
- Press `Ctrl`-`Enter←` to record the check.

Quicken now displays a Current Balance at the bottom right of the screen, right above the Ending Balance. The Current Balance shows you how much money you have in the account at this moment. The Ending Balance includes the post-dated check and shows what you have left in the account after all checks have been issued.

If you look in the Register you will see that Quicken has entered the post-dated transaction at the very end, and has separated it from the other transactions with a double line (see Figure 6-5). Five asterisks (*****) are in the NUM column until the check is printed.

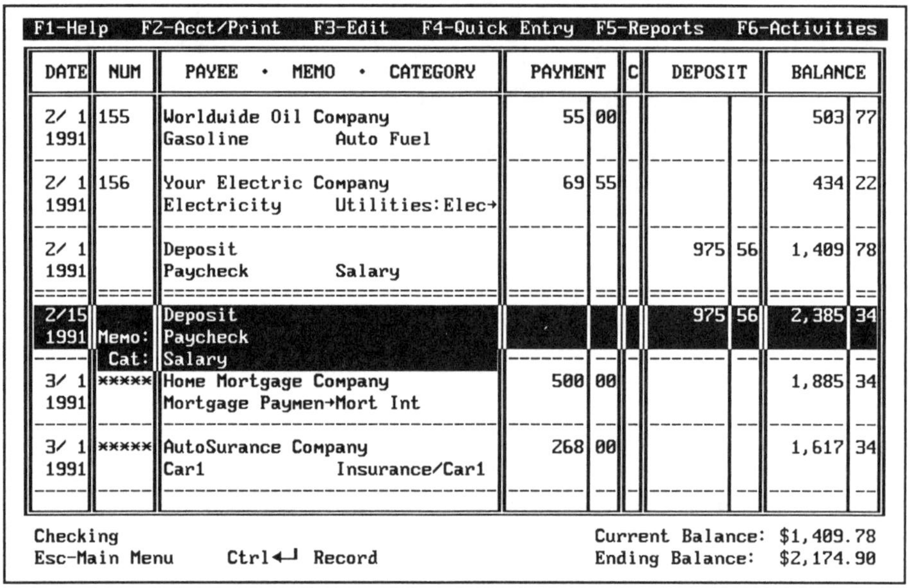

| F1-Help | F2-Acct/Print | F3-Edit | F4-Quick Entry | F5-Reports | F6-Activities |

DATE	NUM	PAYEE · MEMO · CATEGORY	PAYMENT	C	DEPOSIT	BALANCE
2/ 1 1991	155	Worldwide Oil Company Gasoline Auto Fuel	55 00			503 77
2/ 1 1991	156	Your Electric Company Electricity Utilities:Elec→	69 55			434 22
2/ 1 1991		Deposit Paycheck Salary			975 56	1,409 78
2/15 1991	Memo: Cat:	Deposit Paycheck Salary			975 56	2,385 34
3/ 1 1991	*****	Home Mortgage Company Mortgage Paymen→Mort Int	500 00			1,885 34
3/ 1 1991	*****	AutoSurance Company Car1 Insurance/Car1	268 00			1,617 34

Checking   Current Balance: $1,409.78
Esc-Main Menu   Ctrl↵ Record   Ending Balance: $2,174.90

Figure 6-5 — Postdated Transactions.

By writing post-dated checks, you can determine how much money you will need in your account to pay your known expenses. This is helpful if you have two accounts and use one of them for paying bills. You can keep most of your money in an interest-bearing account and transfer only what you need to pay your bills.

Changing a Check

Shortcut Keys:

Ctrl-B	Find previous transaction
Ctrl-F	Find transaction
Ctrl-G	Go to Date
Ctrl-N	Find next transaction
Ctrl-W	Write Checks screen
Arrow keys	Move the cursor one space or line at a time
PgUp	Go to the preceding check
PgDn	Go to the next check
Ctrl-home	Go to the first check
Ctrl-end	Go to the last check
+	Increase date
-	Decrease date

If a check has not been printed you can review and/or change it at the Write Checks screen. After you have printed a check, you can only review it in the Register.

Your checks will be in the same order in which you wrote them. You can use the cursor keys to scroll forward and backward like pages in a book. A blank check signals the end of the list. Small up and down arrows are displayed in the lower right corner of the screen, just above the Checks to Print total, to help you determine where you are.

- If there is no arrow, you have written no checks.

- If there is an up arrow, you are at a blank check and one or more checks are before it.

- If there is a down arrow, you are at the first check you've written and one or more come after it.

- If there are up and down arrows, you have checks before and after the one you are looking at.

Select your account, Ctrl-A, and call the Write Checks screen, Ctrl-W. Use PgDn and PgUp to review the checks, and to find the ones you want to change. You can use the Find Transaction, Ctrl-F, and Go to Date, Ctrl-G, features to find a specific check (for more information, see Chapter 5).

Make any necessary corrections, and press Ctrl-Enter to record the changes. If you do not want to record the changes you made, press esc to cancel the changes (this is useful when memorizing a transaction).

You can also review your unprinted checks at the Register, too, Ctrl-R. They're listed by date and marked with asterisks (*****). If you want to review and change addresses, you have to do that at the Write Checks screen — **address** is not a field in the Register.

Deleting a Check

You can delete a check from the Write Checks screen or the Register. Either way, the check will be permanently removed from the Register and the list of unprinted checks and your balance will be adjusted.

- From the Write Checks screen, display the check you want to delete.

- Press Ctrl-D or select Delete Transaction from the F3-Edit menu. The OK to Delete Transaction window will be displayed.

- Press Enter⏎ to delete or esc to cancel. Type 1 to delete the check, or 2 to return to it.

Voiding a Check

You can only void a check from the Register. A check is usually voided because you made a mistake when you hand wrote it, you stopped payment on it, or the Quicken checks were misprinted and had to be discarded. Voiding the check (instead of deleting it) allows you to keep a record of the check number. This allows you to keep your account accurate. If you have not yet printed a check, you can change or delete it from the Write Check screen.

1. In the Register, position the cursor on the transaction you want to void.

2. Press Ctrl-V or select Void Transaction from the F3-Edit menu. Quicken will insert the word "VOID" in front of the payee name, remove the number from the amount column, place an X in the Cleared column, and adjust the balance (see Figure 6-6).

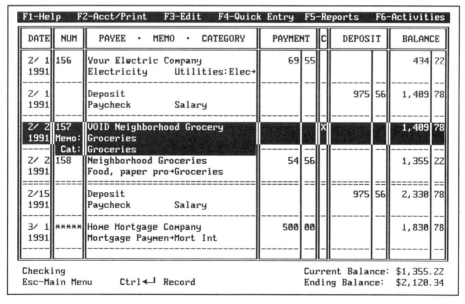

Figure 6-6 — Voiding a Check in the Register.

You can write a check at the Write Checks screen, record it, and press ⌃Ctrl⌄-⌃V⌄ to void it. But it will be recorded in the Register with no check number. There is no point in doing this, because without a number, there is no need to account for the check.

Check Printing

Quicken lets you select the checks you want to print, so you can write all of your payments for the month (or more), then print them as necessary. Quicken will also let you print post-dated checks.

Quicken will remind you if you have unprinted checks. If you have checks that are due to be printed, a message will appear at the bottom of the Main Menu when you start Quicken (see Figure 6-7). If you are using Billminder, you will also see a reminder at the DOS prompt when you start your computer (for more information, see Chapter 7).

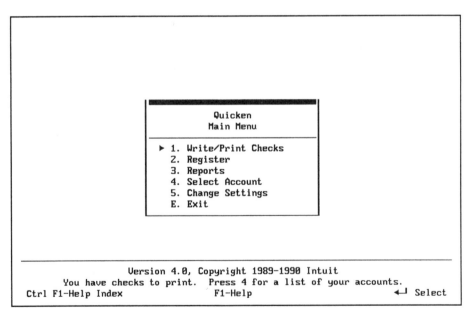

```
                         Quicken
                        Main Menu

              ▶ 1.  Write/Print Checks
                2.  Register
                3.  Reports
                4.  Select Account
                5.  Change Settings
                E.  Exit
```

```
             Version 4.0, Copyright 1989-1990 Intuit
        You have checks to print.  Press 4 for a list of your accounts.
   Ctrl F1-Help Index              F1-Help                    ↵ Select
```

Figure 6-7 — A Checks to Print Message.

To print checks with Quicken, you must have preprinted check forms to fit your printer. Check forms come in several styles and a variety of sizes to fit most printers — impact printers as well as laser printers. Preprinted checks come printed with your name, address, check number, bank name, account number, and other information that is required by financial institutions.

Quicken will print an order form you can use to order checks, window envelopes, and other supplies from Intuit. To print the form, select Order Supplies from the [F6]-Activities menu.

Printer Setup

Quicken is set up to work with three different printers (one each for checks, reports, and alternate) or one printer doing all three jobs. You can set printer options for checks and different options for reports. For more information on printer settings, see Chapter 7.

Quicken's default printer setting is 10 characters per inch, with the printer connected through the LPT1 parallel printer port. If you have a laser printer, or a serial printer, you will need to change these settings. For more information, see the section on Printer Settings in Chapter 7.

Try printing something with Quicken before you change any settings. Quicken is able to work with most printers, except lasers, without having to change anything.

Positioning Checks in the Printer

Insert the checks into your printer just as you would insert your regular continuous form paper. Quicken will let you print a sample check to make sure the check form is correctly aligned in the printer.

If you have a laser printer, Quicken automatically aligns the checks. Change the printer settings to match your laser printer and put a stack of checks (laser printer checks come three to a page) in the tray. For more information on setting up your laser printer, see Chapter 7.

Make sure the printer is turned on and on-line.

Printing a Sample Check

Follow the instructions below to print a sample check. When the check form is correctly aligned, you can tell Quicken to print your checks.

1. Select the appropriate account, [Ctrl]-[A], and press [Ctrl]-[W] to see the Write Checks screen.

2. Select Print Checks from the [F2]-Acct/Print menu or press [Ctrl]-[P] to see the Print Check window (see Figure 6-8). Quicken tells you how many checks are due to be printed, and asks for some information.

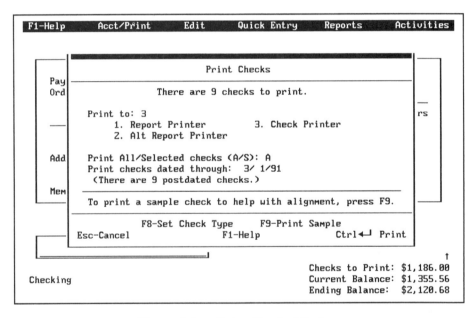

Figure 6-8 — Print Checks Window.

*   **Print to**: Type the appropriate number (1 for Report Printer, 2 for Alternate Report Printer, or 3 for Check Printer) and press [Enter←].

*   **Print All/Selected checks** (A/S): Type A to print all of the checks or S to print selected checks. Press [Enter←].

*   **Print checks dated through**: This line appears only if you have postdated checks. Type the desired date and Quicken will print all checks dated on or before that date.

3. Press ⊞ to select the Type of Checks window (see Figure 6-9). You only need to do this once, Quicken will remember the kind of checks you're using from then on. You won't have to set it again unless you change to another kind of check form. If you have a laser printer, you can also select the number of copies you want printed.

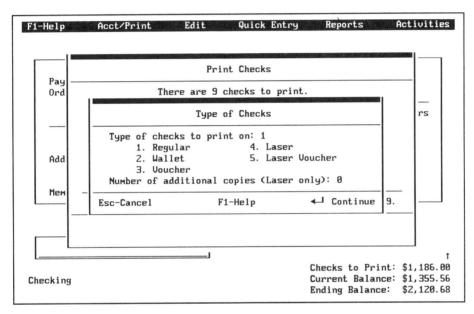

Figure 6-9 — Type of Checks Window.

4. You should print a sample check now to make sure the check form is correctly aligned in the printer. Press ⊞ and Quicken will display a note telling you not to adjust the printer after it finishes printing (see Figure 6-10).

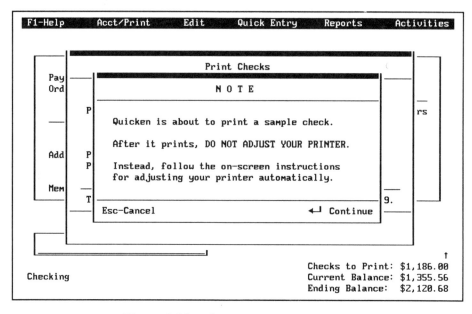

Figure 6-10 — Printing a Sample Check.

5. Press [Enter←] and the printer will print a sample check and the Type Position Number window (see Figure 6-11) will be displayed. If the check prints correctly, Press [Enter←].

6. If it didn't print correctly, look at the "Pointer Line" and the number it points to on the tractor strip. Type the number it is pointing to and press [Enter←]. If the Pointer Line wraps to the next line, the pitch or indent setting of the printer probably needs adjusting.

    • Quicken will advance the check and print another. If it is off by one-half of a line, manually adjust the printer by one half line.

    • If the check is too far to the right or left, reposition the checks by hand.

    • When the sample check prints correctly, press [Enter←] and the Print Checks window will be displayed (see Figure 6-8).

7. Make a note of the correct position for future use.

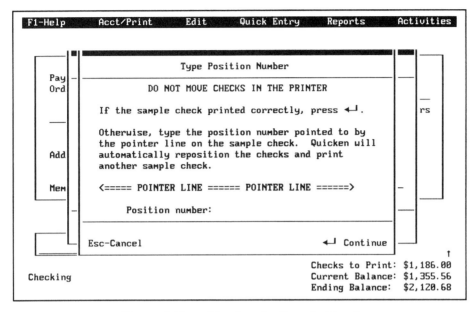

Figure 6-11 — Aligning the Sample Check.

Printing Checks

Now that your checks are correctly aligned in the printer, you can print your checks.

From the Print Checks window (see Figure 6-8), fill in the following:

Print to: Type the appropriate number (1 for Report Printer, 2 for Alternate Report Printer, or 3 for Check Printer) and press [Enter←].

Print All/Selected checks (A/S): You have two choices here.

- Type A to print all of the checks and press [Enter←].

Print checks dated through: Will display if you have postdated checks. Type the desired date or use ⊞ and ⊟ to increase or decrease the date. Quicken will print all checks dated on or before this date. You can specify a date and still select which checks to print.

or

- Type S to print selected checks. The Select Checks to Print window will be displayed (see Figure 6-12). The unprinted checks are listed in chronological order. To print all of the checks listed, do nothing. Use ⎡PgUp⎤ and ⎡PgDn⎤ to position the cursor on the checks you don't want to print and press ⎡space⎤. The word "Print" will disappear from the right-most column. Press ⎡space⎤ again to mark the check for printing. ⎡F9⎤ acts as a toggle; press it once to select all for printing and press it again to select none. When you have selected the checks you want to print, press ⎡Enter◄⏎⎤.

```
 F1-Help      Acct/Print      Edit      Quick Entry      Reports      Activities

                            Select Checks to Print

         Date         Payee                 Memo              Amount

     ▶  3/ 1/91  Home Mortgage Company  Mortgage Payment       500.00   Print
        3/ 1/91  AutoSurance Company    Car1                   268.00   Print
        3/ 1/91  AutoSurance Company    Car2                   193.00   Print
        3/ 1/91  BankCharge             B/C Payment              0.00   Print
        3/ 1/91  Our Telephone Company  Telephone Expenses       0.00   Print
        3/ 1/91  State Bank             Car Payment            175.00   Print
        3/ 1/91  Worldwide Oil Company  Gasoline                 0.00   Print
        3/ 1/91  Your Electric Company  Electricity              0.00   Print
        3/ 1/91  Corner Savings Bank    Transfer from checkin    50.00   Print



               Space Bar-Select/Deselect     F9-Select All
     Esc-Cancel                              F1-Help              ◄⏎ Continue

                                              Checks to Print: $1,186.00
     Checking                                 Current Balance: $1,355.56
                                              Ending Balance:  $2,120.68
```

Figure 6-12 — Selecting Checks to Print.

The Type Check Number window is displayed (see Figure 6-13). Look at the number on the next check and type it in the blank. Or use ⊞ and ⊟ to increase or decrease the number.

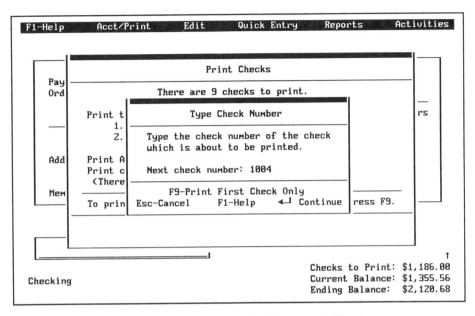

Figure 6-13 — Typing in the First Check Number.

You are ready to print and you again have two choices, to print one check or to print all of the checks.

•   Press [F9] to print only one check. Quicken prints the check and asks if it printed correctly (see Figure 6-14).

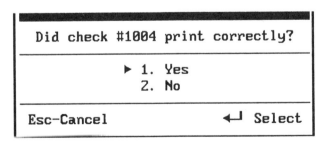

Figure 6-14 — Did the Check Print Correctly?

151

- If the check printed correctly, press $\boxed{\text{Enter} \leftarrow}$ or type 1. Quicken takes you back to the Write Checks screen.

or

- Press $\boxed{\text{Enter} \leftarrow}$ to print all of the checks. Quicken prints the checks and asks if they printed OK (see Figure 6-15).

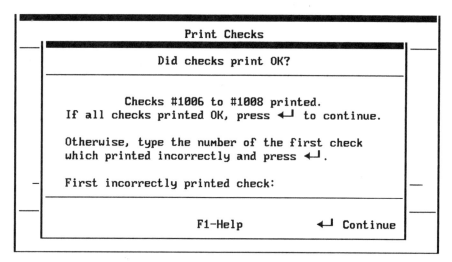

```
                    Print Checks

                 Did checks print OK?


             Checks #1006 to #1008 printed.
      If all checks printed OK, press ←┘ to continue.

     Otherwise, type the number of the first check
     which printed incorrectly and press ←┘.

     First incorrectly printed check:


                 F1-Help        ←┘ Continue
```

Figure 6-15 — Did Checks Print OK?

- If the checks printed correctly, press $\boxed{\text{Enter} \leftarrow}$.
- If they didn't print correctly, because you ran out of checks, or they got jammed in the printer, correct the problem. Type the number of the first check that didn't print correctly. Quicken will mark that check and any subsequent checks as unprinted and return you to the Print Checks window (see Figure 6-8). Answer the questions and try again.

Quicken will print the date you assigned to the check. If you want to change the date when you are printing it, see Other Settings in Chapter 7.

If a problem occurs, you can stop the printing process by pressing $\boxed{\text{esc}}$ and answering the questions to discontinue printing. If your printer has a buffer, you will have to turn off the printer to stop it.

Reprinting Checks

Quicken makes it easy for you to reprint a check at any time.

1. In the Register, position the cursor on the check you want to reprint.

2. In the Num column, type an asterisk (*). If you're in insert mode, delete the check number first. Quicken will place four more asterisks in the column to mark it as unprinted.

3. Go to the Write Checks screen to see the check, Ctrl-W. If you had an address on the check, Quicken erased it when the check was printed. You'll have to type it again, unless it's part of a Memorized Transaction.

4. Press Ctrl-Enter⏎ to record the check.

You can now print the check following the instructions listed in the print checks section.

You can keep Quicken from printing a check by deleting the asterisks in the Num column. You don't have to type in a check number because the asterisks act as a flag when Quicken looks for unprinted checks.

Electronic Bill Paying

CheckFree is an electronic bill payment system. You can use Quicken to interface with CheckFree and let CheckFree pay your bills while you retain complete control and keep up-to-date records (See Figure 6-16).

There is one very important consideration if you are thinking about using CheckFree to pay your bills: Once Quicken is configured for CheckFree, you can no longer use it to print checks. You can continue to use Quicken to account for handwritten checks, deposits, and services charges.

```
Select an Account for Electronic Payments

Select a Quicken account to set up so that you can
make payments electronically, using CheckFree, an
electronic payment service.

The account must be a bank account and it must be
the account you have authorized Checkfree Corporation
to make payments from. (This authorization is part
of the form for registering with Checkfree Corporation.)

If you have more than one account to use with Checkfree,
you should have ID numbers sent to you by Checkfree
Corporation to distinguish your accounts. If you have
only one account to use with CheckFree, its ID number
is your Social Security number.
_____
Esc-Cancel            F1-Help Index
```

Figure 6-16 — Help Screen for CheckFree.

There are several requirements if you decide to use Quicken to pay bills through CheckFree:

- You must have a modem.

- You must set up an account with CheckFree Corporation. Fill out and mail the CheckFree form that came with your Quicken package. CheckFree will then send you an account number, modem baud rates for transmissions, and the telephone number to call for transmissions. At the time of this writing, this service costs $9.00 per month for up to 20 transactions.

- You must change Quicken's settings to allow for electronic payment. To do this, choose Change Settings on the Main Menu and select number 7, Electronic Payment.

If you are new to Quicken, you probably should not use CheckFree right away. Enter the transactions from your checkbook and get your finances organized. The next step is to use Quicken to print checks. When you have mastered your personal finances, you'll be ready to try CheckFree. See your Quicken manual for more information about CheckFree.

Summary

You can use Quicken to write and print checks. You can memorize transactions and set up transaction groups to minimize the time and effort in paying you bills. You can also use an electronic bill paying service.

Chapter 7

Other Features

One of Quicken's strengths is that it can be tailored to your requirements, tastes, and computer system. In this chapter, you'll learn how to

- set up and use other account groups
- change Quicken's many settings to meet your needs
- set up a password
- use Billminder.

Change Settings

The Change Settings menu is the fifth selection on the main menu. Position the cursor on Change Settings and press [Enter←], or type 5 (see Figure 7-1).

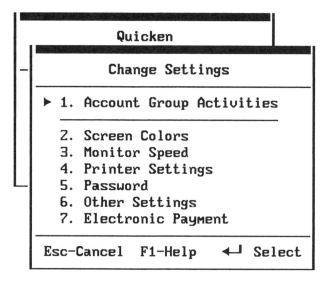

Figure 7-1 — The Change Settings Menu.

Account Groups

Quicken organizes your data in two ways, by account and by account group. You can work with only one account group at a time but it can contain up to 255 accounts. Quicken initially places all of your data in the account group named QDATA. For most users, that's all they need.

You might need to create other account groups, however. If you don't have a hard disk drive, for instance, and your account grows too large for one diskette. If you have a small business and you want to separate it from your personal finances. Another use might be to separate the transactions for each year into separate account groups.

Accounts within a group use the same categories, subcategories, classes, memorized transactions, electronic payees, memorized reports, and transaction groups. You can make transfers between accounts in the same account group and all of the data in a group is available so you can generate reports on selected accounts or all of the accounts.

Set up any additional account groups you want, but remember: you cannot transfer money between accounts in different groups, and you cannot use data from more than one group in a report.

The Account Group Activities menu gives you five selections that let you set up additional account groups, select, back up, restore, delete, rename, copy and shrink an account group, and set a new location for an account group (see Figure 7-2).

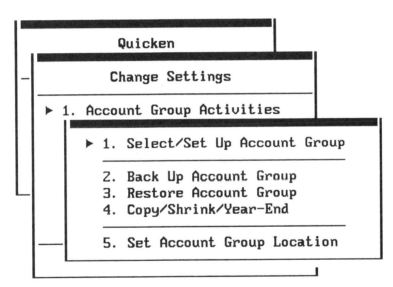

Figure 7-2 — Account Group Activities Menu.

Select/Set Up Account Groups

Shortcut keys:

Ctrl-D   Delete an account group

Ctrl-E   Edit an account group

Ctrl-G   Select/Set Up Account Group (from Main Menu)

F9   Set directory

Quicken remembers which account you last used and will automatically take you there the next time you start the program. If you want to set up a new account group, or work with a different account group, you must select the one you want.

The Select/Set Up Account Group menu lets you select, set up, change, and delete an account group or change its location. You can get to this menu two ways:

• From the Main Menu, press Ctrl-G.

• Select Change Settings on the Main Menu, or type 5, then select Account Group Activities. Position the cursor on Select/Set Up Account Group and press Enter↵, or type 1. The Select/Set Up Account Group window will display (see Figure 7-3).

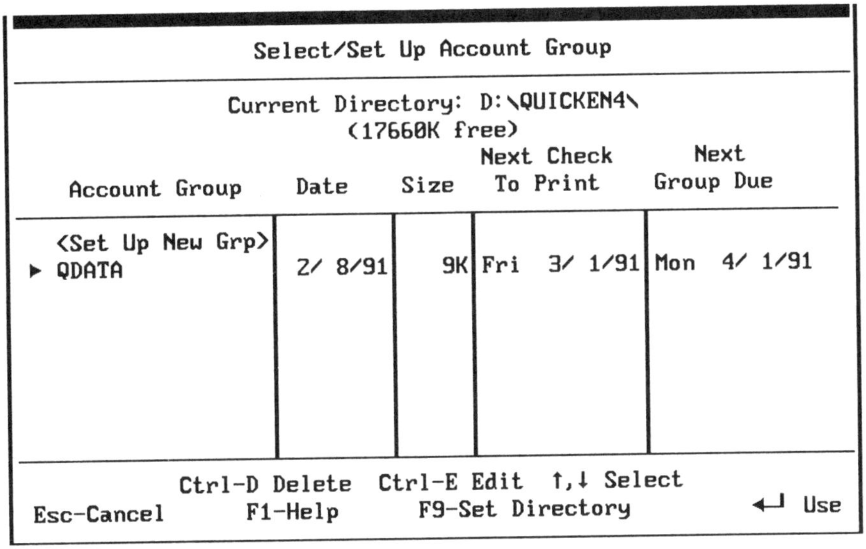

```
┌─────────────────────────────────────────────────────────────┐
│            Select/Set Up Account Group                       │
├─────────────────────────────────────────────────────────────┤
│         Current Directory: D:\QUICKEN4\                      │
│                   (17660K free)                              │
│                             Next Check      Next             │
│    Account Group    Date   Size  To Print   Group Due        │
│  ┌──────────────────────┐                                    │
│    <Set Up New Grp>      │        │                 │        │
│  ▶ QDATA              2/ 8/91   9K│Fri   3/ 1/91│Mon   4/ 1/91│
│  └──────────────────────┘                                    │
│                                                              │
│                                                              │
│                                                              │
│                                                              │
│                                                              │
│        Ctrl-D Delete   Ctrl-E Edit   ↑,↓ Select             │
│  Esc-Cancel      F1-Help      F9-Set Directory      ↵  Use   │
└─────────────────────────────────────────────────────────────┘
```

Figure 7-3 — The Select/Set Up Account Group Window.

The first time you see this window there will be only one account group listed, QDATA. You will have several options at this window.

- **Set up an account group**: Position the cursor on the first line in the Select/Set Up Account Group window — <Set Up New Grp> — and press [Enter◄─┘]. The Set Up Account Group Window will be displayed (see Figure 7-4).

161

```
┌─────────────────────────────────────────────────────────────┐
│ ████████████████████████████████████████████████████████████│
│                                                              │
│                   Set Up Account Group                       │
│ ─────────────────────────────────────────────────────────── │
│                                                              │
│   Enter name for account group:                              │
│     (8 character DOS filename)                               │
│                                                              │
│   Quicken uses categories to track your income and expenses. │
│   Select which type of categories you would like to start with.│
│                                                              │
│   Standard categories to use:                                │
│       1. Home categories          3. Both                    │
│       2. Business categories      4. Neither                 │
│                                                              │
│   Location for data files: D:\QUICKEN4\                      │
│ ─────────────────────────────────────────────────────────── │
│  Esc-Cancel                F1-Help              ↵ Continue   │
└─────────────────────────────────────────────────────────────┘
```

Figure 7-4 — Set Up Account Group Window.

- **Enter name for account group**: Type the name of the account group you want to create, using up to eight characters and DOS conventions. Press [F1] if you need help. Do not include an extension. Quicken will use this name to create four files with the following extensions: .QDT, .QNX, .QMT, and .QDI. Press [Enter◄─┘] to continue. If you typed lower case letters, Quicken will capitalize the group name.

- **Standard categories to use**: Type 1 for home, 2 for business, 3 for both home and business, or 4 for neither. Press [Enter◄─┘] to continue.

- **Location for data files**: If you want your files stored somewhere other than the location Quicken inserted here, type the path, including drive and directory. Press [Enter◄─┘].

- Quicken returns you to the Select/Set Up Account Group window and adds the group you just created to the list.

To select an Account Group, position the cursor on the account group you want to use and press [Enter◄─┘]. The Select Account to Use window will be displayed. Position the cursor on the account you want, press [Enter◄─┘], and the Register for that account will be displayed on the screen.

If this is a new account group, one that you just set up, there will be no accounts listed. Set up your accounts for this group just as you did when you began using Quicken. For more information, see Chapter 4.

To change the name of an account group, position the cursor on the account group you want to use and press [Ctrl]-[E]. The Rename an Account Group window will be displayed (see Figure 7-5).

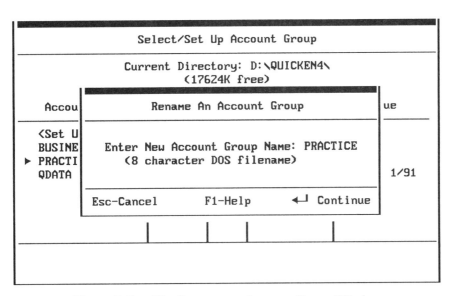

```
                 Select/Set Up Account Group

              Current Directory:  D:\QUICKEN4\
                        (17624K free)

  Accou │       Rename An Account Group        │ ue

  <Set U│                                      │
  BUSINE│   Enter New Account Group Name: PRACTICE
► PRACTI│      (8 character DOS filename)       │
  QDATA │                                      │ 1/91

        │  Esc-Cancel      F1-Help      ◄┘ Continue
```

Figure 7-5 — The Rename an Account Group Window.

Type the new name in the space provided. If the new name is shorter than the old name, be sure to delete the extra characters. If you typed lower case letters, Quicken will capitalize the name. Press [Enter◄┘]. Quicken will rename the account group and return you to the Select/Set Up Account Group window.

To delete an Account Group, position the cursor on the account group you want to delete and press [Ctrl]-[D]. A warning message will appear where Quicken asks you for verification (see Figure 7-6). Type YES to delete the account group or press [esc] to cancel. Press [Enter◄┘]. Quicken removes the account group from the list and returns you to the Select/Set Up Account Group window.

Pressing [Enter◄┘] without typing the word YES is the same as pressing [esc].

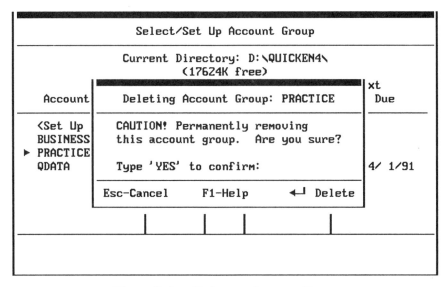

Figure 7-6 — Delete an Account Group.

To set the drive and/or directory, press ⌘F9⌘. For more information, see Set Account Group Location, later in this chapter.

Back Up Account Group

Use this selection when to want to backup any account group to another directory on your hard drive, or to a floppy disk.

Note: It is extremely important to have backup copies of your files. If anything should happen to the original files, you will save a lot of time and effort if you can easily restore data using your backup files. Get in the habit of doing a backup every time you exit Quicken. You can even use this backup feature without having to quit Quicken.

1.   At the Change Settings menu, select Account Group Activities.

2.   Position the cursor on Back Up Account Group and press ⌘Enter←⌘, or type 2. The Select Backup Drive window will be displayed (see Figure 7-7). Type the letter of the disk drive on which you want your files to be backed up. Insert a disk in the drive and press ⌘Enter←⌘. When it finishes, Quicken will return you to the Account Group Activities menu.

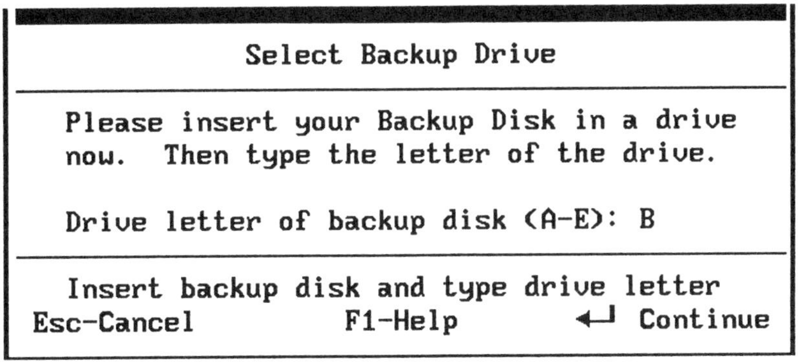

```
┌─────────────────────────────────────────────┐
│                                               │
│            Select Backup Drive                │
│ ───────────────────────────────────────────── │
│   Please insert your Backup Disk in a drive   │
│   now.  Then type the letter of the drive.    │
│                                               │
│   Drive letter of backup disk (A-E): B        │
│ ───────────────────────────────────────────── │
│   Insert backup disk and type drive letter    │
│   Esc-Cancel           F1-Help      ↵ Continue │
│                                               │
└─────────────────────────────────────────────┘
```

Figure 7-7 — Select Backup Drive Window.

3. Position the cursor on Select/Set Up Account Group and press `Enter↵`, or type 1. The Select/Set Up Account Group window will be displayed.

4. Position the cursor on the account group you want to back up and press `Enter↵`. When Quicken finishes, you will see a message telling you that your files were successfully backed up. Press `Enter↵`, and the Select/Set Up Account Group window will again be displayed. You can back up another account group if you wish.

You can back up your current account group from the Main Menu by pressing `Ctrl`-`B`. If you need to format a disk, select Use DOS from the `F6`-Activities menu.

Restore Account Group

You can use this selection to restore account group data should your hard disk crash.

1. At the Change Settings menu, select Account Group Activities.

2. Position the cursor on Restore Account Group and press `Enter↵`, or type 3. The Select Drive to Restore From window will be displayed (see Figure 7-8).

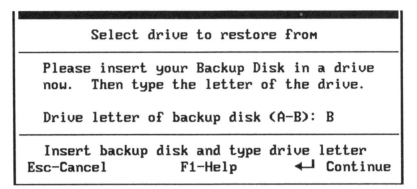

Figure 7-8 — The Select Drive to Restore From Window.

3. Type the letter of the disk drive that contains the disk with the files to be restored and press Enter⏎. The Select Account Group to Restore window will be displayed.

4. Position the cursor on the account group you want to restore and press Enter⏎. You may see a message asking if it's all right to overwrite the existing account group (see Figure 7-9). Press Enter⏎ to restore the files or esc to cancel.

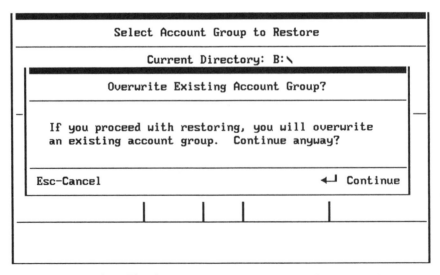

Figure 7-9 — The Overwrite Existing Account Group Window.

Quicken will restore the files and display a message that they were successfully restored. Press Enter⏎ and the Select Account Group to Restore window will display again.

Copy/Shrink/Year-End

Use this selection to copy all or part of a Quicken account group to a new account group. Quicken will let you copy one or more of the following: the Category and Transfer List, the Memorized Transaction List, and the Transaction Group List.

You will want to use this option if your floppy disk is full, if you want to keep each year's records separate from one another, or if you want to copy the lists of categories, memorized transactions, and transaction groups to another account group.

To use the Copy/Shrink/Year-End feature

1.   Select the account group you want to copy (see Select/Set Up Account Group earlier in this chapter).

2.   At the Change Settings menu, select Account Group Activities.

3.   Position the cursor on Copy/Shrink/Year-End and press Enter⏎, or type 4. The Copy Account Group window will be displayed (see Figure 7-10).

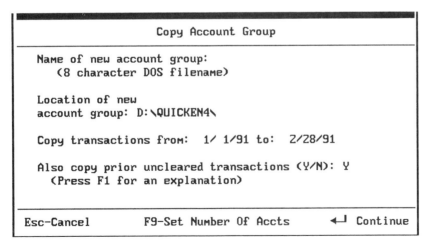

Figure 7-10 — Copy Account Group Window.

To copy and shrink an account group

Type in the following information:

1. **Name of new account group**: Type the name of the new account group using up to eight characters and DOS conventions. If necessary, press [Fl] for help. Press [Enter←].

2. **Location of new account group**: If you want your files stored somewhere other than the location Quicken inserted here, type the path, including drive and directory. Press [Enter←].

3. **Copy transactions from and to**: Use the beginning and ending dates of the range of transactions you want to copy to the new account group. For instance, if you want to separate your records by years, type 1/1/91 and 12/31/91. Type the beginning date, press [Enter←], type the ending date, and press [Enter←].

If you want to change the number of accounts in the new account group, Press [F9] (see Figure 7-11). Quicken normally copies up to 64 accounts, but you can increase it to a maximum of 255 accounts. This allows you to ensure that all accounts will be copied when copying an account group with a lengthy Category and Transfer List.

```
              Copy Account Group

 Name of new account group:

              Set Maximum Accounts In Group


  Maximum number of accounts in new account group: 64


 Esc-Cancel                                 ↵ Continue
```

Figure 7-11 — The Set Maximum Number of Accounts in Group Window.

4. **Also copy prior uncleared transactions (Y/N):**

    •   If you reconcile your bank and credit card accounts, type Y (yes). Quicken will copy all prior transactions not marked with an X in the Cleared column.

    •   Otherwise, type N (no).

    •   **Copy all investment transactions (Y/N):** This line appears only if you have set up one or more investment accounts in this group. Type Y (yes) to retain all of the historical data.

5. Press Enter⏎ and Quicken will copy the information into the new account group. The account group you copied from will remain in your records. The Account Group Copied Successfully window is displayed (see Figure 7-12).

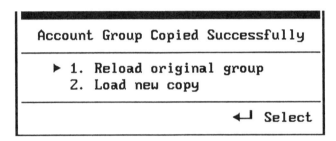

Figure 7-12 — The Account Group Copied Successfully Window.

This window gives you two options:

•   Reload the original group, if you want to work with the old account group.

•   Load the new copy, if you want to enter transactions in the new group.

To copy an account to a different account group

If you are trying to transfer information into an existing account, Quicken will not let you do it in one step. You have to use the export and import features described in Chapter 5.

You can, however, use the procedure discussed above, Copy and Shrink an Account Group, to copy specified transactions into an account that you tell Quicken to create. You must use the Set Directory function, [F9], to set the number of accounts to the maximum of 255. If you don't, all of the items on the Category and Transfer List will not be copied. Remember that your accounts are part of that list and are located at the end. If you only copy 64 items, your bank, credit card, or other accounts may not be copied.

To do year-end procedures

Quicken does not require you to close out your accounts as do most accounting packages. Closing out an account means that individual income and expense transactions for that period are no longer available to you, only the totals of the transactions. Year-end closing takes it all away. This makes it difficult to produce reports covering more than the current year.

If you want to close out an account, you have two choices: You can make a backup copy and continue to use the original account name. Or, you can use the original account group as an archive account and copy specified information into another group.

- Use the Backup procedure to make a copy of the account group. Date it and store it in a safe place, and continue to use the original disk. This is not really closing out the account. You are merely archiving a copy. Because you can still access and edit the old information, this is not considered a good accounting practice for a business.

  Because this file still contains all of your old data, as well as the new, you can generate reports covering more than one reporting period. This can be very convenient for personal finances.

- Use the original account group as an archive account and copy your year-end carryover information into a new account group. You will now have one set of files containing all of your current status and transactions, and a different set of files for each fiscal period, such as 1989, 1990, and 1991, that can be used as read-only files for reports specific to that period.

Don't forget to use the Set Directory function, 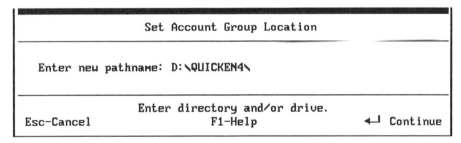, to set the number of accounts to the maximum of 255, so that all of the items on the Category and Transfer List will be copied.

Be careful with uncleared transactions. It may take more than a month before you can reconcile your account and mark transactions as cleared. If you want to archive your records for a calendar year, wait (if you can) until all of the items for that period have cleared the bank. You can then copy complete records, using the Copy/Shrink/Year-End procedure as described above.

Set Account Group Location

This feature lets you change the location of your data. You'll need to do this if you want to store your files on a different drive or directory.

1.   At the Change Settings menu, select Account Group Activities.

2.   Position the cursor on Set Account Group Location and press Enter◄┘ or type 5. The Set Account Group Location window will be displayed (see Figure 7-13).

```
              Set Account Group Location
  ─────────────────────────────────────────────────

   Enter new pathname: D:\QUICKEN4\

  ─────────────────────────────────────────────────
                Enter directory and/or drive.
   Esc-Cancel             F1-Help            ◄┘ Continue
```

Figure 7-13 — Set Account Group Location.

3.   Type the path name, including drive and directory if applicable. Press Enter◄┘ to change the location, or esc to cancel.

You can also change the location from the Select/Set Up Account Group window.

Screen Colors

You can change the colors or shades that Quicken displays on your monitor. Quicken gives you five choices:

- **Monochrome**: Use this if your monitor is one-color and can't display shades.

- **Navy/Azure**:

- **White/Navy**:

- **Red/Gray**: This color combination is helpful if you are color blind.

- **Shades of Gray**: Use this if your one-color monitor can display shades of gray.

At the Change Settings menu, select Screen Colors by typing 2 or by positioning the cursor on Screen Colors and pressing [Enter←]. The Change Color Scheme window will display (see Figure 7-14).

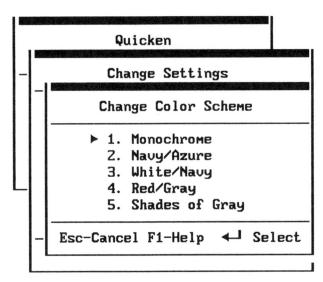

Figure 7-14 — The Change Color Scheme Menu.

Type the appropriate number or position the cursor on the selection you want, and press [Enter←]. The Change Settings Menu will be displayed and your screen colors will change.

Monitor Speed

Quicken works at two speeds: fast or slow. The best one for you depends on your monitor. If you have EGA or VGA, you should use the default fast setting.

If you have a CGA adapter, if your monitor has trouble changing screens, or if you get snow (white specks) on the screen, you will need to change to the slow speed.

1. At the Change Settings menu, select Monitor Speed by typing 3, or by positioning the cursor on Monitor Speed and pressing [Enter←]. The Screen Update window will be displayed.

2. Select Slow, and press [Enter←].

Printer Settings

Depending on the printer(s) you have, you may have to change some settings. Quicken will work with most standard printers but if you have a serial or laser printer, or if your printer is set to a character pitch other than 10, you will have to make some adjustments.

Quicken will work with as many as three different printer settings. You can use onc printer to work in up to three ways; to print checks, print reports in draft mode, and print final reports in letter quality. Or you can use three different printers to each do one of the above tasks.

At the Change Settings menu, select Printer Settings by typing 4, or by positioning the cursor on Change Printer Settings and pressing [Enter←]. A window with three options will be displayed (see Figure 7-15).

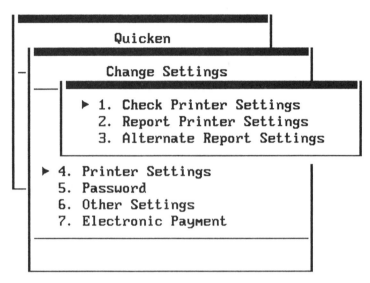

Figure 7-15 — The Printer Settings Menu.

Choose one of the following by typing the number, or by positioning the cursor on the selection you want and pressing Enter←⟋ .

1. Check Printer Settings.

2. Report Printer Settings.

3. Alternate Report Settings.

The Printer List will be displayed (see Figure 7-16). Use ⬆ and ⬇ and PgUp and PgDn to scroll through the list. Position the cursor on the selection and style you want, and press Enter←⟋ .

```
┌─────────────────────────────────────────────────────┐
│███████████████████████████████████████████████████████│
│              Check Printer Settings                   │
│█████████████████████████████████████████████████████  │
│  ┌─────────────────────────────────────────────────┐  │
│  │                 Printer List                    │  │
│  │  ─────────────────────────────────────────────  │  │
│  │    Printer         Printing Style        Pitch  │  │
│  │  ─────────────────────────────────────────────  │  │
│  │ ▶ <Unlisted>   │Checks & Reports - Normal │ 10  │  │
│  │                │Wide Carriage             │ 10  │  │
│  │ Canon LBP-II & │Check Printing            │ 10  │  │
│  │      LBP-III   │Report Printing           │ 10  │  │
│  │                │Report Printing-Compressed│ 17  │  │
│  │                │Report Printing-Lscp,Cmpr │ 17  │  │
│  │ Epson          │Checks & Reports - Normal │ 10  │  │
│  │                │Near Letter Quality       │ 10  │  │
│  │                │Compressed Printing       │ 17  │  │
│  │  ─────────────────────────────────────────────  │  │
│  │ Esc-Cancel  Select Printer and Style  ↵ Select  │  │
│  └─────────────────────────────────────────────────┘  │
└─────────────────────────────────────────────────────┘
```

Figure 7-16 — Printer List.

The Printer Settings window will be displayed (see Figure 7-17). Depending on which selection you made, it will say Check, Report, or Alternate Report Printer Settings. The contents of each window is the same.

```
┌─────────────────────────────────────────────────────────────┐
│▓▓▓▓▓▓▓▓▓▓▓▓▓▓▓▓▓▓▓▓▓▓▓▓▓▓▓▓▓▓▓▓▓▓▓▓▓▓▓▓▓▓▓▓▓▓▓▓▓▓▓▓▓▓▓▓▓▓▓▓▓▓│
│                   Check Printer Settings                     │
│─────────────────────────────────────────────────────────────│
│  Name of printer (optional): Okidata                         │
│  Print to: 2                                                 │
│       1. PRN:        4. LPT3:        7. COM2:                │
│       2. LPT1:       5. AUX:                                  │
│       3. LPT2:       6. COM1:                                 │
│  Indent: 0                                                   │
│─────────────────────────────────────────────────────────────│
│              Settings for this printing style                │
│  Lines per page: 66             Print pitch: 10              │
│  Characters per line: 80        (characters per inch)        │
│  Pause between pages (Y/N): N                                │
│─────────────────────────────────────────────────────────────│
│  Page-oriented (e.g. laser) printer (Y/N): N                 │
│  Supports IBM graphics characters (Y/N): N                   │
│─────────────────────────────────────────────────────────────│
│   F8-Edit Control Codes   F9-Select Printer From List        │
│   Esc-Cancel                  F1-Help          ↵ Continue    │
└─────────────────────────────────────────────────────────────┘
```

Figure 7-17 — Check Printer Settings Window.

If necessary, make changes to the following settings:

- **Name of printer (optional)**: The name of the printer you selected will be displayed here. If you type over or erase it, the settings for this printer will not change. Press [Enter←] to continue.

- **Print to**: Type the number of the printer port you are using. PRN, LPT1, LPT2, and LPT3 are parallel ports; AUX, COM1, and COM2 are serial ports. Press [Enter←] to continue.

Press [F8] (Edit Control Codes) if you want to enter or change control codes for your printer (see Figure 7-18). If you selected a printer from the list provided with Quicken, you probably don't need to do anything here. If you need to enter or change control codes, refer to your printer manual to determine what those codes should be. Press [Enter←] to change the codes or [esc] to cancel.

```
┌─────────────────────────────────────────────────────────────────┐
│ ▬▬▬▬▬▬▬▬▬▬▬▬▬▬▬▬▬▬▬▬▬▬▬▬▬▬▬▬▬▬▬▬▬▬▬▬▬▬▬▬▬▬▬                    │
│                     Printer Control Codes                         │
│  ───────────────────────────────────────────────────────────     │
│  Before printing:                                                 │
│  After printing :                                                 │
│  Start of page  :                                                 │
│  Single checks  :                                                 │
│  Portrait/Centered landscape/Left-align landscape single checks (P/C/L): │
│  ───────────────────────────────────────────────────────────     │
│  Esc-Cancel                   F1-Help                 ◄┘ Continue │
└─────────────────────────────────────────────────────────────────┘
```

Figure 7-18 — Printer Control Codes Window.

Press [F9] to select a printer or print mode from the Printer List. Use [↑] and [↓] and [PgUp] and [PgDn] to scroll through the list. Position the cursor on the selection and style you want and press [Enter◄──].

The following fields were preset when you selected a printer, and you probably won't need to change them.

- **Indent**: If you type a number here, Quicken will move all printing that many characters to the right. Press [Enter◄──] to continue.

- **Lines per page**: Type in the number of lines you want on a report and include the top and bottom margins. Quicken's default is 66 for a regular sheet of eleven-inch paper. Press [Enter◄──] to continue.

- **Print pitch (characters per inch)**: Set this to match the pitch setting of your printer and press [Enter◄──]. Changing this setting will not change the pitch of your printer. You must use printer control codes to do that (Edit Control Codes, [F8]).

- **Characters per line**: Type the number of characters to print on each line and press [Enter◄──]. If your printer has a wide carriage, you changed the indent number, or your printer pitch is other than 10 or 12, you might need to change this setting. Set this to equal the number of printable columns less the amount of any indents.

- **Pause between pages (Y/N)**: Type Y (yes) if you want to use single sheets of paper or N (no) to use continuous form paper, then press [Enter◄──].

- **Page-oriented (e.g. laser) printer (Y/N)**: This setting affects the printing of checks. Type Y (yes) if you are using a laser printer and press [Enter◄──].

- **Supports IBM graphics characters (Y/N)**: Type Y (yes) if your printer supports IBM graphics. Quicken will use them to generate reports. To find out if you printer will support these graphics characters, type Y (yes) and print a report. If unusual symbols (D and M) are printed, instead of – or =, your printer does not support the graphic characters. Change the setting to N (no). Press `Enter◄┘`.

If you selected one of the serial port selections (AUX, COM1, or COM2), the Serial Port Settings window will be displayed. This window contains special settings for most serial printers. Refer to your printer manual to determine what these settings should be.

You can also get to Printer Settings by choosing Change Printer Settings on the Acct/Print menu.

Password

You can use passwords to provide a basic level of protection. Quicken will let you set and change two kinds of passwords for an account group: a Main password and a Transaction Password. If you set up a Main Password, you can control access to an account group. Set up a Transaction Password and you can prevent changes to your account.

Setting the Main Password

You can assign a password to each of your account groups. Once you set up a password for a group, you must type the password to access that group, so make sure you keep a record of the passwords.

Note that a password is assigned to the currently active account group, so make certain you are assigning the password to the correct account group. To set up a Main Password:

1. Select the account group you want to protect (select Account Group Activities on the Change Settings menu, then choose Select/Set Up Account Group).

2. At the Change Settings Menu, type 5 or position the cursor on Password and press `Enter◄┘`. The password menu will be displayed (see Figure 7-19).

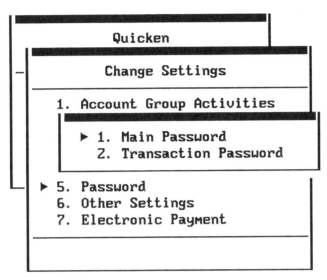

Figure 7-19 — Two Types of Passwords.

3. Select Main Password by typing 1, or by positioning the cursor on Main Password, and pressing [Enter←]. The Set Up Password window will be displayed.

4. Type the name of the password, using up to 16 characters (you can include spaces but Quicken ignores upper and lower case). Press [Enter←]. The Confirm Password window is displayed.

5. Type the password again to confirm, and press [Enter←] to set the password.

Quicken will now prompt you for the password before you can use the account group.

Changing or Removing the Main Password

You can easily change or remove the password as long as you know the original password.

1. Select the account group that has the password you want to change or remove.

2. At the Change Settings Menu, type 5 or position the cursor on Password and press [Enter←]. The password menu will be displayed.

3. Select Main Password by typing 1, or by positioning the cursor on Main Password, and pressing [Enter◄┘]. The Change Password window will be displayed.

4. Type the name of the old password and press [Enter◄┘].

5. To change the password, type the name of the new password. To remove the password, leave it blank. Press [Enter◄┘].

6. If you change to a new password, the Confirm Password window is displayed. Type the password again to confirm, and press [Enter◄┘] to set the password.

Setting a Transaction Password

You can use a Transaction Password to make certain transactions read-only. This means you can look at, print, and make reports on them, but you can't add to, change, or delete them.

1. Select the account group you want to protect (select Account Group Activities on the Change Settings Menu, then choose Select/Set Up Account Group).

2. At the Change Settings Menu, type 5 or position the cursor on Password and press [Enter◄┘]. The password menu will be displayed.

3. Select Transaction Password by typing 2, or positioning the cursor on Transaction Password, and pressing [Enter◄┘]. The Password to Modify Existing Transactions window will be displayed (see Figure 7-20).

4. Type the name of the password, using up to 16 characters. Press [Enter◄┘].

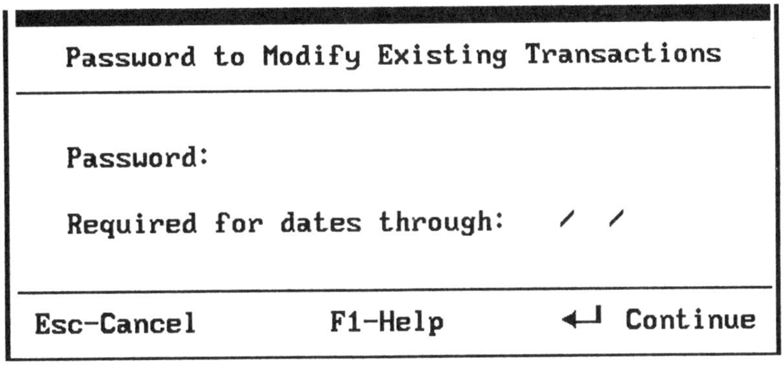

```
┌─────────────────────────────────────────────────────┐
│ �███████████████████████████████████████████████     │
│                                                       │
│   Password to Modify Existing Transactions            │
│  ─────────────────────────────────────────────────   │
│                                                       │
│   Password:                                           │
│                                                       │
│   Required for dates through:    ╱  ╱                 │
│                                                       │
│  ─────────────────────────────────────────────────   │
│   Esc-Cancel          F1-Help        ◄┘ Continue      │
└─────────────────────────────────────────────────────┘
```

Figure 7-20 — Transaction Password.

5. Type the date through which the transaction password will be required (the expiration date) and press [Enter◄─].

    When you assign a Transaction Password, the transactions will be protected until the specified date is reached (expires). For instance, if you set a transaction password and give it the date 7/1/91, all of your transactions are protected from changes until 7/1/91. This means that you can't add a missing or forgotten transaction, make corrections to an existing transaction, or delete a transaction without the password up through 7/1/91. On 7/2/91, however, anybody can do anything to your account. To make the Transaction Password semi-permanent, assign a date that is a long way in the future, such as 12/31/99.

6. The Confirm Password window appears. Type the password again to confirm and press [Enter◄─] to set the password.

When you try to enter a new transaction or make changes to an existing one, Quicken will prompt you for the password before recording the transaction.

Changing or Removing the Transaction Password

You can change or remove a Transaction Password just as you can a Main Password.

1. Select the account group you want (select Account Group Activities on the Change Settings Menu, then choose Select/Set Up Account Group).

2. At the Change Settings Menu, type 5 or position the cursor on Password, and press `Enter←`. The password menu will be displayed.

3. Select Transaction Password by typing 2, or positioning the cursor on Transaction Password, and pressing `Enter←`.

4. The Change Transaction Password window will be displayed. Type the name of the old password, and press `Enter←`.

5. To change the password, type the name of the new password, using up to 16 characters. To remove the password, leave it blank. Press `Enter←`.

6. If necessary, type in a new date through which the transaction password will be required and press `Enter←`.

7. If you change to a new password, the Confirm Password window appears. Type the password again to confirm and press `Enter←` to set the password.

Other Settings

Quicken has several other settings that you can modify. Some have been mentioned elsewhere in this book. You probably should use Quicken with the default settings for a while before you consider changing any of these.

To change these settings:

1. From the Main Menu, type 5 or position the cursor on Change Settings and press `Enter←`.

2. At the Change Settings Menu, type 6 or position the cursor on Other Settings and press [Enter←]. The Other Settings window will be displayed (see Figure 7-21).

```
┌─────────────────────────────────────────────────────────┐
│ ███████████████████████████████████████████████████████ │
│                    Other Settings                        │
│  ─────────────────────────────────────────────────────  │
│  1.  Beep when recording and memorizing (Y/N): Y         │
│  2.  Request confirmation (for example,                  │
│          when changing the Register) (Y/N) : Y           │
│  3.  Require Category on transactions (Y/N)  : N         │
│  4.  Extra message line on check (printed                │
│          on check but not recorded) (Y/N)   : N         │
│  5.  Days in advance to remind of postdated              │
│          checks and scheduled groups (0-30) : 3         │
│  6.  Change date of checks to today's date               │
│          when printed (Y/N)                  : N         │
│  7.  MM/DD/YY or DD/MM/YY date format (M/D)  : M         │
│  8.  Billminder active (Y/N)                 : Y         │
│  9.  Print categories on voucher checks (Y/N): Y         │
│  10. 43 line register/reports (EGA,UGA) (Y/N): N         │
│  11. Show Memo/Category/Both    (M/C/B)      : B         │
│  12. In reports, use category Description/                │
│          Name/Both (D/N/B)                   : D         │
│  13. Warn if a check number is re-used (Y/N) : N         │
│  ─────────────────────────────────────────────────────  │
│  Esc-Cancel           F1-Help           ←┘ Continue      │
└─────────────────────────────────────────────────────────┘
```

Figure 7-21 — The Other Settings Menu.

The following items will be displayed in the window and can be changed as necessary:

1. **Beep when recording and memorizing (Y/N):** Quicken's default setting is Y (yes). When you turn this off, you won't hear the beep when Quicken records, deletes, or memorizes transactions.

2. **Request confirmation (for example, when changing the Register (Y/N)**: Quicken's default setting is Y (yes).

    If you turn this off, Quicken will automatically record a transaction without asking for confirmation. This will save you some keystrokes but you'll lose the option of reconsidering the transaction.

    This setting will also change the way checks page up and down at the Write Checks screen. When you set this to N (no), checks won't scroll up and down but the information will change much more quickly.

3. **Require Category on transactions (Y/N)**: Quicken's default setting is N (no). Change this to Y (yes) and Quicken will prompt you for a category. This is a way to help you to keep your records completely categorized for accurate reports.

4. **Extra message line on check (printed but not recorded (Y/N)**: Quicken's default setting is N (no). If you print checks with Quicken, this option gives you an extra line on the check. The information is printed on the check and can be included in a memorized transaction, but it's not recorded in your Quicken account. Use this to give more information to the payee for his records.

5. **Days in advance to remind of post-dated checks and scheduled groups (0-30)**: Quicken's default setting is 3 days. If you use Quicken to print checks and don't use your computer every day, you might want to change this setting. The point is to ensure that you pay your bills on time and you are the best judge of how much advance notification you need to do this.

6. **Change date of checks to today's date when printed (Y/N)**: Quicken's default setting is N (no) and all checks you print will have the date you typed when you entered them. Change this to Y (yes) and all checks will be printed with today's date.

7. **MM/DD/YY or DD/MM/YY date format (M/D)**: Quicken's default setting M (Month) gives you MM/DD/YY (month/day/year) format. Change this to D (Day) if you want DD/MM/YY (day/month/year) format.

8. **Billminder active (Y/N)**: If you installed Billminder you can activate it or turn it off with this setting. When activated, Billminder reminds you at the DOS prompt if you have checks to be printed, transaction groups due for payment, electronic payments to be transmitted, or reminders about investments.

9. **Print categories on voucher checks (Y/N)**: Quicken's default setting is Y (yes) — category information and the description column will print on voucher checks. Change this to N (no) if you want only the Description information to be printed.

10. **43 line register/reports (EGA, VGA) (Y/N)**: Quicken's default setting is N (no). This setting will allow some high-quality EGA and VGA monitors to display more lines on the screen.

11. **Show Memo/Category/Both (M/C/B)**: Quicken's default setting is Both. Use this setting to decide what will be shown on the screen when you view the Register.

    •   Type **M** (Memo) if you want only the Memo field to be displayed on the second line of a transaction.

    •   Type **C** (Category) if you want only the Category to be displayed on the second line of a transaction.

    •   Type **B** (Both) to show both the Memo and Category fields.

12. **In reports, use category Description/Name/Both (D/N/B)**: Quicken's default setting is Description only.

    •   Type **D** (Description) to label Category information in reports with the description field. If the description field is blank, Quicken will print the name.

    •   Type **N** (Name) to label Category information in reports with the Category name.

    •   Type **B** (Both) to label Category information in reports with both Category name and description.

13. **Warn if a check number is re-used (Y/N)**: Quicken's default setting is N (no). Type Y (yes) and Quicken will warn you that the check number you just typed in has already been used.

Electronic Payment

If you decide to use CheckFree, an electronic bill payment system, you must change Quicken's settings to allow for electronic payment. This selection on the Change Settings menu will let you change your modem and account settings (see Figure 7-22).

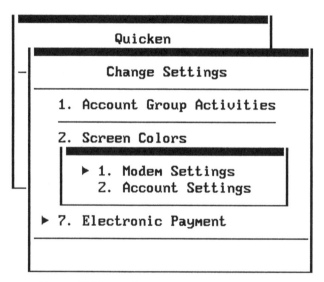

Figure 7-22 — Electronic Payment Settings.

Remember that there are several requirements for using CheckFree:

• You must set up an account with CheckFree Corporation.

• You must have a modem.

• You must change Quicken's settings to allow for electronic payment.

Billminder

This is a feature available to Quicken users with a hard disk. Billminder can remind you if you have checks to be printed, transaction groups due for payment, electronic payments to be transmitted, or of reminders about investments (see Figure 7-23).

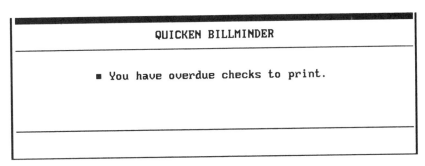

Figure 7-23 — Billminder message.

When you installed Quicken, you had the option of installing Billminder. If you've changed the location of your data files, or you execute other programs and want Billminder to pause after displaying its message, you will have to enter a line in your AUTOEXEC.BAT file.

Quicken added a line to your AUTOEXEC.BAT file when it installed Billminder. Depending on which version of DOS you are using, the line looks like one of the following:

C:\QUICKEN4\BILLMIND C:\QUICKEN4 (For DOS 3.0 or higher)

BILLMIND C:\QUICKEN4 (For DOS lower than 3.0)

If you want Billminder to pause after displaying its message, type **/P** at the end of the line. Billminder will display its message and wait until you press Enter⏎ to continue.

If you have changed the location of your data files, change the directory name in the AUTOEXEC.BAT file (currently QUICKEN4) to reflect where Q.CFG is located. Billminder relies on Q.CFG to tell it the path to the account group files.

If you installed Billminder and now want to turn it off:

- From the Main Menu, type 5 or position the cursor on Change Settings and press ⌜Enter⏎⌝.

- At the Change Settings Menu, type 6 or position the cursor on Other Settings and press ⌜Enter⏎⌝. The Other Settings window will be displayed.

- Position the cursor on number 8, Billminder active (Y/N), and type N (no) to turn Billminder off.

If you installed Billminder and now want to remove it, use your word processor to delete the Billminder line from the AUTOEXEC.BAT file.

If you did not install Billminder, you can do so by reinstalling Quicken. Your data files will not be changed and the installation process will not take as long as it did the first time.

Summary

Customize Quicken to meet your needs by selecting monitor colors and speed, printer specifications, passwords, and various other settings. Use different account groups to keep separate records for each year or to separate home and business transactions.

Chapter 8

Reports

Quicken contains a number of preset forms for personal, business, and investment reports. If none of the preset reports meets your needs, you can customize them to produce almost any kind of report you need, whether it's a transaction, summary budget, or account balances report. You can also memorize a preset or customized report for repeated use. In this chapter, you will learn how to:

- Print a report
- Produce:
  - Personal reports
  - Business reports
  - Investment reports
  - Memorized reports
  - Custom reports
- Set Report Options
- Filter your data.

Quicken's Reports menu (Main Menu, selection 3) gives you access to all of the report forms. After you have typed in your transactions for at least a month, it's time to experiment with some of Quicken's reports. Type a title, or let Quicken give it a generic name, such as Cash Flow Report or Transaction Report. Quicken lets you view reports on the screen before you print them. Limit the first reports you print to cover a period of one month so that you can better understand them and decide if Quicken's preset reports meet your needs.

Producing a Report

Most reports are prepared in the same basic way:

1. Select the account group you want to use in the report (select Account Group Activities on the Change Settings Menu, then choose Select/Set Up Account Group).

2. At the Main Menu, type 3 or position the cursor on Reports and press `Enter←`. The Reports Menu, with eight choices, will appear (see Figure 8-1).

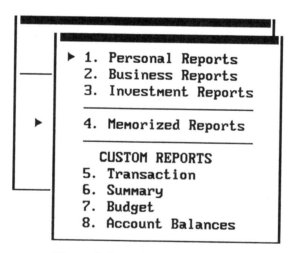

Figure 8-1 — The Reports Menu.

3. Select the report you want to see and/or print.

4. Report title (optional): You can give each report a title if you want. If you leave it blank, Quicken will use the title that is displayed at the top of the report window, such as Cash Flow Report or Monthly Budget Report. Press `Enter◄─┘`.

5. Report on months from: Type the month and year of the first month's transactions to use or use `+` and `-` to increase and decrease the date. Press `Enter◄─┘`. Quicken will begin with transactions from the first day of this month.

6. Report on months through: Type the last month and year of the transactions to use or use `+` and `-` to increase and decrease the date. Press `Enter◄─┘`. Quicken will end the report with transactions from the last day of this month.

For example, if you type 1/91, press `Enter◄─┘`, type 1/91, and press `Enter◄─┘`, your report will show all of the transactions for the month of January 1991.

Some reports, such as the Monthly Budget Report, will have additional windows you need to complete.

If you want to limit your report to certain transactions, you can filter the report by specifying various conditions. For more information, see Filtering Your Data later in this chapter.

You can customize or set options for any report by pressing `F8`. Quicken will display several different windows containing options that fit the type of report you are creating. For more information, see Setting Report Options later in this chapter.

If you customize a preset form or design your own, you can memorize the report for later use. For more information, see Memorized Reports later in this chapter.

Wide Reports

Shortcut keys:

⬅, ➡	Scroll left & right one column at a time
⬆, ⬇	Scroll up and down one line at a time
tab	Scroll right one screen
⇧ Shift - tab	Scroll left one screen
PgUp	Scroll up one screen
PgDn	Scroll down one screen
home	Go to top-left corner
end	Go to bottom-right corner

You will find that some reports will fit on your screen while others are too wide or too long. Small arrows will appear in the lower right corner of the screen to indicate there is more to the report. Use the following keys to see the missing parts.

- Use ⬅ and ➡ to scroll left and right one column at a time.
- Use ⬆ and ⬇ to scroll up and down one line at a time.
- Use tab or Ctrl-➡ to scroll right one screen at a time.
- Use ⇧ Shift - tab or Ctrl-⬅ to scroll left one screen at a time.
- Use PgUp to scroll up one screen at a time and PgDn to scroll down one screen at a time.
- Press home to position the cursor at the top-left corner of the report.
- Press end to position the cursor at the bottom-right corner of the report.

On some reports, columns are set to half-width to allow for more information on the screen. Press F9 to see the full width of the column. Doing this changes the width of the report from 80 characters to 132 characters.

Printing Reports

Quicken gives you the option of sending the report to a printer or to an ASCII file.

To print a report, turn on your printer, put it on-line, and make sure the paper is correctly aligned.

Press [F8] and the Print Report window will be displayed (see Figure 8-2).

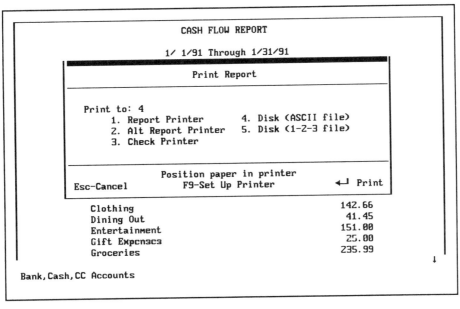

Figure 8-2 — The Print Report Window.

Print to: Type the appropriate number and press [Enter←].

- Type 1 if you want to print the report on your report printer.
- Type 2 if you want to print the report on your alternate report printer.
- Type 3 if you want to print the report on your check printer.
- Type 4 if you want to write the report in ASCII format to a file. Most word processors will be able to read this file.
- Type 5 if you want to write the report to a file in Lotus 1-2-3 format (a .PRN file). You'll be able to use this file in a Lotus (or compatible) spreadsheet (use the Lotus / File / Import command).

Press [Enter←] to print the report, or [F9] if you want to see or change the settings for your printer.

Printing Wide Reports

Quicken will automatically print wide reports in vertical strips so you can tape the sheets of paper together to produce a full-size report.

To fit more information on a sheet of paper, set your printer to print in compressed type (17 characters per inch). Use the Printer Settings option on Change Settings Menu to do this. For more information, see Chapter 7.

Personal Reports

The Personal Reports menu (see Figure 8-3) has five preset personal report forms:
cash flow, monthly budget, itemized categories, tax summary, and net worth.

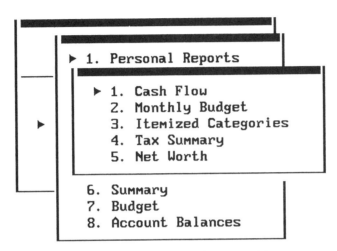

```
 ▶ 1. Personal Reports

     ▶ 1. Cash Flow
       2. Monthly Budget
       3. Itemized Categories
       4. Tax Summary
       5. Net Worth

       6. Summary
       7. Budget
       8. Account Balances
```

Figure 8-3 — The Personal Reports Menu.

Type 1 or position the cursor on Personal Reports and press Enter←. Select the
report you want to prepare by typing the appropriate number, or by positioning
the cursor on your choice and pressing Enter←.

Cash Flow

This report totals by category all of the money you received (inflows) and spent (outflows) and gives you an overall total for all accounts in the current group, including bank, credit card, and cash accounts. Any transfers you made between accounts are excluded.

To prepare a Cash Flow Report:

1. Type 1 or position the cursor on Cash Flow and press [Enter←]. The Cash Flow Report window will appear (see Figure 8-4).

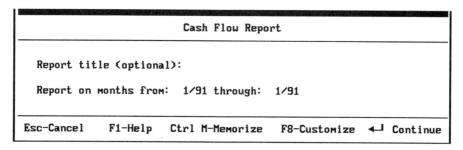

Figure 8-4 — The Cash Flow Report Window.

2. Type a title if you want to give the report a name or leave it blank and Quicken will call it Cash Flow Report. Press [Enter←].

3. Type the beginning date, press [Enter←], type the ending date, and press [Enter←] to continue.

    The prepared report will appear on the screen. Use [PgUp], [PgDn], and the arrow keys to scroll through the report.

4. Press [F8] to see the Print Report window and select your print option. Type the appropriate number and press [Enter←]. For more information on printing, see Printing Reports, earlier in this chapter.

Figure 8-5 shows a sample Cash Flow Report.

```
                      CASH FLOW REPORT
                   1/ 1/91 Through 1/31/91
Bank,Cash,CC Accounts                                    Page 1
2/12/91
                                          1/ 1/91-
                  Category Description     1/31/91
        ---------------------------------- --------------------
        INFLOWS
           Salary Income                       1,951.12
                                              ----------
        TOTAL INFLOWS                          1,951.12

        OUTFLOWS
           Auto Loan Payment                      175.00
           Automobile Fuel                         79.34
           Clothing                               142.66
           Dining Out                              41.45
           Entertainment                          151.00
           Gift Expenses                           25.00
           Groceries                              235.99
           Household Misc. Exp                     41.89
           Insurance                              155.00
           Miscellaneous                           15.93
           Mortgage Interest Exp                  500.00
           Repairs                                 45.49
           Telephone Expense                       92.21
           Water, Gas, Electric:
             Electricity              75.45
             Water, Gas, Electric - Other   29.95
                                       ----------
           Total Water, Gas, Electric             105.40
                                                 ----------
        TOTAL OUTFLOWS                          1,806.36


                                                 ----------
        OVERALL TOTAL                             144.76
                                                 ==========
```

Figure 8-5 — A Sample Cash Flow Report.

Monthly Budget

Shortcut keys:

Ctrl-E	Edit monthly budget detail
Ctrl-M	Memorize a report
F7	Edit budget amounts
F8	Customize report (from Create a Report window)
F8	Print a report (from Report)
F9	Fill remaining months with same budget amount

The Monthly Budget Report compares all the money you received and spent for each account (bank, credit card, and cash) to the amount you budgeted. If you want to prepare a Monthly Budget Report:

1. Type 2, or position the cursor on Monthly Budget, and press Enter⏎. The Monthly Budget Report window will be displayed (see Figure 8-6).

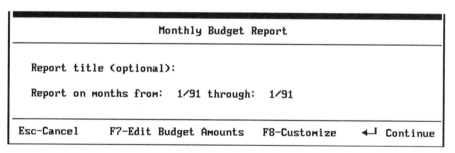

Figure 8-6 — Cash Flow Report Window.

2. Type a name for the report, if desired, and specify which months to include. To produce this report, you must first specify budget amounts for each category.

3. Press [F7] (Edit Budget Amounts) to see the Specify Budget Amounts window (see Figure 8-7). Enter or change your budget amounts for each category. If a category has no budgeted amount, it won't appear on the Monthly Budget Report. If the category has a monthly budgeted amount but you spent nothing for that category, it will appear on the report. For more information on Budgeting, see Chapter 9.

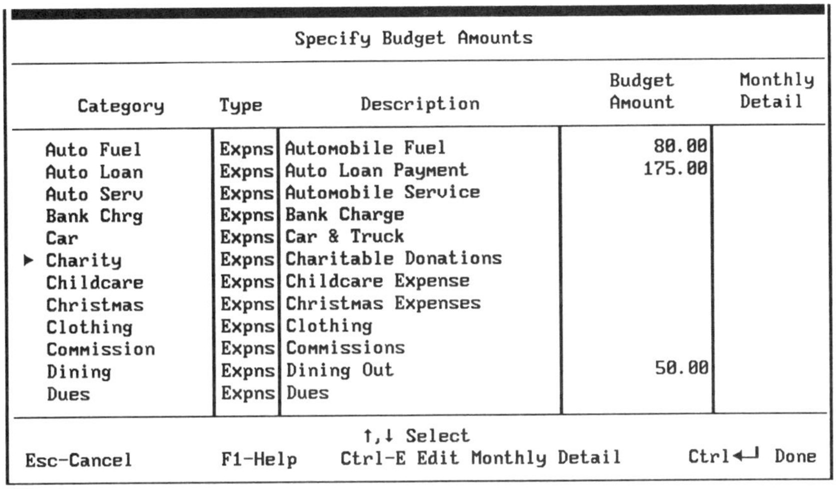

```
┌────────────────────────────────────────────────────────────────────┐
│                       Specify Budget Amounts                         │
├──────────────┬───────┬──────────────────────┬──────────┬────────────┤
│                                               Budget     Monthly     │
│   Category      Type       Description        Amount     Detail      │
├──────────────┼───────┼──────────────────────┼──────────┼────────────┤
│   Auto Fuel   │ Expns │ Automobile Fuel      │   80.00  │            │
│   Auto Loan   │ Expns │ Auto Loan Payment    │  175.00  │            │
│   Auto Serv   │ Expns │ Automobile Service   │          │            │
│   Bank Chrg   │ Expns │ Bank Charge          │          │            │
│   Car         │ Expns │ Car & Truck          │          │            │
│ ► Charity     │ Expns │ Charitable Donations │          │            │
│   Childcare   │ Expns │ Childcare Expense    │          │            │
│   Christmas   │ Expns │ Christmas Expenses   │          │            │
│   Clothing    │ Expns │ Clothing             │          │            │
│   Commission  │ Expns │ Commissions          │          │            │
│   Dining      │ Expns │ Dining Out           │   50.00  │            │
│   Dues        │ Expns │ Dues                 │          │            │
├──────────────┴───────┴──────────────────────┴──────────┴────────────┤
│                          ↑,↓ Select                                  │
│ Esc-Cancel      F1-Help     Ctrl-E Edit Monthly Detail   Ctrl↵ Done  │
└────────────────────────────────────────────────────────────────────┘
```

Figure 8-7 — Specify Budget Amounts Window.

If necessary, the budgeted amounts can be adjusted or changed. Some categories may require different amounts for different months, such as when quarterly or semi-annual insurance payments are due. You may budget money for birthday and Christmas gifts every month or only a few months. Quicken will let you adjust the monthly budget items.

4. Press ⌈Ctrl⌉-⌈E⌉ to see the Monthly Budget Detail window (see Figure 8-8). Enter different amounts in each month or copy an amount from the current month to the end of the year by pressing ⌈F9⌉. Press ⌈Enter←⌋ to return to the Specify Budget Amounts window.

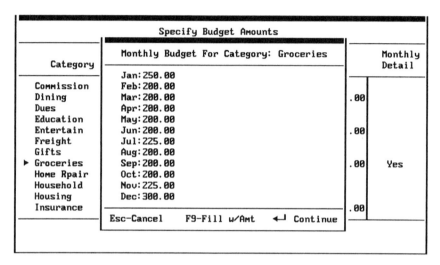

```
                    Specify Budget Amounts
┌─────────────────┬──────────────────────────────────┬──────────┐
│                 │ Monthly Budget For Category: Groceries     Monthly │
│     Category    │                                            Detail  │
├─────────────────┤ Jan: 250.00                        │          │
│  Commission     │ Feb: 200.00                        │          │
│  Dining         │ Mar: 200.00                        │  .00     │
│  Dues           │ Apr: 200.00                        │          │
│  Education      │ May: 200.00                        │          │
│  Entertain      │ Jun: 200.00                        │  .00     │
│  Freight        │ Jul: 225.00                        │          │
│  Gifts          │ Aug: 200.00                        │          │
│ ▶ Groceries     │ Sep: 200.00                        │  .00  Yes│
│  Home Rpair     │ Oct: 200.00                        │          │
│  Household      │ Nov: 225.00                        │          │
│  Housing        │ Dec: 300.00                        │          │
│  Insurance      │                                    │  .00     │
│                 │ Esc-Cancel   F9-Fill w/Amt  ←┘ Continue       │
└─────────────────┴────────────────────────────────────┴─────────┘
```

Figure 8-8 — The Monthly Budget Detail Window.

5. Press ⌈Ctrl⌉-⌈Enter←⌋ to return to the Monthly Budget Report window.

6. When you're ready to print the report, press ⌈F8⌉ to send it to the printer or a file. Figure 8-9 shows a sample Monthly Budget Report.

```
                        MONTHLY BUDGET REPORT
                        1/ 1/91 Through 1/31/91
   Bank,Cash,CC Accounts                                           Page 1
   2/12/91
                                   1/ 1/91    -      1/31/91
                   Category Description   Actual    Budget    Diff
                   ------------------------   -----------------------------------

                   INFLOWS
                     Salary Income       1,951.12  1,951.12     0.00
                                         ----------  ----------  ----------
                   TOTAL INFLOWS         1,951.12  1,951.12     0.00

                   OUTFLOWS
                     Auto Loan Payment     175.00    175.00      0.00
                     Automobile Fuel        79.34     80.00     -0.66
                     Clothing              142.66     75.00     67.66
                     Dining Out             41.45     50.00     -8.55
                     Entertainment         151.00     50.00    101.00
                     Gift Expenses          25.00     25.00      0.00
                     Groceries             235.99    250.00    -14.01
                     Household Misc. Exp    41.89     50.00     -8.11
                     Insurance             155.00     60.00     95.00
                     Medical & Dental        0.00     50.00    -50.00
                     Miscellaneous          15.93     25.00     -9.07
                     Repairs                45.49     50.00     -4.51
                     Telephone Expense      92.21     90.00      2.21
                     Water, Gas, Electric  105.40    120.00    -14.60
                                         ----------  ----------  ----------
                   TOTAL OUTFLOWS        1,306.36  1,150.00    156.36


                                         ----------  ----------  ----------
                   OVERALL TOTAL           644.76    801.12   -156.36
                                         ==========  ==========  ==========
```

Figure 8-9 — A Monthly Budget Report.

Itemized Categories

This report lists all of your transactions by category. Each category, including transfers, is subtotaled, income and expenses are totaled, and an overall total is shown at the end of the report. This report can be filtered to show tax-related categories.

Figure 8-10 shows a sample Itemized Category Report that has been filtered to show only tax-related categories.

```
                          Itemized Category Report
                          1/ 1/91 Through 1/31/91
     All Accounts                                              Page 1
     2/13/91

       Date   Acct     Num    Description     Memo       Category    Clr  Amount
      -----  --------  ------  ----------------  -----------  ----------------  -  ---------

            INCOME/EXPENSE
             INCOME
               Salary Income
               -------------
       1/ 2 Checking         Deposit        Paycheck    Salary       X    975.56
       1/15 Checking         Deposit        Paycheck    Salary       X    975.56
                                                                        ---------
               Total Salary Income                                     1,951.12
                                                                        ---------
             TOTAL INCOME                                              1,951.12


             EXPENSES
               Mortgage Interest Exp
               ---------------------
       1/ 2 Checking 130     Home Mortgage Co January Mor Mort Int    X   -500.00
                                                                        ---------
               Total Mortgage Interest Exp                             -500.00

               Repairs
               -------
       1/15 Checking 142  S Bankcharge        Jimbo's Gar Repairs/Car2 X    -45.49
                                                                        ---------
               Total Repairs                                            -45.49
                                                                        ---------
             TOTAL EXPENSES                                            -545.49


                                                                        ---------
             TOTAL INCOME/EXPENSE                                      1,405.63
                                                                        =========
```

Figure 8-10 — An Intemized Category Report.

Tax Summary

Use the Tax Summary Report to list all tax-related transactions from all of your accounts. The transactions are grouped and subtotaled by category name. The Tax Summary Report is the same as an Itemized Category Report that is filtered to include only tax-related categories (see Figure 8-10).

Net Worth

The Net Worth Report combines all accounts in the current account group to show your net worth as of the day you specify. Net worth is calculated by subtracting the total amount of your liabilities from the total amount of your assets.

Unless you have set up accounts for all of your assets, liabilities, and investments, this report will not reflect your true net worth.

Business Reports

The Business Reports menu has seven preset business report forms: profit & loss statement, cash flow, accounts payable (by vendor), accounts receivable (by customer), job or project, payroll, and balance sheet (see Figure 8-11).

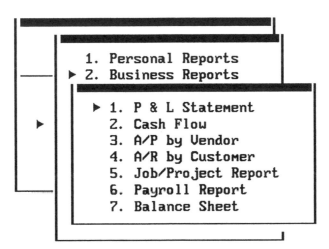

Figure 8-11 — The Business Reports Menu.

P & L Statement

The Profit and Loss Statement is similar to the personal report called Net Worth. While the Net Worth report shows your personal income, expense, and net worth, the P & L Statement shows your business income, expense, and net profit or loss.

Transactions from all of your business accounts are grouped and subtotaled by category. The report shows income transactions, total income, expense transactions, total expense, and overall total (your profit or loss) for the period you specify.

To see your P & L Statement, type a title and a beginning and ending date in the Profit & Loss Statement window (see Figure 8-12).

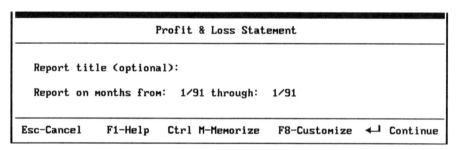

Figure 8-12 — The Profit & Loss Statement Window.

Cash Flow

The business Cash Flow Report is like the personal Cash Flow Report. It totals all of the money your business received and spent by category. It gives you an overall total for all accounts in the current group, including bank, credit card, and cash accounts. Note that any transfers you made between accounts, however, are excluded from the business Cash Flow Report.

A/P by Vendor

This report summarizes the unprinted checks in your bank accounts by payee. Quicken will print a column for each month that has unprinted checks. Use this with your personal accounts if you write postdated checks and want to know how much money you owe for the coming month.

If you do not use Quicken to write your checks, enter your check information at the Write Checks screen and print this report. Assign check numbers to the transactions in the Register when you hand-write the checks.

To see the A/P Report, type a title in the A/P (Unprinted Checks) by Vendor (see Figure 8-13) and press Enter⏎.

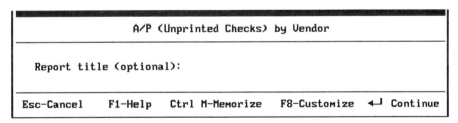

Figure 8-13 — The A/P (Unprinted Checks) by Vendor Window.

Figure 8-14 is a sample A/P (Unprinted Checks) by Vendor Report.

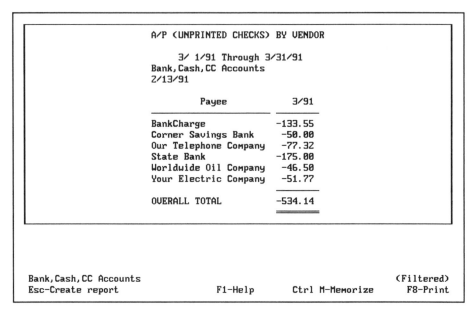

```
                      A/P (UNPRINTED CHECKS) BY VENDOR

                           3/ 1/91 Through 3/31/91
                      Bank,Cash,CC Accounts
                      2/13/91

                              Payee              3/91

                      BankCharge               -133.55
                      Corner Savings Bank       -50.00
                      Our Telephone Company     -77.32
                      State Bank               -175.00
                      Worldwide Oil Company     -46.50
                      Your Electric Company     -51.77

                      OVERALL TOTAL            -534.14


    Bank,Cash,CC Accounts                                        (Filtered)
    Esc-Create report              F1-Help      Ctrl M-Memorize   F8-Print
```

Figure 8-14 — A/P (Unprinted Checks) by Vendor.

A/R by Customer

This report is a summary of outstanding balances for each customer. It is designed for users who want to keep track of individual invoices in Accounts Receivable (A/R). Quicken will automatically select the Other Asset accounts but you can include others.

For this report, Quicken selects transactions that have not been marked as cleared. Make sure that your records are up to date and all paid transactions are marked as cleared with an asterisk (*) in the C (cleared) column.

Type a name for the report in the A/R by Customer window (see Figure 8-15) and press [Enter←]. The Select Accounts to Include window will be displayed (see Figure 8-16) with Other Asset Accounts marked for inclusion. Select any accounts you want to include in or exclude from this report and press [Enter←].

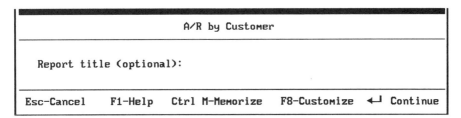

Figure 8-15 — The A/R by Customer Window.

```
┌─────────────────────────────────────────────────────────┐
│                                                         │
│               Select Accounts to Include                │
│─────────────────────────────────────────────────────────│
│                                           Include        │
│      Account      Type      Description   in Report      │
│─────────────────────────────────────────────────────────│
│  ▶ Checking      Bank │ Checking Account              │
│    Petty Cash    Cash │ Petty Cash                    │
│    Accts Rec     Oth A│ Accounts Receivable   Include │
│    Office Equip  Oth A│ Office Equipment      Include │
│    Am Ex         CCard│ American Express              │
│    Acct Pay      Oth L│ Accounts Payable             │
│    Payroll-Fed   Oth L│ Federal W-Holding            │
│    Payroll-FICA  Oth L│ FICA W-Holding               │
│    Sales Tax     Oth L│ Sales Tax Payable            │
│                                                         │
│                                                         │
│─────────────────────────────────────────────────────────│
│               Space Bar-Include/Exclude                  │
│   Esc-Cancel    F1-Help     F9-Select All    ↵ Continue │
└─────────────────────────────────────────────────────────┘
```

Figure 8-16 — The Select Accounts to Include Window.

If you mark several accounts from the Select Accounts to Use window, memorize this report and you'll save time the next time you want to use it.

Job/Project Report

This report uses all of your accounts to total income and expenses for each class. Set up classes for jobs, projects, properties, or departments and you can print a report showing total income and expenses for each.

For more information on how this report can help you, see Reporting by Client, Department, Job, Project, or Property in Chapter 10.

Payroll Report

This report will total income and expenses for each payee by category. To use this report, you must set up categories beginning with the word Payroll.

For more information, see the section on Payroll in Chapter 10.

Balance Sheet

This report shows the total of assets and liabilities in all of your accounts as of the date you specify (see Figure 8-17).

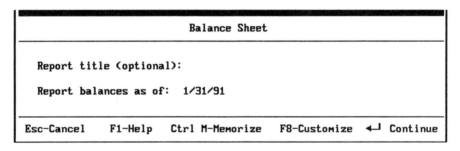

Figure 8-17 — The Balance Sheet Window.

If you have any postdated checks, Quicken adds them to your asset total and lists them as a liability. The Balance Sheet gives totals for assets, liabilities and equity.

Figure 8-18 is a sample Balance Sheet.

```
                        BALANCE SHEET
                        As of 1/31/91
BUSINESS-All Accounts                                    Page 1
2/13/91
                                          1/31/91
                        Acct              Balance
       -------------------------------------  ----------
       ASSETS

         Cash and Bank Accounts
           Checking-Checking Account     2,500.00
           Petty Cash-Petty Cash           120.00
                                        ----------
         Total Cash and Bank Accounts    2,620.00

         Other Assets
           Accts Rec-Accounts Receivable  1,793.79
           Office Equip-Office Equipment   3,600.00
                                        ----------
         Total Other Assets              5,393.79


                                        ----------
       TOTAL ASSETS                      8,013.79
                                        ==========
       LIABILITIES & EQUITY

         LIABILITIES
           Credit Cards
             Am Ex-American Express        336.99
                                        ----------
           Total Credit Cards             336.99

           Other Liabilities
             Acct Pay-Accounts Payable     601.44
             Payroll-Fed-Federal W-Holding 500.00
             Payroll-FICA-FICA W-Holding   500.00
             Sales Tax-Sales Tax Payable    25.00
                                        ----------
           Total Other Liabilities       1,626.44


                                        ----------
         TOTAL LIABILITIES              1,963.43

         EQUITY                         6,050.36
                                        ----------
       TOTAL LIABILITIES & EQUITY       8,013.79
                                        ==========
```

Figure 8-18 — A Sample Balance Sheet.

209

Investment Reports

Quicken provides five preset forms for investment reports: portfolio value, investment performance, capital gains, investment income, and investment transactions (see Figure 8-19).

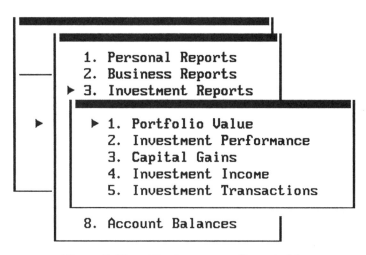

Figure 8-19 — The Investment Reports Menu.

Each Investment Report has a Report Options window with options that pertain to that particular report. Press [F8] from any report window to see the Report Options window.

You can also select filters for each Investment Report. Press [F9] from any report window to see the Filter for that particular report.

Portfolio Value

This report shows the value of each of your securities on a specified date and lists the following information for each security:

- number of shares (to the nearest 0.01)

- price for each share (estimates are marked with *)

- cost basis for the security (0.00 if you entered none for the first transaction of the security)

- unrealized paper gain or loss

- market value on the date specified.

Enter the title, date, options, and accounts to prepare the Portfolio Value Report (see Figure 8-20).

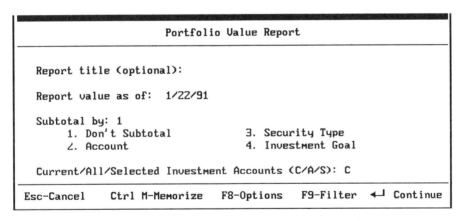

Figure 8-20 — The Portfolio Value Report Window.

Investment Performance

This report lists the average annual total return for your securities during a specified period. Account dividends, interest, other payments you receive, and increases and decreases in the market value of the securities are taken into account when this report is produced.

Enter the title, beginning and ending dates, subtotal criteria, cash flow detail, and accounts to prepare the Investment Performance Report (see Figure 8-21).

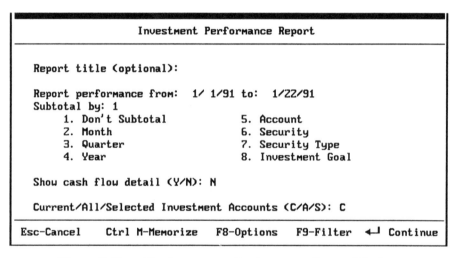

Figure 8-21 — The Investment Performance Report Window.

Capital Gains

The Capital Gains Report will show long and short term capital gains on securities you sold.

At the Capital Gains Report window (see Figure 8-22), enter the title, beginning and ending dates, subtotal criteria, holding period, and account information. Press F8 to set options for this report. Press F9 if you want to filter the report.

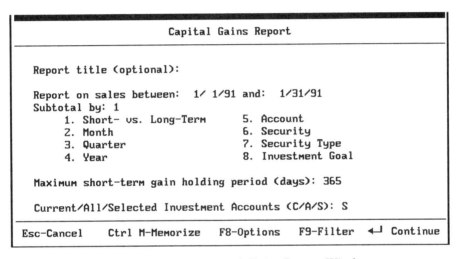

```
                       Capital Gains Report

   Report title (optional):

   Report on sales between:  1/ 1/91 and:  1/31/91
   Subtotal by: 1
         1. Short- vs. Long-Term    5. Account
         2. Month                   6. Security
         3. Quarter                 7. Security Type
         4. Year                    8. Investment Goal

   Maximum short-term gain holding period (days): 365

   Current/All/Selected Investment Accounts (C/A/S): S

   Esc-Cancel    Ctrl M-Memorize   F8-Options   F9-Filter   ↵ Continue
```

Figure 8-22 — The Capital Gains Report Window.

Investment Income

This is a summary report that shows income and expenses for all or for selected investment accounts. Use this report to show capital gains distributions from a mutual fund, dividend and interest income (taxable and nontaxable), realized or unrealized gain or loss, margin interest, and other investment expenses.

Enter a title, beginning and ending dates, subtotal criteria, and account information in the Investment Income Report window (see Figure 8-23). Press [F8] to set options for this report and [F9] if you want to filter the report.

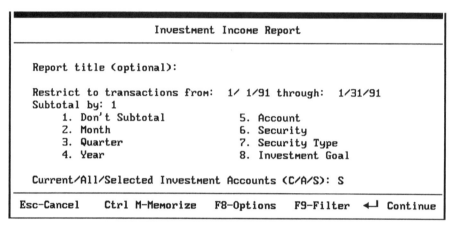

```
                   Investment Income Report

  Report title (optional):

  Restrict to transactions from:  1/ 1/91 through:  1/31/91
  Subtotal by: 1
        1. Don't Subtotal         5. Account
        2. Month                  6. Security
        3. Quarter                7. Security Type
        4. Year                   8. Investment Goal

  Current/All/Selected Investment Accounts (C/A/S): S

 Esc-Cancel    Ctrl M-Memorize    F8-Options    F9-Filter   ↵ Continue
```

Figure 8-23 — The Investment Income Report Window.

Investment Transactions

The Investment Transactions Report lists all transactions within your investment accounts, how they affected the market value or the cost basis of your investments, and the cash balance in your accounts.

At the Investment Transactions Report window, enter a title, beginning and ending dates, subtotal criteria, and account information (see Figure 8-24). Press F8 to set options for this report and F9 if you want to filter the report.

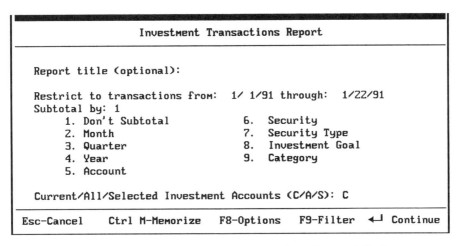

Figure 8-24 — The Investment Transactions Report Window.

Memorized Reports

After you've customized a report with options and filters, you can memorize it for future use. You can recall the format when you want to produce a report without having to reset the options and filters every time.

Quicken memorizes the definition of the report, including all formats, options, and filters you may have used. It does not memorize the date range or budget amounts. You must give the memorized report a meaningful and unique name.

Shortcut keys:

[Ctrl]-[D]	Delete a memorized report
[Ctrl]-[E]	Rename a memorized report
[Ctrl]-[M]	Memorize a report
[F8]	Customize a report
[F9]	Filter a report

To memorize a report:

1. Select the personal, business, or investment report you want to prepare. Type a title and any other information required for that report. Use any desired filters and set any options.

2. When you've finished customizing the report, press [Ctrl]-[M] and the Memorizing Report window will be displayed (see Figure 8-25). Type a title name (Quicken requires a title) and press [Enter←] to memorize the report.

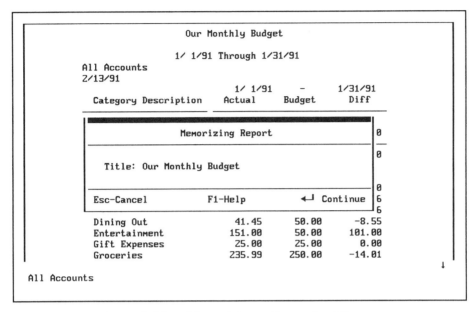

```
                    Our Monthly Budget

                1/ 1/91 Through 1/31/91
    All Accounts
    2/13/91
                            1/ 1/91    -    1/31/91
       Category Description  Actual   Budget    Diff
    _____

    ╔═══════════════════════════════════════════╗ |0
    ║            Memorizing Report              ║ |
    ║                                           ║ |0
    ║                                           ║ |
    ║   Title: Our Monthly Budget               ║ |
    ║                                           ║ |
    ║                                           ║ |0
    ║ Esc-Cancel      F1-Help      ↵ Continue   ║ |6
    ╚═══════════════════════════════════════════╝ |6
       Dining Out        41.45    50.00    -8.55
       Entertainment    151.00    50.00   101.00
       Gift Expenses     25.00    25.00     0.00
       Groceries        235.99   250.00   -14.01       ↓

    All Accounts
```

Figure 8-25 — Memorizing a Customized Report.

If you make changes to a memorized report, you can also memorize the new definition. Use the same name to overwrite the old definition or a different name to create a new one.

Recalling a Memorized Report

You can easily recall a memorized report whenever you want to use it. Remember that you're only recalling the report definition. You will still need to specify a date range so that any data entered since you memorized the report can be included.

To recall a memorized report:

1. Select the account group you used when you memorized the report (select Account Group Activities on the Change Settings Menu, then choose Select/Set Up Account Group).

2. At the Main Menu, type 3 or position the cursor on Reports and press [Enter ↵]. The Reports Menu will be displayed.

3. Type 4 or position the cursor on Memorized Reports and press [Enter←]. The Memorized Reports List will be displayed (see Figure 8-26).

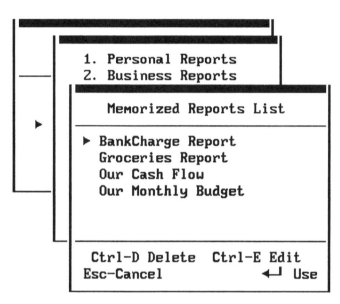

Figure 8-26 — The Memorized Reports List.

4. If you want to change the name of or delete a memorized report, you can do it from this window. Position the cursor on the report you want:

   • Press [Ctrl]-[D] to delete the memorized report.

   • Press [Ctrl]-[E] to rename the memorized report.

5. Position the cursor on the report you want to see and/or print and press [Enter←]. The Memorized Report window will be displayed (see Figure 8-27).

```
                        Memorized Report

                           (Filtered)
        Report title (optional): BankCharge Report

        Report on months from:  1/91 through:  1/91


   Esc-Cancel    F1-Help   Ctrl M-Memorize   F8-Customize  ↵ Continue
```

Figure 8-27 — The Memorized Report Window.

6. You also can customize (press F8) and rememorize (press Ctrl-M) a report from this window.

7. Enter the dates to include in the report and press Enter↵. Quicken will search the transactions and display the report.

Setting Report Options

Quicken will let you customize any preset report form from the Report Options window. Press F8 to display the window. The window will be specific to the type of report you are creating. Some windows will only ask if you want to display cents on your report (see Figure 8-28).

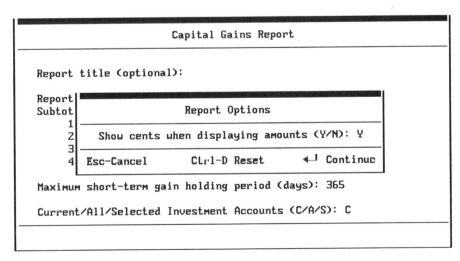

```
                       Capital Gains Report


        Report title (optional):

        Report┌──────────────────────────────────────────────┐
        Subtot│                 Report Options               │
             1│                                              │
             2│   Show cents when displaying amounts (Y/N): Y │
             3│                                              │
             4│ Esc-Cancel        CLrl-D Reset      ↵ Continue│
              └──────────────────────────────────────────────┘
        Maximum short-term gain holding period (days): 365

        Current/All/Selected Investment Accounts (C/A/S): C
```

Figure 8-28 — The Capital Gains Report Options Window.

Other windows will give you more options to select (see Figure 8-29).

```
┌──────────────────────────────────────────────────────────────┐
│█████████████████████████████████████████████████████████████│
│                    Create Transaction Report                 │
│ ─────────────────────────────────────────────────────────── │
│                                                              │
│   Report title (optional):                                   │
│                                                              │
│   Restrict to transactions from:  1/ 1/91 through:  1/31/91  │
│                                                              │
│   Subtotal by: 1                                             │
│        1. Don't Subtotal   5. Month        9.  Category      │
│        2. Week             6. Quarter      10. Class         │
│        3. Two Weeks        7. Half Year    11. Payee         │
│        4. Half Month       8. Year         12. Account       │
│                                                              │
│   Use Current/All/Selected accounts (C/A/S): C               │
│ ─────────────────────────────────────────────────────────── │
│ Esc-Cancel    Ctrl M-Memorize    F8-Options   F9-Filter  ↵ Continue │
└──────────────────────────────────────────────────────────────┘
```

Figure 8-29 — The Create Transaction Report Window.

You will see another Report Options window when you are creating one of the Custom Reports, such as transaction, summary, budget or account balances (see Figure 8-30).

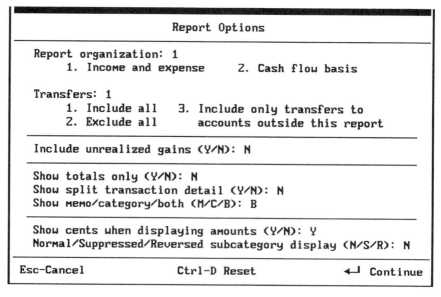

```
┌──────────────────────────────────────────────────────────────┐
│█████████████████████████████████████████████████████████████│
│                        Report Options                        │
│ ─────────────────────────────────────────────────────────── │
│   Report organization: 1                                     │
│        1. Income and expense      2. Cash flow basis         │
│                                                              │
│   Transfers: 1                                               │
│        1. Include all    3. Include only transfers to        │
│        2. Exclude all       accounts outside this report     │
│ ─────────────────────────────────────────────────────────── │
│   Include unrealized gains (Y/N): N                          │
│ ─────────────────────────────────────────────────────────── │
│   Show totals only (Y/N): N                                  │
│   Show split transaction detail (Y/N): N                     │
│   Show memo/category/both (M/C/B): B                         │
│ ─────────────────────────────────────────────────────────── │
│   Show cents when displaying amounts (Y/N): Y                │
│   Normal/Suppressed/Reversed subcategory display (N/S/R): N  │
│ ─────────────────────────────────────────────────────────── │
│ Esc-Cancel              Ctrl-D Reset          ↵ Continue     │
└──────────────────────────────────────────────────────────────┘
```

Figure 8-30 — The Report Options Window.

Set whatever options Quicken offers you and view the report on the screen. Reset the options as necessary to get the desired result.

Filtering Your Data

Some reports will let you filter the data to include only specific transactions. You set the criteria and Quicken includes only those transactions that meet all of the requirements. You can use these filters to prepare very specific reports.

Press [F9] from any Custom Report window and the Filter Report Transaction window will be displayed (see Figure 8-31).

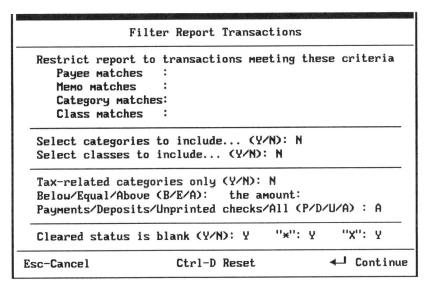

```
                  Filter Report Transactions

    Restrict report to transactions meeting these criteria
         Payee matches    :
         Memo matches     :
         Category matches:
         Class matches    :

    Select categories to include... (Y/N): N
    Select classes to include... (Y/N): N

    Tax-related categories only (Y/N): N
    Below/Equal/Above (B/E/A):    the amount:
    Payments/Deposits/Unprinted checks/All (P/D/U/A) : A

    Cleared status is blank (Y/N): Y     "*": Y     "X": Y

  Esc-Cancel           Ctrl-D Reset           ←┘ Continue
```

Figure 8-31 — The Filter Report Transactions Window.

Enter any or all of the following information:

Payee matches: Type a payee name if you want a report on only that payee. Type the exact name or use Key Word Matches (see Chapter 5 for more information).

Memo matches: Type a memo if you want a report on all transactions with that memo. Type the exact memo or use Key Word Matches.

Category matches: Type the Category name for reports on transactions assigned to that category. Or, type an account name for reports on transactions involving transfers to a specific account. You can use Key Word Matches here, too.

Class matches: Type a Class name for reports on transactions assigned to a specific class. You can use Key Word Matches here, too.

Select categories to include (Y/N): Quicken's default setting is N (no) and all categories are included. Type Y (yes) if you want to select specific categories.

If you select yes, Quicken will display the Select Categories to Include window (see Figure 8-32). Position the cursor on the category you want to exclude and press ⌷space⌷. Accounts are listed so you can include or exclude transfers.

Note: Quicken will remember these selections, and will automatically select them the next time you type **Y** (yes) in this field. You may have to change the settings unless you type **N** (no) or recall a memorized report.

```
┌──────────────────────────────────────────────────────────────────┐
│█████████████████████████████████████████████████████████████████ │
│                   Select Categories To Include                    │
│                                                                    │
│                                                       Include      │
│                                                       in Report    │
│      Category       Type       Description       Tax              │
│                                                                    │
│    Not Categorized                                      Include    │
│  ▶ Bonus           Inc   Bonus Income            ♦      Include    │
│    Canada Pen      Inc   Canadian Pension        ♦      Include    │
│    Div Income      Inc   Dividend Income         ♦      Include    │
│    Family Allow    Inc   Family Allowance        ♦      Include    │
│    Gift Received   Inc   Gift Received           ♦      Include    │
│    Gr Sales        Inc   Gross Sales             ♦      Include    │
│    Int Inc         Inc   Interest Income         ♦      Include    │
│    Invest Inc      Inc   Investment Income       ♦      Include    │
│    Old Age Pension Inc   Old Age Pension         ♦      Include    │
│    Other Inc       Inc   Other Income            ♦      Include    │
│    Rent Income     Inc   Rent Income             ♦      Include    │
│                                                                    │
│                  Space Bar-Include/Exclude                         │
│  Esc-Cancel       F1-Help     F9-Select All         ↵  Continue   │
└──────────────────────────────────────────────────────────────────┘
```

Figure 8-32 — The Select Categories to Include Window.

Tax-related categories only (Y/N): Quicken's default setting is **N** (no). Type **Y** (yes) if you want to restrict the report to tax-related transactions only.

Below/Equal/Above (B/E/A): Type **B**, **E**, or **A** if you want to restrict the report to transactions below, above, or equal to a specific amount. You will be asked to enter the amount.

Payments/Deposits/Unprinted checks/All (P/D/U/A):

- Type **P** (payments) if you want to include only payments. Payments are decreases to Bank, Cash, and Other Asset accounts and increases to Credit Card and Other Liability accounts.

- Type **D** (deposits) if you want to include only deposits.

- Type **U** (unprinted checks) if you want to include only unprinted checks.

- Type **A** (all) if you want to include all transactions.

223

Cleared status is blank (Y/N): "*": "X": Quicken's default setting for all of these is **Y** (yes). Type **N** (no) only if you want to show which transactions are cleared or uncleared.

Enter as many filters as you wish and view the resulting report to see if it has produced the desired results. To reset all of the entries in the window, press [Ctrl]-[D]. Make any necessary changes and memorize the report for future use.

Filter Investment Report Window

If you press [F9] to filter an Investment report, you'll see a different window. Quicken calls it the Filter Investment Report window (Figure 8-33). The one you see may be different than this one because Quicken displays only the options that pertain to the report you've selected.

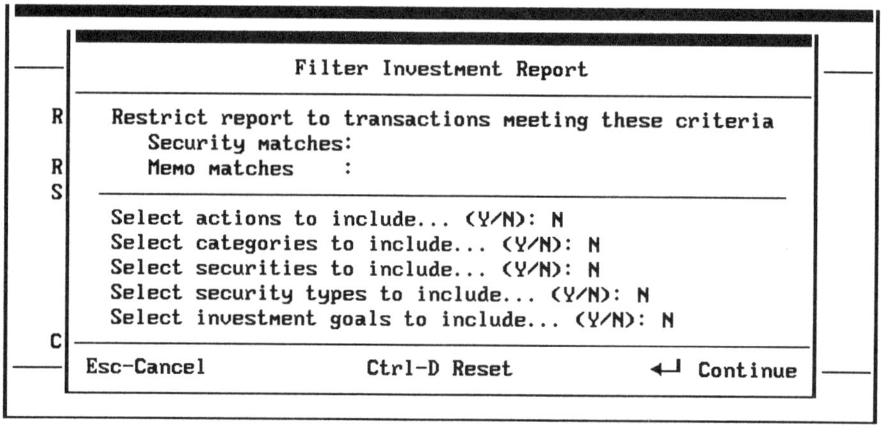

```
                    Filter Investment Report
 R
          Restrict report to transactions meeting these criteria
              Security matches:
 R            Memo matches    :
 S
          ─────────────────────────────────────────────────────
          Select actions to include... (Y/N): N
          Select categories to include... (Y/N): N
          Select securities to include... (Y/N): N
          Select security types to include... (Y/N): N
          Select investment goals to include... (Y/N): N
 C
          ─────────────────────────────────────────────────────
          Esc-Cancel            Ctrl-D Reset          ↵ Continue
```

Figure 8-33 — The Filter Investment Report Window.

Quicken will let you restrict your report to those transactions matching specified security and memo matches. You can also specify actions, categories, securities, security types, and investment goals to include in the report.

Custom Reports

In addition to customizing preset reports, by setting options and using filters, Quicken will let you create four kinds of custom reports: transactions, summary, budget, and account balances. You tell Quicken what transactions to use and how to organize them. You can specify dates of transactions to include, how the report should be totaled, and which accounts to use. You can also include or exclude specific transactions.

Each of these reports is prepared by following the same basic steps.

1. At the Main Menu, type 3 or position the cursor on Reports and press [Enter←].

2. Select the type of custom report you want to prepare: type the number or position the cursor on the report name and press [Enter←]. The Create Report window for that report type will be displayed. Figure 8-34 is an illustration of the Create Transaction Report window.

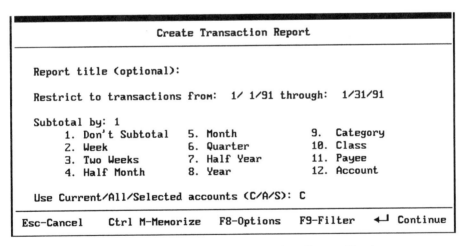

Figure 8-34 — The Create Transaction Report Window.

All of the Create Report windows are similar, but each contains the specific options that pertain to their report type. The following options can appear in these report windows. Enter information you need to create and define your report:

Report title (optional): If you want to title the report, type it here. If you don't name it, Quicken will give it a descriptive name. Remember that you must name the report if you want to memorize it.

Restrict to transactions from and to: or **Report balances on dates from and through**: Type the beginning and ending dates of the transactions you want to include. Quicken inserts the first day of the year and today's date here; use 🔳 and 🔳 to increase or decrease the dates shown.

Row headings (down the left side): Type a number (1 to 4) to indicate whether you want category, class, payee, or account names on the row headings.

Column headings (across the top): Type a number (1 to 12) to indicate what you want on the column headings. Selections include Don't Subtotal, Week, Two Weeks, Half Month, Month, Quarter, Half Year, Year, Category, Class, Payee, and Account.

Subtotal by: Type a number (1 to 12) to indicate how the report should be subtotaled. Selections include Don't Subtotal, Week, Two Weeks, Half Month, Month, Quarter, Half Year, Year, Category, Class, Payee, and Account.

Report at intervals of: Type a number (1 to 8) to indicate how the report balances should be calculated. Selections include Don't Subtotal, Week, Two Weeks, Half Month, Month, Quarter, Half Year, and Year.

Use Current/All/Selected accounts (C/A/S): Quicken's default setting is **C** (current). If you don't change it, your report will include transactions from the current account only.

- Type **A** if you want to include transactions from all accounts.

- Type **S** if you want to select which accounts will be included. When you've completed this window, the Select Accounts to Include window will be displayed and you can select the accounts you want to include. Use the space bar to include or exclude accounts.

3. Press ⌨F8 to set additional options.

4. Press ⌨F9 to restrict the report to specific transactions.

5. When the report is finished but still on the screen, print it by pressing ⌨F8. The Print Report window will be displayed. Tell Quicken where you want to print the report, ready your printer, and press ⌨Enter←.

Transaction Reports

The Transaction Report lists transactions from the Register. You can specify in the Create Transaction Report window which transactions to include and how they should be grouped (see Figure 8-34).

The way in which you choose to subtotal a Transaction Report determines how transactions are sorted, grouped, and subtotaled.

- **Don't Subtotal**: Transactions are listed in chronological order. There are no groups or subtotals.

- **Week**: Transactions are sorted, grouped, and subtotaled by week (Sunday through Saturday).

- **Two Weeks**: Transactions are sorted, grouped, and subtotaled by two-week periods.

- **Half Month**: Transactions are sorted, grouped, and subtotaled by half-month periods (1st through 15th and 16th through the last day).

- **Month**: Transactions are sorted, grouped, and subtotaled by month, starting with the 1st day of the month.

- **Quarter**: Transactions are sorted, grouped, and subtotaled by quarter. A quarter consists of three consecutive months and begins January 1, April 1, July 1, and October 1.

- **Half Year**: Transactions are sorted, grouped, and subtotaled by half year. A half year consists of six consecutive months from January 1 to June 30 and July 1 to December 31.

- **Year**: Transactions are sorted, grouped, and subtotaled by calendar year (January 1 to December 31).

- **Category**: Transactions are sorted, grouped, and subtotaled by category. If you have subcategories, transactions will be sorted, grouped, and subtotaled by subcategories within each category. You can suppress subcategories from the Report Options window (press F8).

- **Class**: Transactions are sorted, grouped, and subtotaled by class. If you have subclasses, transactions will be sorted, grouped, and subtotaled by subclasses within each class.

- **Payee**: Transactions are sorted, grouped, and subtotaled by payee.

- **Account**: Transactions are sorted, grouped, and subtotaled by account.

Figure 8-35 shows a Transaction Report that is not subtotaled.

```
                          TRANSACTION REPORT
                        1/ 1/91 Through 1/31/91
    Checking                                                    Page 1
    2/14/91


     Date   Num      Description        Memo        Category     Clr  Amount
    -----  ------  ----------------  ------------  ------------  -  ---------

            BALANCE 12/31/90                                          0.00

    1/ 1           Opening Balance                 [Checking]     X  1,500.00
    1/ 2           Deposit           Paycheck       Salary        X    975.56
    1/ 2 130       Home Mortgage Compa January Mortga Mort Int    X   -500.00
    1/ 2 131       Cash              Transfer to Sa [Savings]      X   -150.00
    1/ 2 132       Your Electric Compa Electricity  Utilities:Electric X  -75.45
    1/ 2 133       Our Telephone Compa Telephone Expe Telephone   X    -34.76
    1/ 2 134       State Bank        Car Payment    Auto Loan     X   -175.00
    1/ 2 135       Worldwide Oil Compa Gasoline     Auto Fuel     X    -59.34
    1/ 2 136       Neighborhood Grocer Food, paper pr Groceries   X   -105.65
    1/ 2 137       Michael's Insurance Life Insurance Insurance   X   -155.00
    1/ 2 138       Our Telephone Compa Telephone Expe Telephone   X    -57.45
    1/ 2 139       Neighborhood Cable Monthly Cable Utilities/Cable X  -29.95
    1/15 140       Savings Account   Transfer from  [Savings]     X    -50.00
    1/15 141       Savings Account   Transfer from  [Savings]     X    -10.00
    1/15 142  S Bankcharge           B/C Payment    --SPLIT--     X   -147.87
    1/15 143       Neighborhood Grocer Food, paper pr Groceries   X    -47.52
    1/15           Deposit           Paycheck       Salary        X    975.56
    1/21 144       Dinner Theatre    Dinner/Show    Entertain         -136.00
    1/21 145       The News          Newspaper      Entertain          -15.00
    1/21 146       Neighborhood Grocer Food, paper pr Groceries        -42.85
    1/22 147       The Department Stor Clothing/Tyler Clothing/Tyler   -142.66
    1/25 148       The Drug Store    Misc. Supplies Household          -41.89
    1/25 149       Neighborhood Grocer Food, paper pr Groceries        -39.97
                                                                  ---------
            TOTAL  1/ 1/91 -  1/31/91                              1,434.76

            BALANCE  1/31/91                                       1,434.76


            TOTAL INFLOWS                                          3,451.12
            TOTAL OUTFLOWS                                        -2,016.36

                                                                  ---------
            NET TOTAL                                              1,434.76
                                                                  =========
```

Figure 8-35 — A Sample Transaction Report.

Summary Reports

Summary Reports show totals instead of individual transactions for a category, a class, a payee, or an account during a specified period. You can total the report by time period, category, class, payee, or account.

You can use Summary Reports for several things, such as to show monthly spending trends, prepare tax returns and profit and loss statements, manage rental property, and itemize expenses for a certain project or job. Use the Create Summary Report window to produce the kind of report you need (see Figure 8-36).

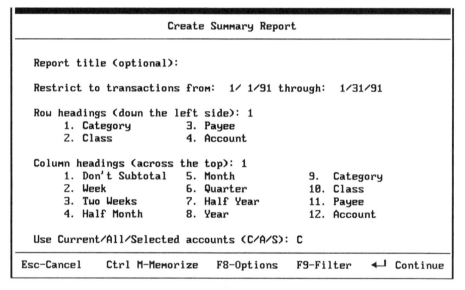

```
                        Create Summary Report

  Report title (optional):

  Restrict to transactions from:  1/ 1/91 through:  1/31/91

  Row headings (down the left side): 1
        1. Category        3. Payee
        2. Class           4. Account

  Column headings (across the top): 1
        1. Don't Subtotal  5. Month         9.  Category
        2. Week            6. Quarter      10. Class
        3. Two Weeks       7. Half Year    11. Payee
        4. Half Month      8. Year         12. Account

  Use Current/All/Selected accounts (C/A/S): C

  Esc-Cancel    Ctrl M-Memorize    F8-Options    F9-Filter    ← Continue
```

Figure 8-36 — The Create Summary Report Window.

Row headings determine what transactions are included and column headings determine how the report is subtotaled.

- **Don't Subtotal**: One column covers the entire time period. There are no groups or subtotals.

- **Week**: One column covers each week (Sunday through Saturday).

- **Two Weeks**: Each column covers a two-week period.

- **Half Month**: Each column covers a half-month period (1st through 15th and 16th through the last day).

- **Month**: Each column covers a month, starting with the 1st day of the month.

- **Quarter**: Each column covers one quarter. A quarter consists of three consecutive months and begins January 1, April 1, July 1, and October 1.

- **Half Year**: Each column covers a half year. A half year consists of six consecutive months from January 1 to June 30 and July 1 to December 31.

- **Year**: Each column covers a calendar year (January 1 to December 31).

- **Category**: Each column covers a single category or subcategory.

- **Class**: Each column covers a single class or subclass.

- **Payee**: Each column covers a single payee.

- **Account**: Each column covers a single account.

In a Summary Report, category descriptions are used instead of category names. Subcategories and subclasses are also listed. Any transactions not assigned to a category, whether income or expense, are listed as Other. Figure 8-37 shows a Summary Report covering a two-month period with categories for row headings and no subtotals.

8 Reports

```
                                    SUMMARY REPORT BY MONTH
Checking                             1/ 1/91 Through 2/28/91                              Page 1
2/15/91

                                                                      OVERALL
                  Category Description          1/91         2/91      TOTAL
          -------------------------------- --------------- --------------- --------------
          INCOME/EXPENSE
            INCOME
              Salary Income                  1,951.12     1,951.12     3,902.24
                                            ----------   ----------   ----------
            TOTAL INCOME                     1,951.12     1,951.12     3,902.24

            EXPENSES
              Auto Loan Payment                175.00       175.00       350.00
              Automobile Fuel                   79.34        55.00       134.34
              Clothing                         142.66         0.00       142.66
              Dining Out                        41.45        35.00        76.45
              Entertainment                    151.00        43.34       194.34
              Gift Expenses                     25.00         0.00        25.00
              Groceries                        235.99       149.27       385.26
              Household Misc. Exp               41.89         0.00        41.89
              Insurance                        155.00         0.00       155.00
              Medical & Dental                   0.00        50.00        50.00
              Miscellaneous                     15.93        57.54        73.47
              Mortgage Interest Exp            500.00       500.00     1,000.00
              Repairs                           45.49         0.00        45.49
              Telephone Expense                 92.21        29.77       121.98
              Water, Gas, Electric:
                Electricity                     75.45        69.55       145.00
                Water, Gas, Electric - Other    29.95        29.95        59.90
                                            ----------   ----------   ----------
                Total Water, Gas, Electric     105.40        99.50       204.90
                                            ----------   ----------   ----------
            TOTAL EXPENSES                    1,806.36     1,194.42     3,000.78

                                            ----------   ----------   ----------
            TOTAL INCOME/EXPENSE               144.76       756.70       901.46

          TRANSFERS
            TO Savings                        -210.00       -50.00      -260.00
                                            ----------   ----------   ----------
          TOTAL TRANSFERS                     -210.00       -50.00      -260.00

          BALANCE FORWARD
            Checking                         1,500.00         0.00     1,500.00
                                            ----------   ----------   ----------
          TOTAL BALANCE FORWARD              1,500.00         0.00     1,500.00

                                            ----------   ----------   ----------
          OVERALL TOTAL                      1,434.76       706.70     2,141.46
                                            ==========   ==========   ==========
```

Figure 8-37 — A Sample Summary Report.

232

Budget Reports

A Budget Report compares the amount you budgeted for an income or expense item against the amount you actually spent or received, Transactions must be assigned to categories if you are to produce a meaningful report.

The Create Budget Report window shows what information you can specify (see Figure 8-38). Subtotaling a Budget Report is very similar to subtotaling a Summary Report.

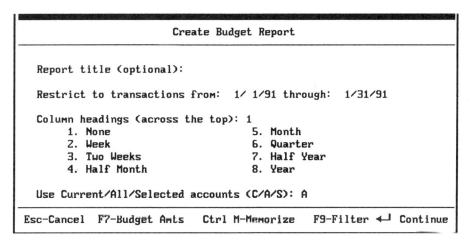

Figure 8-38 — The Custom Budget Report Window.

You must specify budget amounts before you can produce this report. Press F7 to see the Specify Budget Amounts window (Figure 8-39). Enter the amounts you have budgeted for specific categories for each month. Press Ctrl-E to edit the monthly detail column for categories where amounts differ between months of the year.

```
┌─────────────────────────────────────────────────────────────────────┐
│███████████████████████████████████████████████████████████████████████│
│                        Specify Budget Amounts                          │
│───────────────────────────────────────────────────────────────────────│
│                                                         Budget   Monthly│
│       Category      Type        Description             Amount   Detail │
│───────────────────────────────────────────────────────────────────────│
│  ▶ Bonus            Inc  │Bonus Income        │              │          │
│    Canada Pen       Inc  │Canadian Pension    │              │          │
│    Div Income       Inc  │Dividend Income     │              │          │
│    Family Allow     Inc  │Family Allowance    │              │          │
│    Gift Received    Inc  │Gift Received       │              │          │
│    Gr Sales         Inc  │Gross Sales         │              │          │
│    Int Inc          Inc  │Interest Income     │              │          │
│    Invest Inc       Inc  │Investment Income   │              │          │
│    Old Age Pension  Inc  │Old Age Pension     │              │          │
│    Other Inc        Inc  │Other Income        │              │          │
│    Rent Income      Inc  │Rent Income         │              │          │
│    Salary           Inc  │Salary Income       │              │          │
│───────────────────────────────────────────────────────────────────────│
│                             ↑,↓ Select                                  │
│  Esc-Cancel      F1-Help   Ctrl-E Edit Monthly Detail    Ctrl↵  Done    │
└─────────────────────────────────────────────────────────────────────┘
```

Figure 8-39 — The Specify Budget Amounts Window.

Figure 8-40 shows a Budget Report for a two-month period. Although budgeted amounts are for a period of one month, Quicken adjusts the figure if the time period you specified is different.

```
                      BUDGET REPORT
                 1/ 1/91 Through 2/28/91
All Accounts                                             Page 1
2/14/91
                               1/ 1/91    -     2/28/91
            Category Description   Actual     Budget     Diff
            ------------------------  ------------------------------
            INCOME/EXPENSE
              INCOME
                Salary Income      3,902.24   3,902.24      0.00
                                   ----------  ----------  ----------
              TOTAL INCOME         3,902.24   3,902.24      0.00

              EXPENSES
                Auto Loan Payment    350.00     350.00      0.00
                Automobile Fuel      134.34     160.00    -25.66
                Clothing             142.66     150.00     -7.34
                Dining Out            76.45     100.00    -23.55
                Entertainment        194.34     100.00     94.34
                Gift Expenses         25.00      50.00    -25.00
                Groceries            385.26     450.00    -64.74
                Household Misc. Exp   41.89     100.00    -58.11
                Insurance            155.00     120.00     35.00
                Medical & Dental      50.00     100.00    -50.00
                Miscellaneous         73.47      50.00     23.47
                Repairs               45.49     100.00    -54.51
                Telephone Expense    121.98     180.00    -58.02
                Water, Gas, Electric 204.90     240.00    -35.10
                                   ----------  ----------  ----------
              TOTAL EXPENSES       2,000.78   2,250.00   -249.22

                                   ----------  ----------  ----------
            TOTAL INCOME/EXPENSE   1,901.46   1,652.24    249.22
                                   ==========  ==========  ==========
```

Figure 8-40 — The Sample Budget Report.

Account Balances

Use the Account Balances Report to calculate your net worth. The Create Account Balances Report window lets you specify the time period, intervals of reporting, and accounts to use (see Figure 8-41).

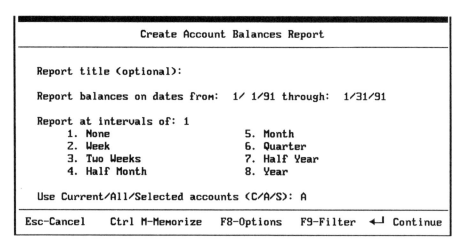

```
                    Create Account Balances Report

  Report title (optional):

  Report balances on dates from:   1/ 1/91 through:   1/31/91

  Report at intervals of: 1
           1. None                  5. Month
           2. Week                  6. Quarter
           3. Two Weeks             7. Half Year
           4. Half Month            8. Year

  Use Current/All/Selected accounts (C/A/S): A

  Esc-Cancel    Ctrl M-Memorize    F8-Options    F9-Filter  ↵ Continue
```

Figure 8-41 — The Account Balances Report Window.

If you chose to use selected accounts in preparing this report, the Select Account to Include window will be displayed. You can mark accounts for inclusion or exclusion.

Press F8 to select the format of this report: net worth or balance sheet (see Figure 8-42). Quicken's default setting is net worth. There is only one difference between the two formats; the balance sheet format adds a line in the liabilities section to show Equity.

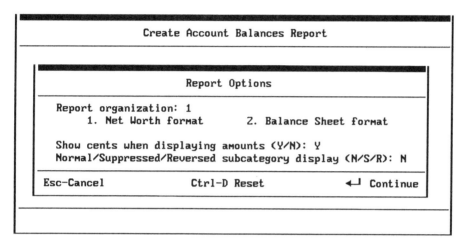

```
        Create Account Balances Report

        ┌─────────────────────────────────────────┐
        │              Report Options              │
        │                                          │
        │  Report organization: 1                  │
        │     1. Net Worth format    2. Balance Sheet format │
        │                                          │
        │  Show cents when displaying amounts (Y/N): Y │
        │  Normal/Suppressed/Reversed subcategory display (N/S/R): N │
        │                                          │
        │  Esc-Cancel      Ctrl-D Reset      ↵ Continue │
        └─────────────────────────────────────────┘
```

Figure 8-42 — The Account Balances Report Options Window.

Figure 8-43 shows the net worth format of the Account Balances Report.

```
                        ACCOUNT BALANCES REPORT
                             As of 2/28/91
   All Accounts                                                    Page 1
   2/14/91
                                                   2/28/91
                               Acct                Balance
          --------------------------------------  ----------
          ASSETS
            Cash and Bank Accounts
              Checking-Checking Account            2,141.46
              Petty Cash-Cash on hand                 50.00
              Savings-Savings Account                560.00
                                                   ----------
            Total Cash and Bank Accounts           2,751.46

            Other Assets
              IBM PC Computer-Personal Computer     1,500.00
                                                   ----------
            Total Other Assets                      1,500.00

                                                   ----------
          TOTAL ASSETS                              4,251.46

          LIABILITIES
            Credit Cards
              BankCharge-1234 5678 9012 3456          736.98
                                                   ----------
            Total Credit Cards                        736.98

                                                   ----------
          TOTAL LIABILITIES                           736.98

                                                   ----------
          OVERALL TOTAL                             3,514.48
                                                   ==========
```

Figure 8-43 — A Sample Account Balances Report.

Summary

Quicken's report forms and customizing features let you produce and print the reports you need. Quicken provides preset forms for personal, business, and investment reports. You can customize them or use them in their original configurations. You can produce custom transaction, summary, budget and account balance reports by setting options and filtering the data. You can also memorize a customized report for future use.

Chapter 9

Home Applications

N ow that you have learned how to set up and use accounts, categories, subcategories, classes, and subclasses, you can use these tools to help you with a variety of applications, such as

- budgeting
- cash management
- home improvements
- loans and mortgages
- personal income taxes
- managing rental properties.

Budgeting

Quicken can make it easy for you to have a workable and realistic budget. The best way to prepare such a budget is to sit down, analyze your income and expenses, prioritize all of your expenses, and make it come out even. Quicken can help you do this job quickly and easily.

To use Quicken's budgeting process most effectively, you must do the following:

Determine the Income and Expense Categories To Use

Begin with the standard category list of home, business, or both that Quicken provides. Add or change categories, as necessary, to make the list of categories applicable to your needs.

For instance, Quicken provides two categories for your monthly mortgage payment: Mortgage Interest and Mortgage Principal. To correctly assign your mortgage payment, you must consult the Amortization Schedule each month for the exact amounts to be applied to each category. To save time and still have accurate records, set up a new category for the total mortgage payment and, if needed, make periodic adjusting transactions.

Don't use subcategories if you want an accurate report of income and expenses. Quicken ignores subcategories in a Budget Report (subcategories will appear in a Summary Report) and includes them in the total for the category listed first. You can split transactions, but assign each line to only one category.

Quicken lists categories in alphabetical order by name. If you want related categories to appear next to each other on reports, give them names that are alphabetically similar. For example, give all categories pertaining to your home or business a name that begins with the same first character or two. You can use numbers, letters, and any characters except " / ", " : ", and " [ ] ". Categories for expenses related to your house could be named H-Utilities, H-Mortgage, and

H-Repairs. Differentiate car expenses by assigning expenses to A_Loan, B_Loan, A_Repairs, and B_Repairs. If you want to keep track of specific medical and dental records, set up categories such as Med_Adams (For Dr. Adams, the pediatrician), Med_Peters (for Dr. Peters, the family doctor), Den_Williams (for Dr. Williams, the family dentist), and Den_Roberts (for Dr. Roberts, the orthodontist).

To force a category to appear last in a report, use an underline (_) as the first character of the name.

Assign Your Transactions To Categories

You can make changes to your records. If you change the name of a category, Quicken will update all of the affected transactions with the new information. You can assign or reassign categories in existing transactions and Quicken will update your records.

You can set Quicken to remind you to assign a transaction to a category. Use the Change Settings menu to select Other Settings. Type **Y** (yes) at number 3, Require Category on all transactions.

Determine Budget Amounts

Set up budget amounts for some or all of the categories you're using. In Chapter 8, you learned how to set up a table of budget amounts for use in preparing budget reports.

1.   From the Main Menu, select number 3 (Reports). Then choose either number 1 (Personal Reports), then number 2 (Monthly Budget), or choose number 7 (Custom Budget).

2.   Press [F7] (Edit Budget Amounts) to see the Specify Budget Amounts window, then enter or change your budget amounts for each category (see Figure 9-1).

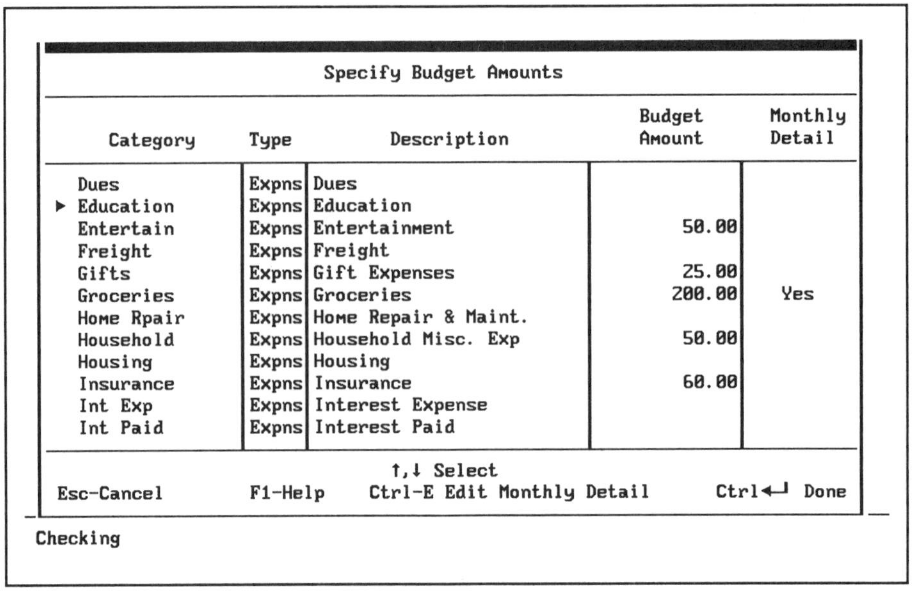

```
                   Specify Budget Amounts
                                                 Budget    Monthly
       Category     Type        Description      Amount    Detail

    Dues           Expns  Dues
  ▶ Education       Expns  Education
    Entertain      Expns  Entertainment           50.00
    Freight        Expns  Freight
    Gifts          Expns  Gift Expenses           25.00
    Groceries      Expns  Groceries              200.00     Yes
    Home Rpair     Expns  Home Repair & Maint.
    Household      Expns  Household Misc. Exp      50.00
    Housing        Expns  Housing
    Insurance      Expns  Insurance               60.00
    Int Exp        Expns  Interest Expense
    Int Paid       Expns  Interest Paid

                        ↑,↓ Select
   Esc-Cancel      F1-Help    Ctrl-E Edit Monthly Detail     Ctrl↵ Done

  Checking
```

Figure 9-1 — The Specify Budget Amounts Window.

3. Press ⌈Ctrl⌉-⌈E⌉ to see the Monthly Budget Detail window. You can specify different monthly amounts for a category with this window. Enter different amounts in each month or copy the same amount from the current month to the end of the year by pressing ⌈F9⌉. Use this for income and expenses that occur on an irregular or periodic basis.

If your income or expenses change, you can easily add to or change budgeted amounts.

Produce Reports

Quicken has three personal reports that are useful for home budgeting: the Cash Flow Report, the Budget Report, and the Itemized Category Report.

The Budget Report compares the money you spent with the amount you budgeted. You only see a total for each category, not individual transactions. If a category has no budgeted amount, it won't appear on the report. If the category has a monthly budgeted amount but you spent nothing for that category, it will appear on the report. If you want a category to appear on the report but you don't want to budget an amount, enter zero (0.00) in the budgeted amount column.

The Personal Monthly Budget Report shows a column for actual income and expenses, one for budgeted amounts, and another column showing the difference. It should meet your needs most of the time. Use the Custom Budget Report if you want to see subtotals for a period other than monthly.

Use the Cash Flow Report to see how you are spending your money. It shows your income (inflows), how much you spent on each category (outflows), and the difference between the two.

The Itemized Category Report will list every transaction in each category. Transfers are listed in a separate section of the report. This report will help you to identify the transactions that helped or hurt your budget.

Print out reports on a regular basis to see how you're doing. If a category named Other appears on any report, it means that Quicken found one or more transactions that were not assigned to a category. For more information about reports and how to customize them, see Chapter 7.

Cash Management

If you have an interest-bearing checking account, you can use Quicken to manage the payment of bills so you will maximize your earned interest.

Write checks on a regular basis and postdate them to the date on which they should be paid. Regular monthly bills can be entered in advance with a transaction group or by recalling a memorized transaction. Other bills can be written as they are received.

Print and mail the checks in one of these ways:

- Print all of the checks and keep them in a safe place. Check the stack every few days and mail those that are due.

- Let Quicken remind you when checks are due to be printed and mailed.

- You decide which checks to print and mail. Print the checks with the date you specified or have Quicken print today's date on the checks.

Home Improvements

If you own your home, it's very difficult to keep track of all of the improvements you've made over a period of years. These improvements can made a difference on the amount of profit you make, and the tax you may pay on the sale of that property. Quicken makes it easier for you to keep accurate records of all of the improvements you made.

The IRS differentiates between home improvements and normal maintenance and repairs. Some of the improvements that qualify are additional rooms, alarm systems, appliances, built-in furniture and bookcases, cabinets, carpeting, drapes and other window treatments, fireplaces, heating systems, patios, siding, skylights, smoke detectors, termite proofing, and wall coverings. Consult an accountant or tax adviser to determine if your project qualifies.

Set up an Other Asset account for your property (see Figure 9-2). Give it a meaningful name, especially if you own more than one property.

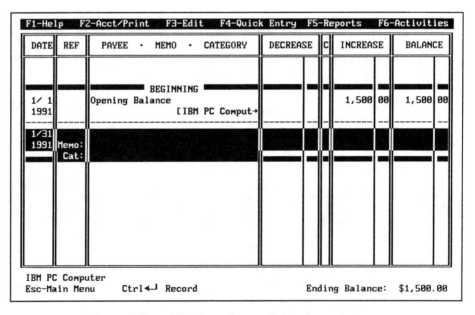

Figure 9-2 — A Register for an Other Asset Account.

Use the purchase price as the opening balance.

Enter each improvement as a transaction in the Register. If you pay for the improvement with a check or credit card, enter it as a transfer transaction when you enter the check or credit card purchase and Quicken will make the entry in the Other Asset account.

Set up and use categories and classes that allow you to specifically identify these improvements. This is important and could save you much time and effort later.

Update the account periodically if necessary, to show increases or decreases in market value.

Loans and Mortgages

Quicken can help you keep track of mortgage and other loan balances.

Set up an Other Liability for each loan you want to track (see Figure 9-3). Decide if you want the loan balance to reflect principal and interest or only principal.

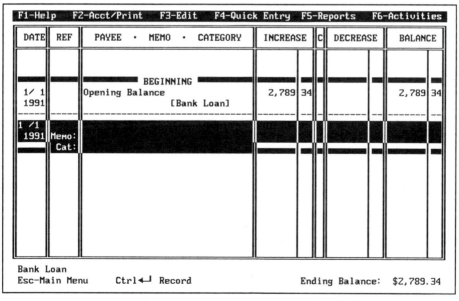

Figure 9-3 — A Register for an Other Liability Account.

To determine the opening balance:

- Pick a starting point, such as January 1, and use the loan balance at that date as the opening balance.
- Or start now and use the current balance as the opening balance.

If your Other Liability account reflects principal only, record each payment as a split transaction, and assign the correct amounts to the Other Asset account and to an Interest Paid account.

Update the account periodically as necessary.

Managing Investments and Other Assets

Quicken can help you to organize and track investments, such as stocks, bonds, IRAs, certificates of deposits, and personal assets.

Investments can be organized into three groups:

- Those investments, such as stocks and bonds, that have a fluctuating unit price or are in a brokerage account.
- Those investments that don't fluctuate in price, such as CDs.
- Personal assets, such as your house and car.

Use an investment account (see Figure 9-4) for stocks, bonds, annuities, mutual funds, IRA accounts, and Keough accounts.

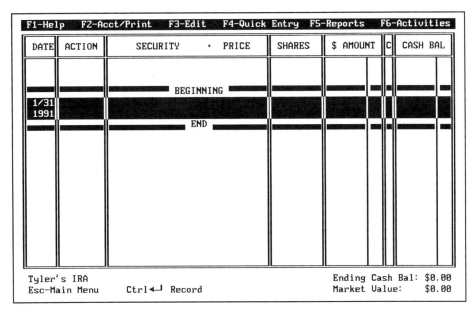

Figure 9-4 — A Register of an Investment Account.

Use an Other Asset account for certificates of deposit, Treasury bills, fixed annuities, money market accounts, retirement plans, rental properties, whole life policies (the cash surrender value), collectibles and antiques, precious metals, and personal assets such as your home, car, and jewelry. You can put all of these in a single account or set up a separate account for each. You probably should set up separate accounts for your home (to keep track of improvements) and for your jewelry and other valuables (to keep records for insurance purposes).

If you group several items in one account, enter each item as a separate transaction and include:

- The name of the item.
- The date you bought it.
- The purchase price of the item.
- The name of the seller.

Use classes to further identify your investments and other assets.

Managing Rental Properties

If you own one or more rental properties, Quicken can be a big help in tracking income and expenses related to each property.

To make the best use of Quicken's features:

1. Set up a list of categories for each income and expense you want to track.

    Look at the expenses you have for the rental properties and set up categories for each of them. You may have rental income, late fees (income), advertising expenses, management fees, legal fees, commissions, repairs, supplies, taxes, utilities, and other expenses. Use meaningful and descriptive names for the categories.

2. Set up a class for each rental property.

    If you have more than one rental property, set up a separate class for each and give them meaningful and descriptive names. If the property has more than one unit, use subclasses to identify them.

3. Assign every transaction to a category and class.

    Use the categories and classes in every transaction. If you pay for repairs or utilities to one property, use the category and class to specify the exact property.

    If you write a check that covers expenses for more than one property, use the Split Transaction window to assign specific amounts to separate properties.

    When you deposit rental income, assign it to a category and class, too. If the deposit is for more than one property or unit, use the Split Transaction window to assign specific amounts to separate units or properties.

4. Print reports periodically.

Use the Job/Property Report and the Summary Report to prepare reports for rental properties.

If you have only one property, use the Summary Report. Filter the report by typing in the class name at Class Matches. This report will automatically subtotal by class.

If you have more than one property, use the Job/Property Report on the Business Reports Menu.

Net Worth

Set up accounts for all of your assets and liabilities and Quicken can help you to determine your Net Worth. Banks and other lending institutions usually want this information if you are applying for a loan.

Set up accounts for all of your assets, such as checking accounts, savings accounts, money market accounts, investments, and personal possessions. Liability accounts should include credit card accounts, home mortgages, and other loans.

Prepare reports, such as Net Worth Report, to show your net worth as of today or at different intervals.

Paycheck Deposits

If you want to keep more accurate records of your income, use a split transaction when you enter the deposit of your paycheck.

Quicken has standard categories you can use: Salary (Salary Income), Tax Fed (Federal Tax), Tax FICA (Social Security Tax), and Tax State (State Tax). If deductions are made for hospitalization insurance or an HMO, you can use Insurance or Medical to record the expense. Or you can set up new categories. Do the same if you have other deductions, such as disability insurance, retirement plans, and local taxes.

To enter a deposit as a split transaction:

1. Type the deposit as usual, until you reach the category field. Press `Ctrl`-`S` to open the Split Transaction window.

2. Type Salary (or other category you set up) and the gross amount on the first line. If you entered the amount of the deposit in the Register, that amount will appear in the split window. Remember to type the full dollar and cents amount to record each line.

3. Type each deduction on a separate line including the category name, description, and amount. Type a minus sign before the amount to designate it as a negative amount. Each line will reduce the amount in the last column.

4. When you've entered all of the deductions, the amount in the split should equal the amount of the deposit (see Figure 9-5).

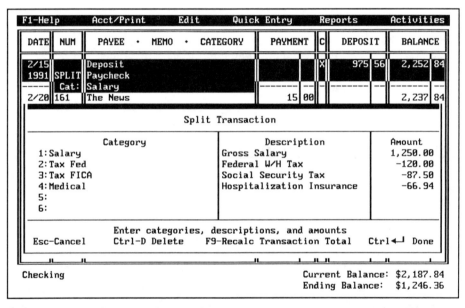

Figure 9-5 — A Paycheck Deposit as a Split Transaction.

5. Press ⌘Ctrl⌐-⌐Enter←⌐ to close the split window and press it again to record the transaction.

6. Press ⌐Ctrl⌐-⌐M⌐ to memorize the transaction for future use. If your paycheck differs each time, memorize the split transaction without amounts and enter them when you recall the transaction.

For more information on split transactions and memorizing transactions, see Chapter 5.

Personal Income Taxes

Quicken can help you prepare your income taxes by producing reports that show your income and tax-related expenses.

If your taxes are not complicated, set up and use categories that help you identify tax-related transactions. Make sure you mark them as tax-related so you can produce Transaction Reports and Summary Reports on tax-related categories.

Set up class names and descriptions to match each form you use, such as 1040, 2106, 8606, A (for Schedule A), and B (for Schedule B). Use them with categories to produce a Summary Report listing all categories for each tax form.

Set up class names and descriptions to match line numbers on the various forms you use, such as 1040-7, 1040-22, A-1a, and A-7. You can then produce a Summary Report showing the totals for each line on a specific tax form.

If you choose to set up and use classes that match line items on the various forms and schedules you use when filing your taxes, be aware that line items on tax forms can change. You'll have to check the numbers every year and make changes when necessary.

Quicken will work with various tax software programs such as TurboTax. Look at the manual that comes with the tax software for further information on how to use it with Quicken.

Summary

Quicken can be used for various home applications. Budgeting, managing cash and rental properties, tracking home improvements, loans, and mortgages, and personal income taxes are only some of the tasks that can be done easily and more efficiently with Quicken.

Chapter 10

Business Applications

Q uicken can be used by businesses for many different applications. Things such as accounts payable, accounts receivable, bookkeeping, payroll, and petty cash, and for reporting income and expenses by job, property, or client. The key to using Quicken effectively is to set up the right categories and classes. A set of business categories is included (see Appendix B) which can be modified, if necessary, to meet the needs of your business.

This chapter covers some of the business uses of Quicken. Whether your business is small or large, profit-making or nonprofit, you can use Quicken's features and preset reports to

- organize your finances
- perform accounting functions
- create reports
- customize Quicken to meet your specific needs.

Cash Basis Bookkeeping

Cash basis accounting is used by many small businesses, especially those where inventory is not a factor. In the cash basis form of accounting, income and expenses are reported when they are received or paid and no adjustments are made for prepaid, unearned, or accrued items. Revenue is recorded when the money is received and expenses are deducted when they are paid. Cash Flow Reports are not connected with cash basis accounting.

Quicken can help you with most of the routine bookkeeping work, eliminate bookkeeping errors, and save time. To make the best use of Quicken, you should do the following:

1. Establish a Chart of Accounts:

    You can use Quicken's standard list of categories (see Appendix B) and modify it, if necessary, to meet your needs. Categories can be added as you need them.

    If you already have an accounting system, set up Quicken categories to match those accounts. Use the account number as the category name and use that same number and account name as the category description.

    For example:

Category	Description
4100	4100-Sales
4110	4110-Returns
4120	4120-Discounts
5100	5100-Cost of Sales

    If you use the same number of digits in naming the categories, your reports will print with that information in ascending numerical order.

2. Assign each transaction to a category:

To have accurate and complete records, assign every transaction to a category. You can set Quicken to remind you to assign a category to every transaction. For more information, see Chapter 7.

Accounts Payable

In cash based accounting, expenses are recognized when you pay them. You can use Quicken to help you keep track of your accounts payable if you remember to enter a bill as an unprinted check as soon as you receive it.

When you receive a bill, write a check in your checking account or recall a memorized check in the amount of the bill. Postdate the check for the date you'll mail it. If you don't use Quicken for writing and printing checks, enter the transaction in the Register and place an asterisk (*) in the Num column to designate is as unprinted. Enter any discount for early payment on a separate line in the Split Transaction window.

Quicken considers any unprinted check as a payable. You can prepare reports on payables in several ways:

- Print part of the Register to see what your cash requirements are for the next few days. Press Ctrl - P and set the date range you want to print.

- Create a A/P by Vendor from the Business Reports Menu. This report will list all postdated checks (your accounts payable) for the dates you have specified and subtotal them by month.

- Create a Transaction Report, type a title, set the date range, and subtotal by week to see your accounts payable in weekly terms. Use selected accounts if you have data in other accounts you would like to include in the report.

A transaction is removed from Quicken's list of accounts payable when you print a check or replace the asterisks (*) in the Num column with a check number.

Accounts Receivable

If you use a cash basis accounting system and want to track accounts receivable, set up an Other Asset account for receivables (see Figure 10-1). Record each invoice as an Increase when you mail it but postdate it, giving it the date on which you expect to be paid. You can enter the actual date of the invoice in the Memo field and the invoice number in the Ref or Memo column.

```
 F1-Help   F2-Acct/Print   F3-Edit   F4-Quick Entry  F5-Reports   F6-Activities

  DATE   REF     PAYEE  ·  MEMO  ·  CATEGORY    DECREASE  C  INCREASE    BALANCE

                           BEGINNING
  1/ 1         Opening Balance                             1,793 79   1,793 79
  1991                              [Accts Rec]

  2/15 1001   Heartbeat of Brevard                     *              1,793 79
  1991 SPLIT  1/15/91
       Cat:  Other Inc
  2/23
  1991                          END



 Accts Rec
 Esc-Main Menu      Ctrl↵  Record                 Ending Balance:  $1,793.79
```

Figure 10-1 — Accounts Receivable – an Other Asset Account.

Record the payment as a transfer to your bank account and as a decrease when you receive it. Use the Split Transaction window for this and for entering credits for goods returned or discounts for early payment. Press [F9] to recalculate the transaction total. If there is no total, the invoice was paid in full and you can type an asterisk (*) in the **C** (Cleared) column. If there is an Increase amount, the customer owes you money, and if there is a Decrease amount, you owe the customer money.

If you want totals to appear in the Register for invoices and payments, enter payments as a Decrease in a separate transaction. That way you will have one transaction to record the invoice and another to record the payment.

To create reports on Accounts Receivable:

1. Create a Transaction Report, type a title, set the date range to include all receivables, and subtotal by week to see your accounts receivable in weekly terms.

2. Create an A/R by Customer Report from the Business Reports Menu. This report will list all uncleared transactions (your accounts receivable) for the dates you have specified and subtotal them by month.

3. Create a Summary Report to see your receivables by customer. Type a title, set the date range, subtotal by month, specify Class as the row heading and Month as the column heading.

4. Create a Customer Payment History. You must type the date of each payment in the Memo field to produce this report. Create a Transaction Report, type a title, set the date range to include all invoices, and subtotal by payee.

Use the Business Cash Flow Report for income and expense reporting.

Produce Reports

Quicken has two types of reports that will help you with your bookkeeping chores: Profit and Loss Statement and Transactions (by Income and Expense Category) Report.

Profit and Loss Statement. This report will show the following totals:

- each income category and total income
- each expense category and total expenses
- income and expense

Transaction Report by Income and Expense Category. At the Create Transaction Report, enter the date range you want the report to cover and subtotal the report by category. The report will provide totals for the following:

- all transactions for each category
- income
- expenses
- income and expenses
- transfers
- overall total

If your reports show a category named Other, it means you've entered one or more transactions that were not assigned to a category. Remember that you can customize any report by filtering it, [F9], and setting options, [F8]. You can also memorize a report for future use, using [Ctrl]-[M]. For more information on reports, see Chapter 8.

Accrual Accounting

In the accrued basis of accounting, adjustments are made for accrued and deferred items such as accounts receivable, accounts payable, and prepaid insurance. Accrued basis accounting is also known as the double-entry system of accounting and is used by large and more complex businesses.

If you have an accrual based accounting system, you can use Quicken to help you track individual transactions in some income and expense accounts.

Accounts Payable

Set up an Other Liability account for your accounts payable. When you receive an invoice, enter a transaction in the account Register and assign it to an appropriate expense category. When you pay the bill, enter it as a transfer in your bank account (see Figure 10-2).

```
┌─────────────────────────────────────────────────────────────────────────┐
│ F1-Help  F2-Acct/Print  F3-Edit  F4-Quick Entry  F5-Reports  F6-Activities│
│ ┌──────┬──────┬────────────────────────────┬──────────┬──┬─────────┬──────────┐ │
│ │ DATE │ REF  │ PAYEE  ·  MEMO  ·  CATEGORY│ INCREASE │C │ DECREASE│ BALANCE  │ │
│ ├──────┼──────┼────────────────────────────┼──────────┼──┼─────────┼──────────┤ │
│ │ 1/ 8 │      │Alan's Print Shop           │  154 77  │  │         │  756 21  │ │
│ │ 1991 │      │Printing of Inv→Office      │          │  │         │          │ │
│ ├──────┼──────┼────────────────────────────┼──────────┼──┼─────────┼──────────┤ │
│ │ 1/10 │      │Jeff's Electronic Repairs   │   98 34  │  │         │  854 55  │ │
│ │ 1991 │      │Typewriter/Serv→Repairs     │          │  │         │          │ │
│ ├──────┼──────┼────────────────────────────┼──────────┼──┼─────────┼──────────┤ │
│ │ 2/ 1 │      │Alan's Print Shop           │          │  │  154 77 │  699 78  │ │
│ │ 1991 │      │A/P             [Checking]  │          │  │         │          │ │
│ ├──────┼──────┼────────────────────────────┼──────────┼──┼─────────┼──────────┤ │
│ │ 2/ 1 │      │Jeff's Electronics Repair   │          │  │   98 34 │  601 44  │ │
│ │ 1991 │      │A/P             [Checking]  │          │  │         │          │ │
│ ├──────┼──────┼────────────────────────────┼──────────┼──┼─────────┼──────────┤ │
│ │ 2/23 │Memo: │                            │          │  │         │          │ │
│ │ 1991 │Cat:  │                            │          │  │         │          │ │
│ └──────┴──────┴────────────────────────────┴──────────┴──┴─────────┴──────────┘ │
│ Acct Pay                                                                  │
│ Esc-Main Menu      Ctrl↵ Record              Ending Balance:  $601.44     │
└─────────────────────────────────────────────────────────────────────────┘
```

Figure 10-2 — Accounts Payable – an Other Liability Account.

If you take a discount for early payment of an invoice, enter the amount of the discount as a negative amount (use the split transaction window) and assign it to the same category as the invoice amount. You can enter the discount as part of the original transaction or as a separate transaction.

You can create two reports on accounts payable.

Accounts Payable Summary: Use the Summary Report, type a title, specify the date range you want to include, set row headings as payee, but do not subtotal. Filter the report to blank cleared status, and use only your accounts payable account.

Payment Detail by Vendor: Use the Transaction Report, type a title, specify the date range you want to include, subtotal by payee, filter the report to blank cleared status, and use only your accounts payable account.

Accounts Receivable

Set up an Other Asset account for your accounts receivable. Every time you send an invoice to a customer, enter a transaction in the account Register. Enter the following information: date, invoice number in the Ref or Memo fields, payee name, amount of invoice as an Increase, assign it to an appropriate income category, and record the transaction..

When you receive payment, enter it in your bank account as a deposit and as a transfer to the Other Asset account using the Split Transaction window. If you offer a discount for early payment of an invoice and your customer takes it, enter the amount of the discount as a negative amount (use the split transaction window) and assign it to the same category as the invoice amount. You can enter the discount as part of the original transaction or as a separate transaction.

If you use an accrual basis method of accounting, you can prepare a standard Profit and Loss Statement for income and expense reporting.

Business Budgeting

Use Quicken to compare your actual income and expenses with budgeted amounts. See the section on Budgeting in Chapter 9 for more information.

Cash Flow and Cash Position

Forecasting cash flow can help a company predict cash surpluses and deficits. Quicken can help you to forecast your cash flow if you enter all of your expected payments and all of your expected deposits.

Set up an Other Asset account and record all expected deposits in it. Write postdated checks in your bank account for all expected payments.

Create a Forecast Cash Flow report by selecting Transaction Report. Type a title, set a date range to cover from tomorrow forward, subtotal by week, and select which accounts to include (your checking account and Other Asset deposits account). Press [Ctrl]-[M] to memorize the report.

Asset and Liability Accounting

You can use Quicken to keep track of assets and liabilities such as capital equipment, loans, and depreciation of assets.

Set up an Other Asset and Other Liability account for each asset and liability you want to track. You can group some items, like office furniture or equipment, in one account.

Record an asset when you purchase it and enter it in your bank or credit card account as a transfer transaction. To record depreciation, enter the transaction in the Register of the depreciation account. Quicken will create a corresponding transaction in the Other Asset account.

To keep track of liabilities, set up an Other Liability account for a loan. Record payments on a loan as a transfer when you write the check and Quicken will create the corresponding transaction.

Use Quicken's Balance Sheet and Account Balances Report to create reports on assets and liabilities. Create a report on depreciation with the Summary Report. Use the Register, report on categories, subtotal by month, and use category for row headings and month for column headings.

Payroll

Quicken is not a complete payroll software package but it can make a simple payroll system easier and quicker. You can use Quicken to do the following things: write and print payroll checks and employer tax liability checks; keep track of employee payroll taxes and other deductions and of employer payroll tax liabilities; create and print reports on payroll expenses that can be used when filling out tax forms and preparing other documents.

Note: Quicken's Payroll Report looks for categories that begin with the word Payroll. If you don't set up your categories and Other Liabilities accounts with this word, the report will not give you the information you need.

If you want to use Quicken to help you with the payroll process, you must do two things:

1.   Set up Payroll categories:

You must create categories that begin with the word Payroll (see Figure 10-3). You may need to include payroll and other payroll expense categories, such as Federal withholding taxes, two for FICA taxes (one for the employee's deduction and one for the employer contribution), state and local withholding taxes, and Federal and state unemployment compensation taxes.

```
 F1-Help        Acct/Print       Edit       Quick Entry      Reports       Activities

  DATE  NUM   PAYE┌──────────────────────────────────────────────────────────────────┐
                  │                 Category and Transfer List                       │═
  1/15 1224  James│                                                                  │5
  1991 SPLIT Januar│     Category     Type         Description         Tax          │
 ─────      Cat: Payrol│                                                             │
  1/19      Deposi│    E-Fed         Sub    Employee Federal W/H        ♦           │5
  1991      Accoun│  ▶ E-FICA        Sub    Employee FICA               ♦           │
 ─────     ──────│    E-Medical     Sub    Medical Deductions          ♦           │
  1/31      James │    Gross         Sub    Gross Salary                ♦           │5
  1991 SPLIT Januar│    Checking      Bank   Checking Account                       │
 ─────     ──────│    Am Ex         CCard  American Express                        │
  1/31      John S│    Petty Cash    Cash   Petty Cash                             │5
  1991 SPLIT Januar│    Accts Rec     Oth A  Accounts Receivable                    │
 ─────     ──────│    Office Equip   Oth A  Office Equipment                       │
  2/ 1 ××××× Alan's│    Acct Pay      Oth L  Accounts Payable                      │8
  1991      A/P   │    Payroll-Fed    Oth L  Federal W-Holding                     │
 ─────     ──────│    Payroll-FICA   Oth L  FICA W-Holding                        │
  2/ 1 ××××× Jeff's│    Payroll-Medical Oth L Medical Insurance                   │4
  1991      A/P   │                                                                 │
 ─────     ──────│       Ctrl-D Delete   Ctrl-E Edit   Ctrl-P Print               │
                  │   Esc-Cancel              F1-Help              ↵ Use           │═
  Checking        └──────────────────────────────────────────────────────────────────┘
                                                    Ending Balance:   $1,623.34
```

Figure 10-3 — Payroll Categories.

To increase the accuracy of your records, create subcategories to help define payroll expenses for your company. Use a category named Payroll and subcategories for FICA (employee and employer), Federal, state, or local tax withheld, and medical deductions. Use a prefix to differentiate between company-paid and employee-paid expenses.

Another way to name your categories is to use the word Payroll and account numbers from your chart of accounts, such as Payroll-5001.

2. Set up Payroll Other Liability accounts:

    You must create Other Liability accounts that begin with the word Payroll. Set up an account for each type of employee deduction, such as federal withholding, FICA (the account can be used for both employee and employer contributions), state or local withholding, medical or state disability insurance premiums, and pension or savings plans. Set up an account for each employer payroll expense, such as FICA, Federal and state unemployment taxes, pension or retirements plans, and medical or disability insurance plans.

Record every deduction, and payroll-related expense as a negative transfer from your payroll checking account to the Other Liability accounts. When you pay these liabilities, the total of those accounts will decrease.

Writing Payroll Checks

If you're using Quicken to print payroll checks, always write them from the Write Checks screen. Enter the date and employee name.

Use the Split Transaction window, Ctrl-S, when writing payroll checks. List every deduction, one on each line, for each paycheck and assign it to a category and/or subcategory or an account (transfer). Enter gross pay as a positive amount first, followed by each deduction as negative amounts (see Figure 10-4).

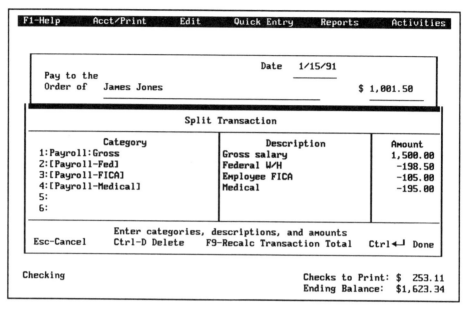

Figure 10-4 — Writing a Payroll Check Using a Split Transaction.

To record the rest of the payroll transactions, such as employer tax expenses, enter a hyphen (–) in the Description column of every unused line up to line 16. Quicken will print only the first 16 lines on a voucher check. Begin on line 17 and enter the rest of the payroll expenses, such as employer FICA, unemployment taxes, and employer-paid medical premiums and retirement. These items will be entered twice: once as a positive amount to a category and subcategory; once as a negative amount transfer to an Other Liability account. The two entries offset each other and there is no change in the amount of the check.

Press [F9] to calculate the amount of the check. Press [Ctrl]-[Enter←] twice, the first time to close the split window and the second time to record the transaction.

Entering Payroll Checks in the Register

If you hand write payroll checks, record them in the Register. Enter the net amount of the check before opening the split window. In the split window, enter the gross salary and deductions as discussed above, with one exception: Because you are not printing this check, you don't have to go to line 17 to enter the remaining items.

If you end up with a remainder in the amount column, you made a mistake somewhere. Check your calculations and make sure you typed the right number. Don't forget to type a minus sign before an amount if the amount is negative.

Memorizing Payroll Checks

You can save time and keystrokes by memorizing your payroll transactions. Type the first one with only the category and transfer information and memorize it using `Ctrl`-`M`. Recall the template, `Ctrl`-`T`, for each payroll check and fill in the date, name, and dollar amounts. As you finish each paycheck, memorize the complete transaction for further use. Decide whether you should memorize it with or without dollar amounts. See Chapter 5 for more information.

Payroll Transaction Group

When all of the payroll checks have been written and memorized, create a transaction group, using `Ctrl`-`J`, for future use. Include all of the checks in the same transaction group and you'll save time and keystrokes every time you do payroll. For more information on Transaction Groups, see Chapter 5.

Transfers and Tax Liability

When you enter payroll deductions and other liabilities as a transfer, Quicken makes a corresponding entry in the appropriate Other Liability account. The transaction, written from the Write Checks screen or the Register, decreases the amount in your checking account. The corresponding entry in the Other Liability account increases the balance of the account.

The Other Liability accounts, such as for Federal withholding, FICA, and state and local withholding taxes, can give you the information you need to pay the payroll taxes. If you enter detailed split transactions every time you do payroll, the account will give you accurate records of your tax liabilities.

When you write a check to pay a tax liability such as FICA or Federal withholding taxes, assign the transaction as a transfer to the corresponding Other Liability account. When recorded, the transaction will appear in both accounts and keep your records accurate.

Printing Payroll Checks

If you use voucher checks, Quicken will print up to 16 lines of wage and deduction information. See the section on Check Printing in Chapter 6 for more information.

Payroll Reports

Quicken's Payroll Report looks for categories that begin with the word Payroll. You can use the Summary Report and Transaction Report to calculate amounts you need for various tax forms, including Form W-2, Form W-3, Form 940, and Form 941.

When you prepare a report, subtotal it different ways and filter it to match certain conditions to get different amounts. Be sure to check the totals manually to ensure accuracy.

Form W-2, Wage and Tax Statement

To get Social Security wages:

- Use the Summary Report
- Report on payee
- Subtotal by category
- Restrict to "category matches Payroll."

To get Federal income tax withheld; Wages, tips, and other compensation; Social security tax withheld; State income tax withheld; State wages, tips, etc.; Local income tax; or Local wages:

- Use the Summary Report
- Report on payee
- Subtotal by category
- Restrict to "category matches Payroll"
- Restrict to the bank account from which you write payroll checks.

Form W-3, Transmittal of Income and Tax Statements

To get Federal income tax withheld; Wages, tips, and other compensation; or Social security tax withheld:

- Use the Summary Report
- Restrict to "category matches Payroll."

To get Social Security wages:

- Use the Summary Report
- Report on payee
- Do not subtotal
- Restrict to "category matches Payroll:Gross" (Gross pay subcategory).

Form 940 (1989) Federal Unemployment (FUTA) Tax

To get Total payments (Part I, line 1) and Total FUTA tax deposited (Part II, line 2):

- Use the Summary Report
- Report on category
- Do not subtotal
- Restrict to "category matches Payroll."

To get Payments for services... (Part I, line 3):

- Use Transaction Report
- Subtotal by payee
- Restrict to "category matches Payroll:Gross" (Gross pay subcategory).

To get Record of Quarterly Federal Tax Liability for Unemployment (Part IV):

- Use Transaction Report
- Use only the Payroll-FUTA account
- Subtotal by quarter
- Restrict to payments (Filter Report Transactions window).

Form 941 (1990) Employer's Quarterly Federal Tax

To get Taxable social security wages paid:

- Use Summary Report
- Report on payee
- Do not subtotal
- Restrict to "category matches Payroll:Gross" (Gross pay subcategory).

To get Total wages (line 2); Total income tax withheld (line 3); Total deposits (line 17):

- Use Summary Report
- Restrict to "category matches Payroll."

To get Record of Tax Liability:

- Use Summary Report
- Report on category
- Subtotal by frequency of payroll
- Restrict to "category matches Payroll-Federal" (Federal tax withholding account).

Petty Cash

Use Quicken to track your Petty Cash by setting up a cash account. For more information, see Chapter 4.

Reporting by Client, Department, Job, Project, or Property

Quicken can help you keep track of income and expenses related to different clients, departments, jobs, projects, or properties. There are four things you must do to accomplish this.

1. Establish a list of categories — Use your chart of accounts as a basis for the list of categories. See the section on Cash Basis Bookkeeping earlier in this chapter.

2. Establish a list of classes — Use whatever you want to report on as the basis for your list of classes. If you want to report by clients, set up a list of classes for each client. If you want to report by departments, set up a list of classes for each department. For more information on managing Rental Properties, see Chapter 9.

3. Assign each transaction to a category and a class — If you want accurate and complete records, you should assign every transaction to a category. You can set Quicken to remind you to assign a category to every transaction. For more information, see Chapter 7.

4. Produce Reports — Quicken has three types of reports that will help you: Job/Project, Summary, and Transaction.

    - Job/Project: This report will show the following totals for a job, project, or client:

        - all transactions for each category

        - income

        - expenses

        - income and expenses

        - transfers

        - overall total.

    - Income and Expense Summary: Use this report for a single job, project, or client by filtering it to match a class name, to show the following totals:

        - each income category and total income

        - each expense category and total expenses

        - income and expense

        - transfers

        - overall total.

- Transaction (for a Job, Project, or Client by Income and Expense category): At the Create Transaction Report, enter the date range you want the report to cover and subtotal the report by time period (to report a payment history for a period of time) or subtotal by class (to report a payment history for multiple jobs, projects, or clients). The report will provide totals for the following:

  - all transactions for each category

  - income

  - expenses

  - income and expenses

  - transfers

  - overall total.

If your reports show a category named Other, it means you've entered one or more transactions that were not assigned to a category. Remember that you can customize any report by filtering it, F9, and setting options, F8. You can also memorize a report, using Ctrl-M, for future use. For more information on reports, see Chapter 8.

IRS Form 1099

Quicken can help you keep track of non-employee compensation expenses that must be reported to the Internal Revenue Service on a Form 1099.

Set up a class named 1099 and assign all pertinent transactions to that class. Or type **1099** in the Memo field. Print a Transaction Report and filter it to transactions assigned to match the class or memo field 1099.

Summary

Businesses using either cash or accrual accounting can also use Quicken. Accounts payable, accounts receivable, asset and liability accounts, payroll, petty cash, and taxes are some of the tasks made easier if you set up the right categories and classes. You can also produce reports on income and expenses by job, property, or client.

Appendix A

Keys

Quick Keys by Function

Account, select or set up	`Ctrl`-`A`
Account Group, select or set up (from Main Menu)	`Ctrl`-`G`
Back up (from Main Menu)	
All Accounts	`Ctrl`-`B`
All Accounts and Exit	`Ctrl`-`E`
Calculator	`Ctrl`-`O`
Category, select or set up	`Ctrl`-`C`
Class, select or set up	`Ctrl`-`L`
Delete item	`Ctrl`-`D`

Edit item	`Ctrl`-`E`
Find transaction	`Ctrl`-`F`
Find Next	`Ctrl`-`N`
Find Previous	`Ctrl`-`B`
Go To	
Date	`Ctrl`-`G`
Register	`Ctrl`-`R`
Transfer	`Ctrl`-`X`
Write Checks	`Ctrl`-`W`
Memorize transaction or report	`Ctrl`-`M`
Print	`Ctrl`-`P`
Recall memorized transaction	`Ctrl`-`T`
Quick recall of memorized transactions	`Ctrl`-`E`
Split transaction	`Ctrl`-`S`
Transaction group, select	`Ctrl`-`J`

Quick Keys by Quick Key

`Ctrl`-`A`	Account, select or set up
`Ctrl`-`B`	Back up All Accounts (from Main Menu)
`Ctrl`-`B`	Find Previous
`Ctrl`-`C`	Category, select or set up
`Ctrl`-`D`	Delete item
`Ctrl`-`E`	Back up All Accounts and Exit (from Main Menu)
`Ctrl`-`E`	Edit item
`Ctrl`-`E`	Quick recall of memorized transactions
`Ctrl`-`F`	Find transaction
`Ctrl`-`G`	Account Group, select or set up (from Main Menu)
`Ctrl`-`G`	Go To Date

`Ctrl`-`J`	Transaction group, select
`Ctrl`-`L`	Class, select or set up
`Ctrl`-`M`	Memorize transaction or report
`Ctrl`-`N`	Find Next
`Ctrl`-`O`	Calculator
`Ctrl`-`P`	Print
`Ctrl`-`R`	Go To Register
`Ctrl`-`S`	Split transaction
`Ctrl`-`T`	Recall memorized transaction
`Ctrl`-`W`	Go To Write Checks
`Ctrl`-`X`	Go To Transfer

Other Helpful Keys

`F1`	Help key
`Ctrl`-`F1`	Help index
`esc`	Returns you to the previous activity or menu
Arrow keys	Move the cursor one line or space at a time
`↓`	Next transaction
`↑`	Previous transaction
`tab`	Move the cursor from blank to blank in windows
`⇧ Shift`-`tab`	Move the cursor backward through blanks in windows
`home`	Move the cursor to beginning of current field. Press twice to move to the beginning of the first field
`end`	Move the cursor to end of current field. Press twice to move to the end of the last field
`Ctrl`-`home`	Move the cursor to first check or top of register
`Ctrl`-`end`	Move the cursor to last check or bottom of Register
`PgDn`	Move the cursor to next check or screen

Appendix A

`PgUp`	Move the cursor to preceding check or screen
`Ctrl`-`PgDn`	Move the cursor to next month in the Register
`Ctrl`-`PgUp`	Move the cursor to previous month in the Register
`+` (Plus)	Increase date or check number
`-` (minus)	Decrease date or check number
..	Represents the unknown portion of a field
?	Represents an unknown character
~	Used in reports to exclude certain transactions
"	Repeats Category and Class name in a Split
`F10` or `Ctrl`-`Enter`	Record the transaction

Appendix **B**

Standard Categories

Standard Home Categories

Category Name	Category Description
Bonus	Bonus Income
Canada Pen	Canadian Pension
Div Income	Dividend Income
Family Allow	Family Allowance
Gift Received	Gift Received
Int Inc	Interest Income
Invest Inc	Investment Income
Old Age Pen	Old Age Pension

Appendix B

Other Inc	Other Income
Salary	Salary Income
Auto Fuel	Automobile Fuel
Auto Loan	Auto Loan Payment
Auto Serv	Automobile Service
Bank Chrg	Bank Charge
Charity	Charitable Donations
Childcare	Child Care Expense
Christmas	Christmas Expense
Clothing	Clothing
Dining	Dining Out
Dues	Dues
Education	Education
Entertain	Entertainment
Gifts	Gift Expense
Groceries	Groceries
Home Rpair	Home Repair & Maint.
Household	Household Misc. Exp
Housing	Housing
Insurance	Insurance
Int Exp	Interest Expense
Invest Exp	Investment Expense
Medical	Medical & Dental
Misc	Miscellaneous
Mort Int	Mortgage Interest Exp
Mort Prin	Mortgage Principal
Other Exp	Other Expenses

Recreation	Recreation Expense
RRSP	Reg Retirement Sav Plan
Subscriptions	Subscriptions
Supplies	Supplies
Tax Fed	Federal Withholding Tax
Tax FICA	Social Security Tax
Tax Other	Misc. Taxes
Tax Prop	Property Tax
Tax State	State Withholding Tax
Telephone	Telephone Expense
UIC	Unemploy. Ins. Commission
Utilities	Water, Gas, Electric

Standard Business Categories

Category Name	Category Description
Gr Sales	Gross Sales
Other Inc	Other Income
Rent Income	Rent Income
Ads	Advertising
Car	Car & Truck
Commission	Commissions
Freight	Freight
Int Paid	Interest Paid
L&P Fees	Legal & Prof Fees
Late Fees	Late Payment Fees
Office	Office Expenses
Rent Paid	Rent Paid

Repairs	Repairs
Returns	Returns & Allowances
Taxes	Taxes
Travel	Travel Expenses
Wages	Wages & Job Credits

Both

Category Name	Category Description
Bonus	Bonus Income
Canada Pen	Canadian Pension
Div Income	Dividend Income
Family Allow	Family Allowance
Gift Received	Gift Received
Gr Sales	Gross Sales
Int Inc	Interest Income
Invest Inc	Investment Income
Old Age Pen	Old Age Pension
Other Inc	Other Income
Rent Income	Rent Income
Salary	Salary Income
Ads	Advertising
Auto Fuel	Automobile Fuel
Auto Loan	Auto Loan Payment
Auto Serv	Automobile Service
Bank Chrg	Bank Charge
Car	Car & Truck
Charity	Charitable Donations

Childcare	Child Care Expense
Christmas	Christmas Expense
Clothing	Clothing
Commission	Commissions
Dining	Dining Out
Dues	Dues
Education	Education
Entertain	Entertainment
Freight	Freight
Gifts	Gift Expense
Groceries	Groceries
Home Rpair	Home Repair & Maint.
Household	Household Misc. Exp
Housing	Housing
Insurance	Insurance
Int Exp	Interest Expense
Int Paid	Interest Paid
Invest Exp	Investment Expense
L&P Fees	Legal & Prof Fees
Late Fees	Late Payment Fees
Medical	Medical & Dental
Misc	Miscellaneous
Mort Int	Mortgage Interest Exp
Mort Prin	Mortgage Principal
Office	Office Expenses
Other Exp	Other Expenses
Recreation	Recreation Expense
Rent Paid	Rent Paid

Appendix B

Repairs	Repairs
Returns	Returns & Allowances
RRSP	Reg Retirement Sav Plan
Subscriptions	Subscriptions
Supplies	Supplies
Tax Fed	Federal Withholding Tax
Tax FICA	Social Security Tax
Tax Other	Misc. Taxes
Tax Prop	Property Tax
Tax State	State Withholding Tax
Taxes	Taxes
Telephone	Telephone Expense
Travel	Travel Expenses
UIC	Unemploy. Ins. Commission
Utilities	Water, Gas, Electric
Wages	Wages & Job Credits

Appendix C

Menu Map

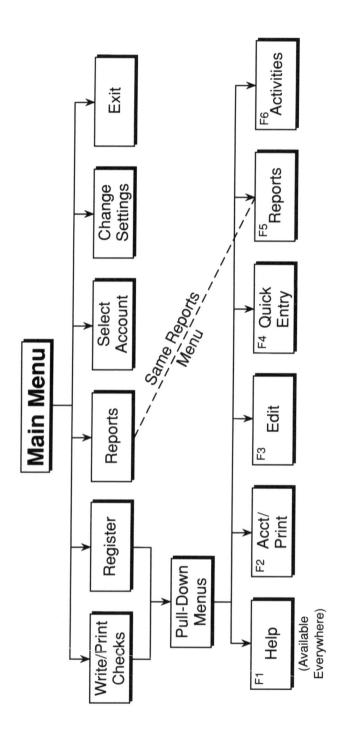

Index

A

account, 2, 3
account balances report, custom, 236
account description, 21
account groups, 3, 21, 158
    back up account group, 164
    copy account group, 167
    default account group, 21, 23
    delete account group, 163
    location of account group, 171
    QDATA, 21, 23
    restore account group, 165
    select account group, 158
    set up account group, 158
    shrink account group, 167
    year-end, 167
account
    account description, 21
    account name, 20
    account types, 20
    adding account, 60
    back up accounts, 48
    bank account, 20
    beginning balance, 21
    cash account, 59
    changing account, 62
    credit card account, 20
    deleting account, 62
    investment account, 59
    name, 20
    other asset account, 59, 244, 261
    other liability account, 59, 245, 261
    select account, 41, 47
    set up account, 18, 47
    types, 20, 57
accounts payable, 255, 258
accounts payable by vendor report, 205
accounts receivable, 256, 260
accounts receivable by customer report, 206
accrual basis, 258
adding account, 60
adding category, 65
adding classes, 71
adding transaction group, 127
adding transactions, 81
annuities, 246
asset accounting, 261
autoexec.bat, 10, 187
AUX device, 176

B

back up account group, 164
back up accounts, 48
backup drive, 22
balance, 89
balance sheet, 208
bank account, 20
beeping, 183
beginning balance, 21
Billminder, 12, 185, 187
bonds, 246
Both categories, 18, 278
budget report, custom, 233
budgeting, business, 260
budgeting, home, 240
Business categories, 18, 277

C

calculator, 4, 30, 54
capital gains report, 213
cash account, 59
cash basis, 254
cash flow, 260
cash flow report, 196
cash flow report, business, 205
. cash management, home, 243
cash position, 260
categories, 63
    adding category, 65
    Both categories, 18
    Business categories, 18
    changing category, 67
    deleting category, 67
    Home categories, 18
    Neither categories, 18
    requiring categories, 68
    using categories, 74
category, 2, 3, 96
Category and Transfer List, 4, 64
certificates of deposit, 246
CGA, 173
Change Settings, 158
change transaction, 89
changing account, 62
changing category, 67
changing classes, 73
changing transaction group, 127
characters/line, 177
chart of accounts, 254
check register, 133
CheckFree, 153
checks, 53
    deleting check, 142
    printing check, 144, 149
    printing checks, 36
    reprinting check, 153
    voiding check, 143
    writing checks, 36, 133
class, 3
Class List, 4

classes, 70
    adding classes, 71
    changing classes, 73
    deleting classes, 73
    using classes, 74
cleared transaction, 110
colors, 172
COM devices, 176
config.sys, 10
confirmations, 184
copy account group, 167
credit card account, 20
cursor movement, 29
custom account balances report, 236
custom budget report, 233
custom summary report, 230
custom transaction report, 225
customizing Quicken, 43

D

data files, location, 18
date format, 184
default account group, 21, 23
delete account, 62
delete account group, 163
delete category, 67
delete check, 142
delete classes, 73
delete transaction, 90
delete transaction group, 128
delete transfer, 94
DOS, 54

E

editing keys, 29, 34
EGA, 173, 185
electronic bill paying, 153, 186
executing transaction group, 125
exiting (quitting) Quicken, 22, 45
export data, 48
exporting data, 118

F

filtering, 221
finding transactions, 84
first time reconciliation, 107
Form 1099, 270
FUTA tax, 267

G

go to date, 50, 87
go to transfer, 50, 93

H

help, 27, 46
help topics, 28
home budgeting, 240
home cash management, 243
Home categories, 18, 275
home improvements, 244

I

IBM graphics characters, 178
import data, 48
importing data, 118
income tax, 251
indenting, 177
Install, 10
investment account, 59
investment income report, 214
investment performance report, 212
investment transactions report, 215
IRA, 246
itemized category report, 202

J

job/project report, 208

K

Keough, 246
key word match, 88

L

laser printer, 173
liability accounting, 261
lines per page, 177
loan account, 245
location of account group, 171
LPT devices, 176

M

main menu, 17, 35
memorized report, 216
memorized transaction, 100
memorized transaction, change, 104
memorized transaction, delete, 105
memorized transaction, print, 106
memorized transaction, recall, 103
menus, 4, 282
missing transaction, 111
monitor, 173
monitor type, 10, 15
monthly budget report, 198
mortgage account, 245
mutual funds, 246

N

Neither categories, 18
net worth, 249
net worth report, 203

O

other asset account, 59, 244, 261
other liability account, 59, 245, 261

P

passwords, 178
pasting calculator totals, 33
paychecks, 249
payroll, 261
payroll checks, 263
payroll checks, printing, 266
payroll report, 208
payroll reports, 266
payroll taxes, 265

petty cash, 268
petty cash fund, 91
pitch, 177
portfolio value report, 211
post-dated check, 139
print register, 47
printer control codes, 176
printer list, 175
printer settings, 47, 173
printing check, 144, 149
printing checks, 36
printing register, 116
printing reports, 193
PRN device, 176
profit and loss statement, 204, 257
pull-down menus, 45

Q

QDATA, 21, 23
quarterly federal tax, 268
Quick Entry, 50
quick keys, 4, 29, 271
Quicken Interchange Format (QIF), 118

R

recalling transaction group, 125
reconcile register, 106
reconciliation, 53
reconciliation, first time, 107
register, 3, 53, 77
    category, 3
    print register, 47
    printing register, 116
    shortcut keys, 38
rename account group, 163
rental property, 248
report options, 219
reports, 40, 52, 190
reports, printing, 193
reprinting check, 153
requiring categories, 69
restore account group, 165

S

screen, 172
select account, 41, 47
select account group, 160
serial printer, 173
set up account, 18, 47
set up account group, 158
set up transaction group, 122
settings, 43
settings, printer, 47
shortcut keys, 38
shrink account group, 167
split transaction, adding, 95
split transaction, change, 98
split transaction, delete, 98
split transaction, transfer, 98
split transfer, 94
stocks, 246
subcategories, 68
subclasses, 73
summary report, custom, 230
supplies, ordering, 53

T

tax summary report, 203
transaction, 2, 49, 80
    adding transactions, 81
    balance, 89
    change transaction, 89
    delete transaction, 90
    finding transactions, 84
    memorized transaction, 100
transaction group, 121
    adding transaction group, 127
    changing transaction group, 127
    deleting transaction group, 128
    executing transaction group, 125
    recalling transaction group, 125
    set up transaction group, 121
transaction report, 258
transaction report, custom, 225

transfer
    change transfer, 93
    delete transfer, 94
    split transfer, 94
transfer funds, 91
transfer split transaction, 98

U

using categories, 74
using classes, 74

V

VGA, 173, 185
video monitor, 173
video screen, 172
voiding check, 143

W

W-2, 266
W-3, 267
wide reports, 192
wide reports, printing, 194
Write Checks, 4